CALIFORNIA Common Core Math

POWERED BY GO MATH!

HOUGHTON MIFFLIN HARCOURT

CALIFORNIA Common Core Math

POWERED BY GO MATH!

HOUGHTON MIFFLIN HARCOURT

Printed in the U.S.A.

ISBN 978-0-547-89402-7

5 6 7 8 9 10 0868 21 20 19 18 17 16 15 14 13

4500419647 B C D E F G

Table of Contents

Operations and Algebraic Thinking

Write and interpret numerical expressions. Analyze patterns and relationships.

Common Core Standards CC.5.OA.1, CC.5.OA.2, CC.5.OA.3

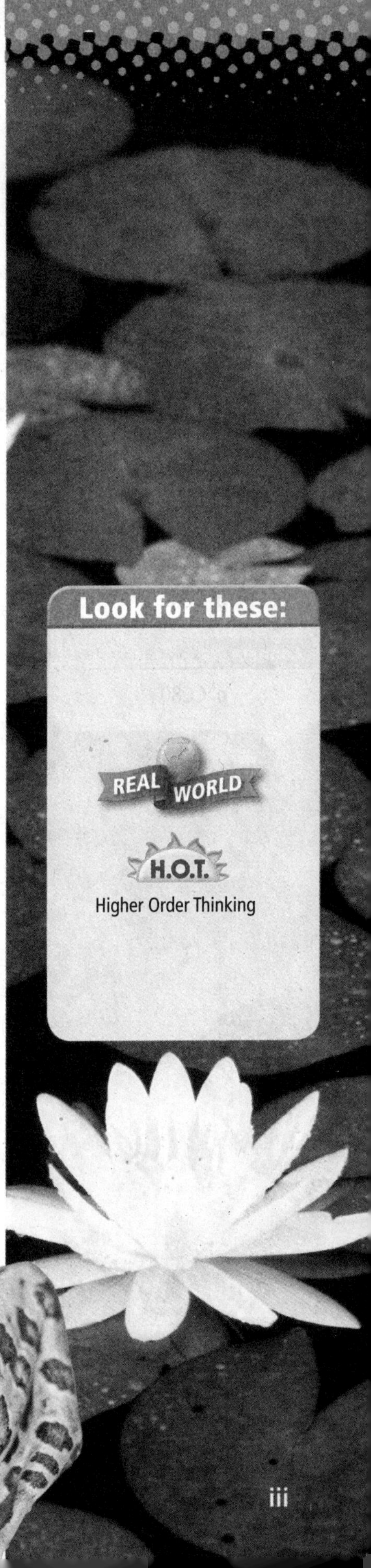

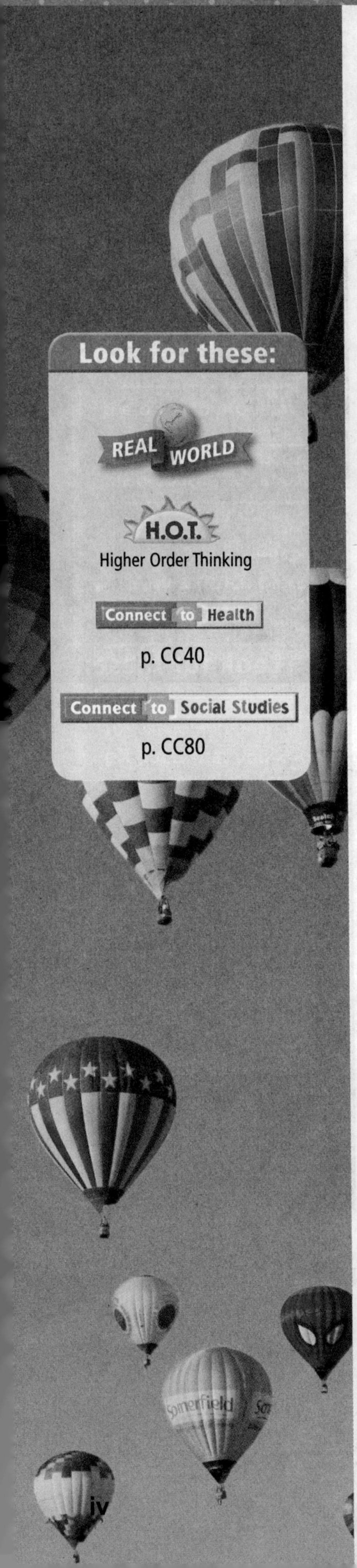

Look for these:

REAL WORLD

H.O.T.
Higher Order Thinking

Connect to Health

p. CC40

Connect to Social Studies

p. CC80

Number and Operations in Base Ten

Understand the place value system. Perform operations with multi-digit whole numbers and with decimals to hundredths.

Common Core Standards CC.5.NBT.1, CC.5.NBT.2, CC.5.NBT.3a, CC.5.NBT.5, CC.5.NBT.6, CC.5.NBT.7

Number and Operations–Fractions

Use equivalent fractions as a strategy to add and subtract fractions. Apply and extend previous understandings of multiplication and division to multiply and divide fractions.

Common Core Standards CC.5.NF.2, CC.5.NF.3, CC.5.NF.4a, CC.5.NF.4b, CC.5.NF.5a, CC.5.NF.5b, CC.5.NF.6, CC.5.NF.7a, CC.5.NF.7b, CC.5.NF.7c

Measurement and Data

Convert like measurement units within a given measurement system. Represent and interpret data. Geometric measurement: understand concepts of volume and relate volume to multiplication and to addition.

Common Core Standards CC.5.MD.1, CC.5.MD.2, CC.5.MD.3a, CC.5.MD.3b, CC.5.MD.4, CC.5.MD.5a, CC.5.MD.5b, CC.5.MD.5c

Geometry

Graph points on the coordinate plane to solve real-world and mathematical problems.

Common Core Standards CC.5.G.1, CC.5.G.2

Look for these:

REAL WORLD

H.O.T.
Higher Order Thinking

Connect to Art
p. CC220

Connect to Reading
p. CC185

Name ______________________

Evaluate Numerical Expressions

Essential Question In what order must operations be evaluated to find the solution to a problem?

COMMON CORE STANDARD CC.5.OA.1
Write and interpret numerical expressions.

CONNECT Remember that a numerical expression is a mathematical phrase that uses only numbers and operation symbols.

$(5 - 2) \times 7$ $\quad 72 \div 9 + 16$ $\quad (24 - 15) + 32$

To **evaluate**, or find the value of, a numerical expression with more than one operation, you must follow rules called the **order of operations.** The order of operations tells you in what order you should evaluate an expression.

Order of Operations
1. Perform operations in parentheses.
2. Multiply and divide from left to right.
3. Add and subtract from left to right.

UNLOCK the Problem REAL WORLD

A cake recipe calls for 4 cups of flour and 2 cups of sugar. To triple the recipe, how many cups of flour and sugar are needed in all?

Evaluate $3 \times 4 + 3 \times 2$ to find the total number of cups.

A Heather did not follow the order of operations correctly.

Heather

$3 \times 4 + 3 \times 2$ First, I added.

$3 \times 7 \times 2$ Then, I multiplied.

42

Explain why Heather's answer is not correct.

____

B Follow the order of operations by multiplying first and then adding.

Name ______

$3 \times 4 + 3 \times 2$

So, ______ cups of flour and sugar are needed.

Evaluate Expressions with Parentheses To evaluate an expression with parentheses, follow the order of operations. Perform the operations in parentheses first. Multiply from left to right. Then add and subtract from left to right.

Example

Each batch of cupcakes Lena makes uses 3 cups of flour, 1 cup of milk, and 2 cups of sugar. Lena wants to make 5 batches of cupcakes. How many cups of flour, milk, and sugar will she need in all?

Write the expression. $5 \times (3 + 1 + 2)$

First, perform the operations in parentheses. $5 \times$ (______)

Then multiply. ______

So, Lena will use ______ cups of flour, milk, and sugar in all.

- **H.O.T.** **What if** Lena makes 4 batches? Will this change the numerical expression? **Explain.**

____

Try This! **Rewrite the expression with parentheses to equal the given value.**

A $6 + 12 \times 8 - 3$; value: 141

- Evaluate the expression without the parentheses. ______
- Try placing the parentheses in the expression so the value is 141.

Think: Will the placement of the parentheses increase or decrease the value of the expression?

- Use order of operations to check your work.

$6 + 12 \times 8 - 3$

B $5 + 28 \div 7 - 4$; value: 11

- Evaluate the expression without the parentheses. ______
- Try placing the parentheses in the expression so that the value is 11.

Think: Will the placement of the parentheses increase or decrease the value of the expression?

- Use order of operations to check your work.

$5 + 28 \div 7 - 4$

Name ______________________________

Share and Show

Evaluate the numerical expression.

1. $10 + 36 \div 9$

Think: I need to divide first.

______

2. $10 + (25 - 10) \div 5$

______

3. $9 - (3 \times 2) + 8$

______

Math Talk MATHEMATICAL PRACTICES Raina evaluated the expression $5 \times 2 + 2$ by adding first and then multiplying. Will her answer be correct? **Explain.**

On Your Own

Evaluate the numerical expression.

4. $(4 + 49) - 4 \times 10$ ______

5. $5 + 17 - 100 \div 5$ ______

6. $36 - (8 + 5)$ ______

7. $125 - (68 + 7)$ ______

8. $(4 \times 6) - 12$ ______

9. $3 \times (22 - 2)$ ______

10. $23 + (16 - 7)$ ______

11. $(25 - 4) \div 3$ ______

Rewrite the expression with parentheses to equal the given value.

12. $100 - 30 \div 5$
value: 14

______

13. $12 + 17 - 3 \times 2$
value: 23

______

14. $9 + 5 \div 5 + 2$
value: 2

______

UNLOCK the Problem REAL WORLD

15. A movie theater has 4 groups of seats. The largest group of seats, in the middle, has 20 rows, with 20 seats in each row. There are 2 smaller groups of seats on the sides, each with 20 rows and 6 seats in each row. A group of seats in the back has 5 rows, with 30 seats in each row. How many seats are in the movie theater?

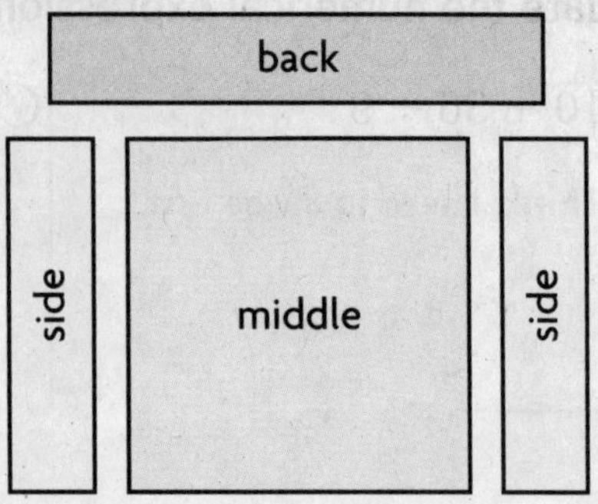

a. What do you need to know? ______

______

b. What operation can you use to find the number of seats in the back group of seats? Write the expression. ______

c. What operation can you use to find the number of seats in both groups of side seats? Write the expression.

______

d. What operation can you use to find the number of seats in the middle group? Write the expression.

______

e. Write an expression to represent the total number of seats in the theater.

______

______

f. How many seats are in the theater? Show the steps you use to solve the problem.

______

______

16. ★ **Test Practice** In the wild, an adult giant panda eats about 30 pounds of food each day. Which expression shows how many pounds of food 6 pandas eat in 3 days?

Ⓐ $3 + (30 \times 6)$

Ⓑ $3 \times (30 \times 6)$

Ⓒ $(30 \times 6) \div 3$

Ⓓ $(30 \times 6) - 3$

17. ★ **Test Practice** Which expression has a value of 6?

Ⓐ $(6 \div 3) \times 4 + 8$

Ⓑ $27 - 9 \div 3 \times (4 + 1)$

Ⓒ $(18 + 12) \times 6 - 4$

Ⓓ $71 - 5 \times (9 + 4)$

Name ______________________________

Grouping Symbols

Essential Question In what order must operations be evaluated to find a solution when there are parentheses within parentheses?

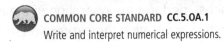

COMMON CORE STANDARD CC.5.OA.1
Write and interpret numerical expressions.

UNLOCK the Problem REAL WORLD

Mary's weekly allowance is $8 and David's weekly allowance is $5. Every week they each spend $2 on lunch. Write a numerical expression to show how many weeks it will take them together to save enough money to buy a video game for $45.

- Underline Mary's weekly allowance and how much she spends.
- Circle David's weekly allowance and how much he spends.

Use parentheses and brackets to write an expression.

You can use parentheses and brackets to group operations that go together. Operations in parentheses and brackets are performed first.

STEP 1 Write an expression to represent how much Mary and David save each week.

- How much money does Mary save each week?

  Think: Each week Mary gets $8 and spends $2.

  (____________)

- How much money does David save each week?

  Think: Each week David gets $5 and spends $2.

  (____________)

- How much money do Mary and David save together each week? ______________________

STEP 2 Write an expression to represent how many weeks it will take Mary and David to save enough money for the video game.

- How many weeks will it take Mary and David to save enough for a video game?

  Think: I can use brackets to group operations a second time. $45 is divided by the total amount of money saved each week.

  __________ ÷ [______________________________]

MATHEMATICAL PRACTICES

Math Talk **Explain** why brackets are placed around the part of the expression that represents the amount of money Mary and David save each week.

Evaluate Expressions with Grouping Symbols When evaluating an expression with different grouping symbols (parentheses, brackets, and braces), perform the operation in the innermost set of grouping symbols first, evaluating the expression from the inside out.

Example

John gets \$6 for his weekly allowance and spends \$4 of it. His sister Tina gets \$7 for her weekly allowance and spends \$3 of it. Their mother's birthday is in 4 weeks. If they spend the same amount each week, how much money can they save together in that time to buy her a present?

- Write the expression using parentheses and brackets. $4 \times [(\$6 - \$4) + (\$7 - \$3)]$
- Perform the operations in the parentheses first. $4 \times [$ ______ $+$ ______ $]$
- Next perform the operations in the brackets. $4 \times$ ______
- Then multiply. ______

So, John and Tina will be able to save ____________ for their mother's birthday present.

- H.O.T. **What if** only Tina saves any money? Will this change the numerical expression? **Explain.**

____

Try This! **Follow the order of operations.**

A $4 \times \{[(5 - 2) \times 3] + [(2 + 4) \times 2]\}$

- Perform the operations in the parentheses. $4 \times \{[3 \times 3] + [$ ______ $\times$ ______ $]\}$
- Perform the operations in the brackets. $4 \times \{9 +$ ______ $\}$
- Perform the operations in the braces. $4 \times$ ______
- Multiply. ______

B $32 \div \{[(3 \times 2) + 7] - [(6 - 4) + 7]\}$

- Perform the operations in the parentheses. $32 \div \{[$ ______ $+$ ______ $] - [$ ______ $+$ ______ $]\}$
- Perform the operations in the brackets. $32 \div \{$ ______ $-$ ______ $\}$
- Perform the operations in the braces. $32 \div$ ______
- Divide. ______

Name ______________________________

Share and Show

Evaluate the numerical expression.

1. $12 + [(15 - 5) + (9 - 3)]$

   $12 + [10 + \_\_\_\_]$

   $12 + \_\_\_\_$

   ____

2. $5 \times [(26 - 4) - (4 + 6)]$

   ____

3. $36 \div [(18 - 10) - (8 - 6)]$

   ____

On Your Own

Evaluate the numerical expression.

4. $4 + [(16 - 4) + (12 - 9)]$

   ____

5. $24 - [(10 - 7) + (16 - 9)]$

   ____

6. $16 \div [(13 + 7) - (12 + 4)]$

   ____

7. $5 \times [(7 - 2) + (10 - 8)]$

   ____

8. $[(17 + 8) + (29 - 12)] \div 6$

   ____

9. $[(6 \times 7) + (3 \times 4)] - 28$

   ____

10. $3 \times \{[(12 - 8) \times 2] + [(11 - 9) \times 3]\}$

    ____

11. $\{[(3 \times 4) + 18] + [(6 \times 7) - 27]\} \div 5$

    ____

UNLOCK the Problem REAL WORLD

12. Dan has a flower shop. Each day he displays 24 roses. He gives away 10 and sells the rest. Each day he displays 36 carnations. He gives away 12 and sells the rest. What expression can you use to find out how many roses and carnations Dan sells in a week?

a. What information are you given? ____________

____

____

b. What are you being asked to do? ____________

____

____

c. What expression shows how many roses Dan sells in one day? ____________

d. What expression shows how many carnations Dan sells in one day? ____________

e. Write an expression to represent the total number of roses and carnations Dan sells in one day. ____________

f. Write the expression that shows how many roses and carnations Dan sells in a week. ____________

13. Evaluate the expression to find out how many roses and carnations Dan sells in a week.

____

14. ★ **Test Practice** Which expression has a value of 4?

Ⓐ $[(4 \times 5) + (9 + 7)] + 9$

Ⓑ $[(4 \times 5) + (9 + 7)] \div 9$

Ⓒ $[(4 \times 5) - (9 + 7)] \times 9$

Ⓓ $[(4 + 5) + (9 + 7)] - 9$

FOR MORE PRACTICE:
Standards Practice Book

Name ______________________

Numerical Expressions

Essential Question How can you use a numerical expression to describe a situation?

COMMON CORE STANDARD CC.5.OA.2
Write and interpret numerical expressions.

UNLOCK the Problem REAL WORLD

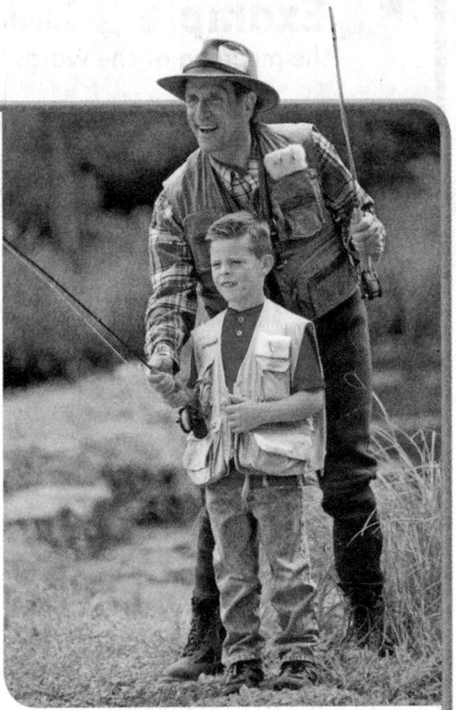

A **numerical expression** is a mathematical phrase that has numbers and operation signs but does not have an equal sign.

Tyler caught 15 small bass, and his dad caught 12 small bass in the Memorial Bass Tourney in Tidioute, PA. Write a numerical expression to represent how many fish they caught in all.

Choose which operation to use.

You need to join groups of different sizes, so use addition.

15 small bass	plus	12 small bass
↓	↓	↓
15	+	12

So, 15 + 12 represents how many fish they caught in all.

Example 1 Write an expression to match the words.

A Addition

Emma has 11 fish in her aquarium. She buys 4 more fish.

fish	plus	more fish
↓	↓	↓
11	+	4

B Subtraction

Lucia has 128 stamps. She uses 38 stamps on party invitations.

stamps	minus	stamps used
↓	↓	↓
128	−	______

C Multiplication

Karla buys 5 books. Each book costs $3.

books	multiplied by	cost per book
↓	↓	↓
______	×	______

D Division

Four players share 52 cards equally.

cards	divided by	players
↓	↓	↓
______	÷	______

MATHEMATICAL PRACTICES
Math Talk Describe what each expression represents.

Expressions with Parentheses The meaning of the words in a problem will tell you where to place the parentheses in an expression.

Example 2 Which expression matches the meaning of the words?

- Underline the events for each day.
- Circle the number of days these events happened.

Doug went fishing for 3 days. Each day he put $15 in his pocket. At the end of each day, he had $5 left. How much money did Doug spend by the end of the trip?

Think: Each day he took $15 and had $5 left. He did this for 3 days.

($15 − $5) ← **Think:** What expression can you write to show how much money Doug spends in one day?

3 × ($15 − $5) ← **Think:** What expression can you write to show how much money Doug spends in three days?

MATHEMATICAL PRACTICES

Math Talk Explain how the expression of what Doug spent in three days compares to the expression of what he spent in one day?

Example 3 Which problem matches the expression $20 − ($12 + $3)?

Kim has $20 to spend for her fishing trip. She spends $12 on a fishing pole. Then she finds $3. How much money does Kim have now?

List the events in order.

First: Kim has $20.

Next: ______________.

Then: ______________.

Do these words match the expression? __________

Kim has $20 to spend for her fishing trip. She spends $12 on a fishing pole and $3 on bait. How much money does Kim have now?

List the events in order.

First: Kim has $20.

Next: ______________.

Then: ______________.

Do these words match the expression? __________

Share and Show

Circle the expression that matches the words.

1. Teri had 18 worms. She gave 4 worms to Susie and 3 worms to Jamie.

   (18 − 4) + 3   18 − (4 + 3)

2. Rick had $8. He then worked 4 hours for $5 each hour.

   $8 + (4 × $5)   ($8 + 4) × $5

Name ______________________________

Write an expression to match the words.

3. Greg drives 26 miles on Monday and 90 miles on Tuesday.

____

4. Lynda has 27 fewer fish than Jack. Jack has 80 fish.

____

Write words to match the expression.

5. $34 - 17$

____

____

6. $6 \times (12 - 4)$

____

____

MATHEMATICAL PRACTICES

Math Talk Is $4 \times 8 = 32$ an expression? **Explain** why or why not.

On Your Own

Write an expression to match the words.

7. José shared 12 party favors equally among 6 friends.

____

8. Braden has 14 baseball cards. He finds 5 more baseball cards.

____

9. Isabelle bought 12 bottles of water at \$2 each.

____

10. Monique had \$20. She spent \$5 on lunch and \$10 at the bookstore.

____

Write words to match the expression.

11. $36 \div 9$

____

____

12. $35 - (16 + 11)$

____

____

Draw a line to match the expression with the words.

13. Fred catches 25 fish. Then he releases 10 fish and catches 8 more. •

Nick has 25 pens. He gives 10 pens to one friend and 8 pens to another friend. •

Jan catches 15 fish and lets 6 fish go. •

Libby catches 15 fish and lets 6 fish go for three days in a row. •

• $3 \times (15 - 6)$

• $15 - 6$

• $25 - (10 + 8)$

• $(25 - 10) + 8$

Problem Solving REAL WORLD

Use the rule and the table for 14.

Aquarium Fish

Type of Fish	Length (in inches)
Lemon Tetra	2
Strawberry Tetra	3
Giant Danio	5
Tiger Barb	3
Swordtail	5

▲ The rule for the number of fish in an aquarium is to allow 1 gallon of water for each inch of length.

14. Write a numerical expression to represent the total number of lemon tetras that could be in a 20-gallon aquarium.

15. H.O.T. Write a word problem for an expression that is three times as great as (15 + 7). Then write the expression.

16. **What's the Question?** Lu has 3 swordtails in her aquarium. She buys 2 more swordtails.

17. H.O.T. Tammy gives 45 stamps to her 9 friends. She shares them equally among her friends. Write an expression to match the words. How many stamps does each friend get?

18. **Test Practice** Josh has 3 fish in each of 5 buckets. Then he releases 4 fish. Which expression matches the words?

Ⓐ $(3 \times 4) - 5$

Ⓑ $(5 \times 4) - 3$

Ⓒ $(5 \times 3) - 4$

Ⓓ $(5 - 3) \times 4$

SHOW YOUR WORK

Name ______________________________

Numerical Patterns

COMMON CORE STANDARD CC.5.OA.3
Analyze patterns and relationships.

Essential Question How can you identify a relationship between two numerical patterns?

UNLOCK the Problem REAL WORLD

On the first week of school, Joel purchases 2 movies and 6 songs from his favorite media website. If he purchases the same number of movies and songs each week, how does the number of songs purchased compare to the number of movies purchased from one week to the next?

- How many movies does Joel purchase each week?

  ____

- How many songs does Joel purchase each week?

  ____

STEP 1 Use the two rules given in the problem to generate the first 4 terms in the sequence for the number of movies and the sequence for number of songs.

- The sequence for the number of movies each week is:

  +2 +2 +2

  2, ____, ____, ____, . . .

- The sequence for the number of songs each week is:

  +6 +6 +6

  6, ____, ____, ____, . . .

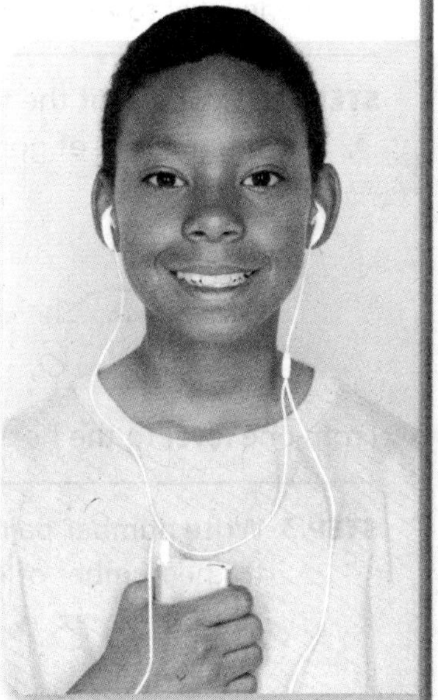

STEP 2 Write number pairs that relate the number of movies to the number of songs.

Week 1: 2, 6   Week 2: ______________

Week 3: ______________   Week 4: ______________

STEP 3 For each number pair, compare the number of movies to the number of songs. Write a rule to describe this relationship.

Think: For each related number pair, the second number is _______ times as great as the first number.

Rule: ________________________________

So, from one week to the next, the number of songs Joel purchased is _______ times as many as the number of movies purchased.

Example

When Alice completes each level in her favorite video game, she wins 3 extra lives and 6 gold coins. What rule can you write to relate the number of gold coins to the number of extra lives she has won at any level? How many extra lives will Alice have won after she completes 8 levels?

Level	0	1	2	3	4	8
Extra Lives	0	3	6	9	12	
Gold Coins	0	6	12	18	24	48

Add ______. (Extra Lives)

Add ______. (Gold Coins)

Multiply by ______ or divide by ______.

STEP 1 To the left of the table, complete the rule for how you could find the number of extra lives won from one level to the next.

← difference between consecutive terms

0, 3, 6, 9, 12

From one level to the next, Alice wins ______ more extra lives.

STEP 2 To the left of the table, complete the rule for how you could find the number of gold coins won from one level to the next.

← difference between consecutive terms

0, 6, 12, 18, 24

From one level to the next, Alice wins ______ more gold coins.

STEP 3 Write number pairs that relate the number of gold coins to the number of extra lives won at each level.

Level 1: 6, 3 Level 2: ______

Level 3: ______ Level 4: ______

STEP 4 Complete the rule to the right of the table that describes how the number pairs are related. Use your rule to find the number of extra lives at level 8.

Think: For each level, the number of extra lives is ______ as great as the number of gold coins.

Rule: ____________________

So, after 8 levels, Alice will have won ______ extra lives.

MATHEMATICAL PRACTICES

Math Talk Explain how your rule would change if you were relating extra lives to gold coins instead of gold coins to extra lives.

Name ______________________________

Share and Show

Use the given rules to complete each sequence. Then, complete the rule that describes how nickels are related to dimes.

1.

	Number of coins	1	2	3	4	5
Add 5.	Nickels (¢)	5	10	15	20	
Add 10.	Dimes (¢)	10	20	30	40	

Multiply by ______.

Complete the rule that describes how one sequence is related to the other. Use the rule to find the unknown term.

2. Multiply the number of books by ______ to find the amount spent.

Day	1	2	3	4	8
Number of Books	3	6	9	12	24
Amount Spent ($)	12	24	36	48	

3. Divide the weight of the bag by ______ to find the number of marbles.

Bags	1	2	3	4	12
Number of Marbles	10	20	30	40	
Weight of Bag (grams)	30	60	90	120	360

On Your Own

Complete the rule that describes how one sequence is related to the other. Use the rule to find the unknown term.

4. Multiply the number of eggs by ______ to find the number of muffins.

Batches	1	2	3	4	9
Number of Eggs	2	4	6	8	18
Muffins	12	24	36	48	

5. Divide the number of meters by ______ to find the number of laps.

Runners	1	2	3	4
Number of Laps	4	8	12	
Number of Meters	1,600	3,200	4,800	6,400

6. H.O.T. Suppose the number of eggs used in Exercise 4 is changed to 3 eggs for each batch of 12 muffins, and 48 eggs are used. How many batches and how many muffins will be made?

____

Problem Solving REAL WORLD

SHOW YOUR WORK

7. Emily has a road map with a key that shows an inch on the map equals 5 miles of actual distance. If a distance measured on the map is 12 inches, what is the actual distance? Write the rule you used to find the actual distance.

____

____

8. To make a shade of lavender paint, Jon mixes 4 ounces of red tint and 28 ounces of blue tint into one gallon of white paint. If 20 gallons of white paint and 80 ounces of red tint are used, how much blue tint should be added? Write a rule that you can use to find the amount of blue tint needed.

____

____

____

9. H.O.T. In the cafeteria, tables are arranged in groups of 4, with each table seating 8 students. How many students can sit at 10 groups of tables? Write the rule you used to find the number of students.

____

____

10. What is the unknown number in Sequence 2 in the chart? What rule could you write that relates Sequence 1 to Sequence 2?

Sequence Number	1	2	3	5	7
Sequence 1	5	10	15	25	35
Sequence 2	15	30	45	75	?

Ⓐ 70; Multiply by 2.

Ⓑ 100; Add 25.

Ⓒ 105; Multiply by 3.

Ⓓ 150; Add 150.

Name ____________________________

Problem Solving • Find a Rule

Essential Question How can you use the strategy *solve a simpler problem* to help you solve a problem with patterns?

COMMON CORE STANDARD CC.5.OA.3
Analyze patterns and relationships.

UNLOCK the Problem REAL WORLD

On an archaeological dig, Gabriel separates his dig site into sections with areas of 15 square feet each. There are 3 archaeological members digging in every section. What is the area of the dig site if 21 members are digging at one time?

15 sq ft

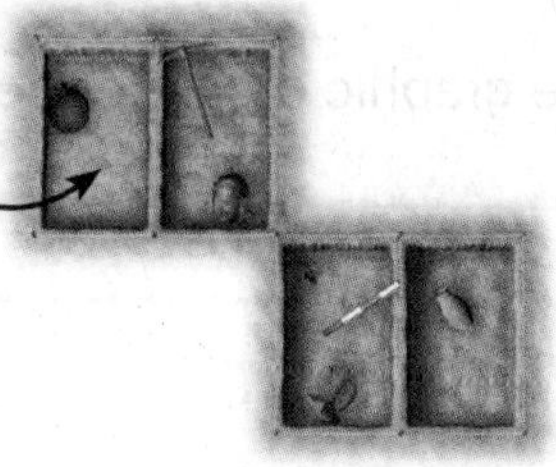

Read the Problem

What do I need to find?

I need to find the

____

____

____________________.

What information do I need to use?

I can use the area of each section, which is

____________________, that

there are ______ members in each section, and that there are 21 members digging.

How will I use the information?

I will use the information to search for patterns to solve

a ____________ problem.

Solve the Problem

	Sections	1	2	3	4	5	6	7
Add 3.	Number of Members	3	6	9	12	15	18	21
Add 15.	Area (in square feet)	15	30	45	60	75	90	

Multiply by ______.

Multiply by ______.

Possible Rules:

- Multiply the number of sections by ______ to find the number of members.
- Multiply the number of members by ______ to find the total area. Complete the table.

So, the area of the dig site if 21 members are digging is ______ square feet.

MATHEMATICAL PRACTICES

Math Talk Explain how you can use division to find the number of members if you know the dig site area is 135 square feet.

Try Another Problem

Casey is making a design with triangles and beads for a costume. In his design, each pattern unit adds 3 triangles and 18 beads. If Casey uses 72 triangles in his design, how many times does he repeat the pattern unit? How many beads does Casey use?

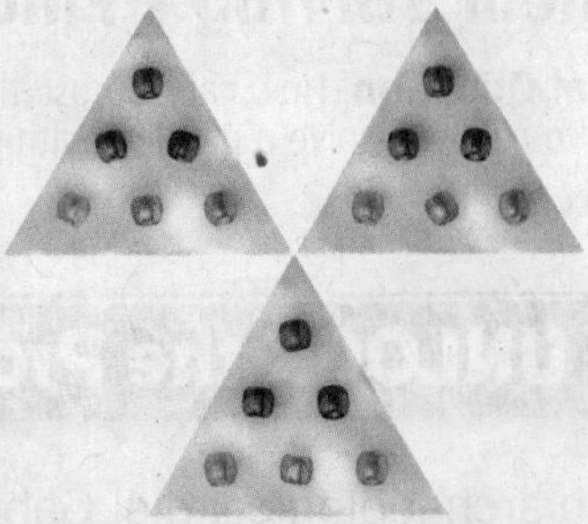

Use the graphic organizer below to solve the problem.

Read the Problem

What do I need to find?	What information do I need to use?	How will I use the information?

Solve the Problem

So, Casey repeats the pattern unit ______ times and uses ______ beads.

- What rule could you use to find an unknown number of beads if you know the related number of triangles?

____

____

Name ________________________________

Share and Show

1. Max builds rail fences. For one style of fence, each section uses 3 vertical fence posts and 6 horizontal rails. How many posts and rails does he need for a fence that will be 9 sections long?

1 Section

2 Sections

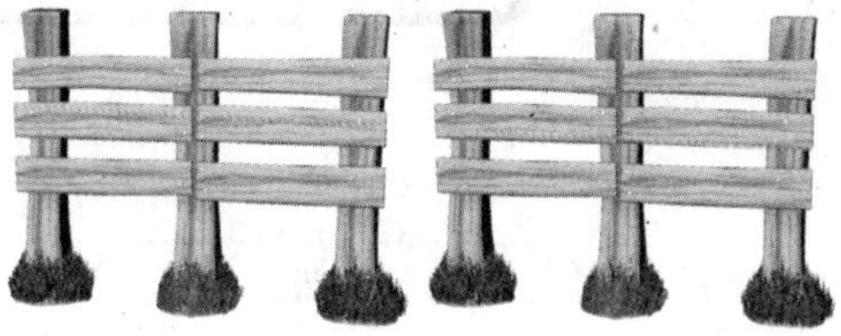

3 Sections

First, think about what the problem is asking and what you know. As each section of fence is added, how does the number of posts and the number of rails change?

Next, make a table and look for a pattern. Use what you know about 1, 2, and 3 sections. Write a rule for the number of posts and rails needed for 9 sections of fence.

Number of Sections	1	2	3	9
Number of Posts	3	6	9	
Number of Rails	6	12	18	

Possible rule for posts: ________________________

____

Possible rule for rails: ________________________

____

Finally, use the rule to solve the problem.

2. H.O.T. **What if** another style of rail fencing has 6 rails between each pair of posts? How many rails are needed for 9 sections of this fence?

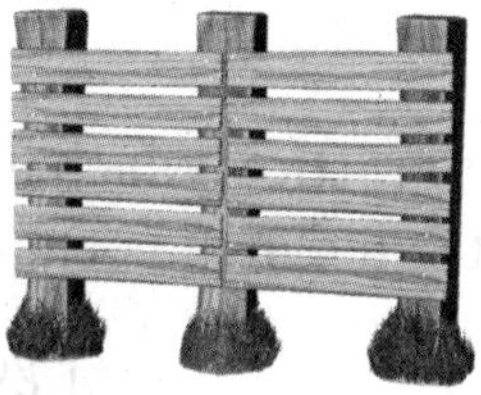

Number of Sections	1	2	3	9
Number of Posts	3	6	9	
Number of Rails	12	24	36	

Possible rule: ________________________

____

3. Leslie is buying a coat on layaway for $135. She will pay $15 each week until the coat is paid for. How much will she have left to pay after 8 weeks?

Number of Weeks	1	2	3	8
Amount paid ($)	15	30	45	

____

On Your Own

Choose a STRATEGY

- Act It Out
- Draw a Diagram
- Make a Table
- Solve a Simpler Problem
- Work Backward
- Guess, Check, and Revise

4. Jane works as a limousine driver. She earns $50 for every 2 hours that she works. How much does Jane earn in one week if she works 40 hours per week? Write a rule and complete the table.

Possible rule: ______________________

Hours Worked	2	4	6	40
Jane's Pay ($)	50	100	150	

5. H.O.T. Rosa joins a paperback book club. Members pay $8 to buy 2 tokens, and can trade 2 tokens for 4 paperback books. Rosa buys 30 tokens and trades them for 60 paperback books. How much money does she spend? Write a rule and complete the table.

Tokens	2	4	6	8	30
Cost ($)	8	16	24	32	
Books	4	8	12	16	60

Possible rule: ______________________

____

____

6. H.O.T. Paul is taking a taxicab to a museum. The taxi driver charges a $3 fee plus $2 for each mile traveled. How much does the ride to the museum cost if it is 8 miles away?

____

7. Test Practice Which expression could describe the next figure in the pattern, Figure 4?

Figure 1 Figure 2 Figure 3

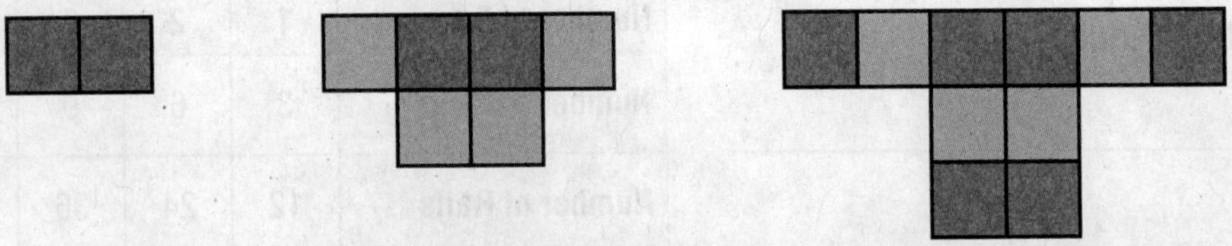

2 squares 6 squares 10 squares

Ⓐ 2×5

Ⓑ $2 + 4 + 4$

Ⓒ $2 + 4 + 4 + 4$

Ⓓ 16

 FOR MORE PRACTICE: Standards Practice Book

Name ______________________________

Graph and Analyze Relationships

Essential Question How can you write and graph ordered pairs on a coordinate grid using two numerical patterns?

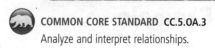

COMMON CORE STANDARD CC.5.OA.3
Analyze and interpret relationships.

UNLOCK the Problem — REAL WORLD

Sasha is making hot cocoa for a party. For each mug of cocoa, he uses 3 tablespoons of cocoa mix and 6 fluid ounces of hot water. If Sasha uses an entire 18-tablespoon container of cocoa mix, how many fluid ounces of water will he use?

- How many tablespoons of cocoa mix does Sasha add for each mug of cocoa?

  ____

- How many fluid ounces of water does Sasha add for each mug of cocoa?

  ____

STEP 1 Use the two given rules in the problem to generate the first four terms for the number of tablespoons of cocoa mix and the number of fluid ounces of water.

Cocoa Mix (tbsp)	3				18
Water (fl oz)	6				

STEP 2 Write the number pairs as ordered pairs, relating the number of tablespoons of cocoa mix to the number of fluid ounces of water.

(3, 6) ______ ______ ______

STEP 3 Graph and label the ordered pairs. Then write a rule to describe how the number pairs are related.

- What rule can you write that relates the amount of cocoa mix to water?

  ____

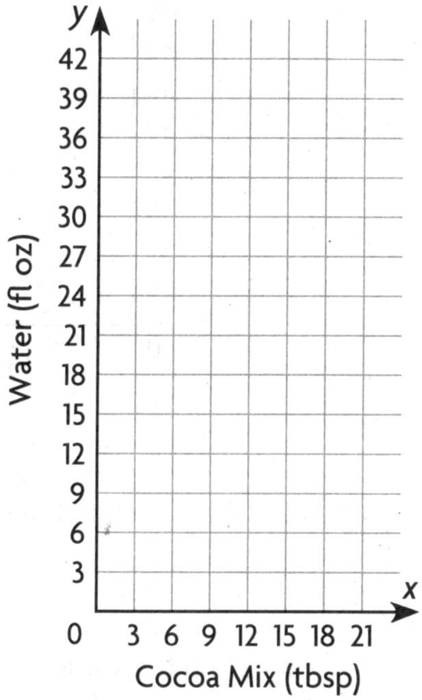

So, Sasha will use ______ fluid ounces of water if he uses the entire container of cocoa mix.

- Write the final number pair as an ordered pair. Then graph and label it. What pattern do you see with the ordered pairs? **Explain.**

____

____

____

Example

Jon is customizing an audio sound system. He needs to buy $3\frac{1}{2}$ feet of cable wire, but it is sold in inches. He knows there are 12 inches in 1 foot. How many inches of wire will he need?

Feet	1	2	3	4
Inches	12			

Rule: Multiply the number of feet by ______.

STEP 1 Write the number pairs as ordered pairs, relating the number of feet to the number of inches.

______ ______ ______ ______

STEP 2 Graph the ordered pairs.

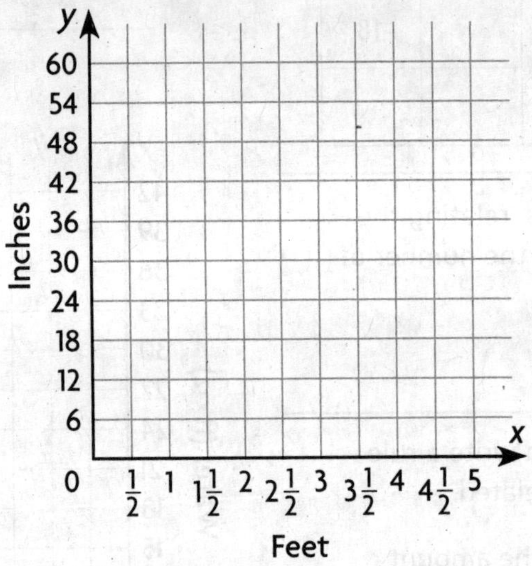

STEP 3 Use the graph to find the number of inches in $3\frac{1}{2}$ feet.

Think: $3\frac{1}{2}$ is between the whole numbers ______ and ______.

Locate $3\frac{1}{2}$ on the *x*-axis.

STEP 4 Multiply the *x*-coordinate times 12 to find the *y*-coordinate.

Think: $3\frac{1}{2} \times 12 =$ ______

Graph the point. What is the ordered pair for the point?

______

So, Jon needs to buy ______ inches of cable wire.

Name ____________________________

Share and Show

Graph and label the related number pairs as ordered pairs. Then complete and use the rule to find the unknown term.

1. Multiply the number of tablespoons by ______ to find its weight in ounces.

Butter (tbsp)	1	2	3	4	5
Weight (oz)	2	4	6	8	

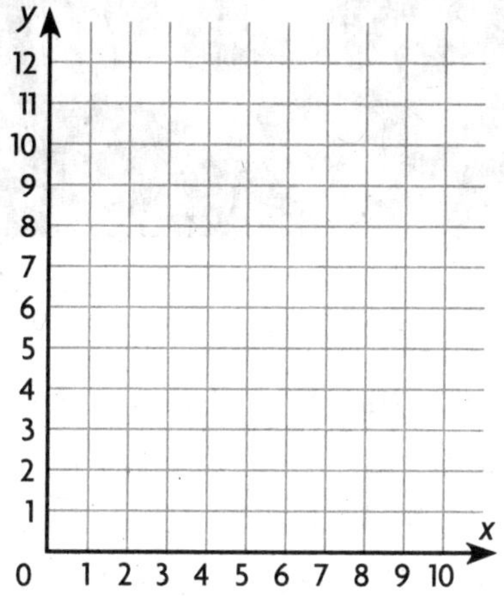

2. Multiply the number of hours by ______ to find the distance in miles.

Time (hr)	1	2	3	4
Distance walked (mi)	3	6	9	

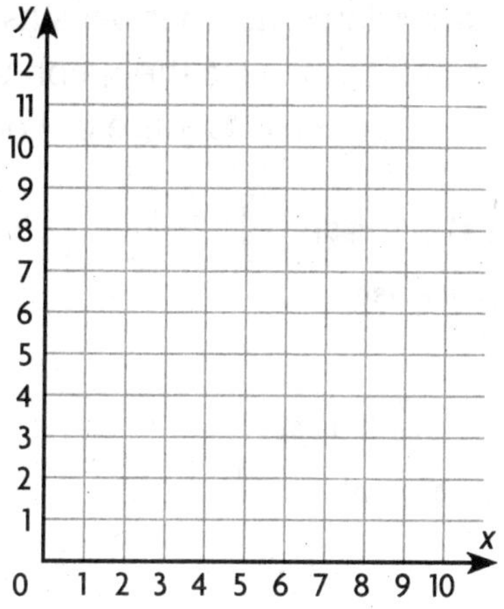

On Your Own

Graph and label the related number pairs as ordered pairs. Then complete and use the rule to find the unknown term.

3. Multiply the number of inches by ______ to find the distance in miles.

Map (in.)	2	4	6	8	10
Miles	10	20	30	40	

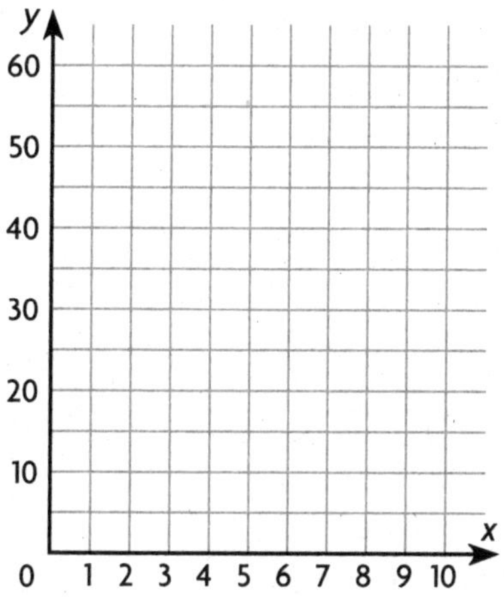

4. Multiply the number of centiliters by ______ to find the equivalent number of milliliters.

Centiliters	1	2	3	4	5
Milliliters	10	20	30	40	

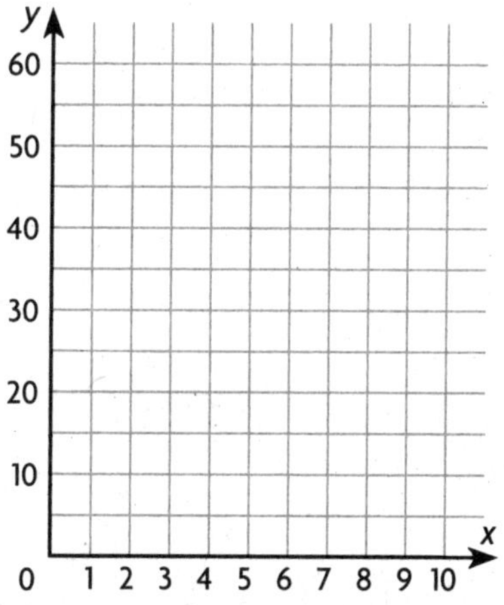

Problem Solving REAL WORLD

H.O.T. Sense or Nonsense?

5. Elsa solved the following problem.

Lou and George are making chili for the Annual Firefighter's Ball. Lou uses 2 teaspoons of hot sauce for every 2 cups of chili that he makes, and George uses 3 teaspoons of the same hot sauce for every cup of chili in his recipe. Who has the hotter chili, George or Lou?

Write the related number pairs as ordered pairs and then graph them. Use the graph to compare who has the hotter chili, George or Lou.

Lou's chili (cups)	2	4	6	8
Hot sauce (tsp)	2	4	6	8

George's chili (cups)	1	2	3	4
Hot sauce (tsp)	3	6	9	12

Lou's chili: (2, 2), (4, 4), (6, 6), (8, 8)

George's chili: (1, 3), (2, 6), (3, 9), (4, 12)

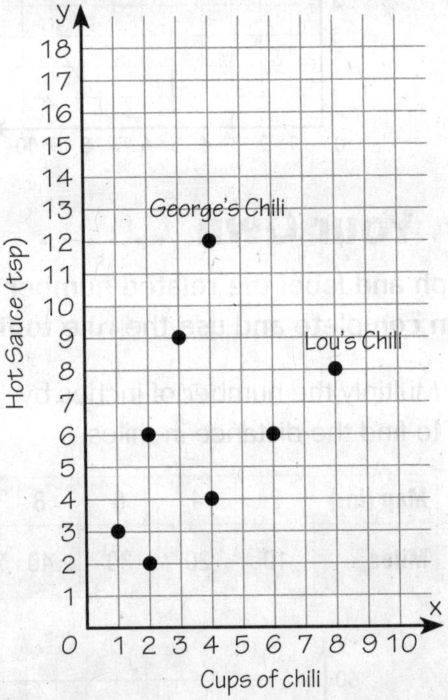

Elsa said that George's chili was hotter than Lou's, because the graph showed that the amount of hot sauce in George's chili was always 3 times as great as the amount of hot sauce in Lou's chili. Does Elsa's answer make sense, or is it nonsense? **Explain.**

Name ______________________

Place Value and Patterns

Essential Question How can you describe the relationship between two place-value positions?

COMMON CORE STANDARD CC.5.NBT.1
Understand the place value system.

Investigate

Materials ■ base-ten blocks

You can use base-ten blocks to understand the relationships among place-value positions. Use a large cube for 1,000, a flat for 100, a long for 10, and a small cube for 1.

Number	1,000	100	10	1
Model	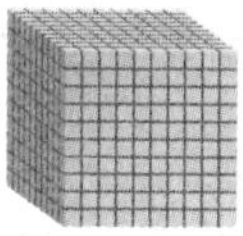	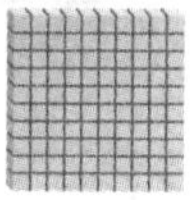		
Description	large cube	flat	long	small cube

Complete the comparisons below to describe the relationship from one place-value position to the next place-value position.

A.
- Look at the long and compare it to the small cube.

  The long is ______ times as much as the small cube.

- Look at the flat and compare it to the long.

  The flat is ______ times as much as the long.

- Look at the large cube and compare it to the flat.

  The large cube is ______ times as much as the flat.

B.
- Look at the flat and compare it to the large cube.

  The flat is ______ of the large cube.

- Look at the long and compare it to the flat.

  The long is ______ of the flat.

- Look at the small cube and compare it to the long.

  The small cube is ______ of the long.

Math Talk MATHEMATICAL PRACTICES How many times as much is the flat compared to the small cube? the large cube to the small cube? **Explain.**

Draw Conclusions

1. **Describe** the pattern you see when you move from a lesser place-value position to the next greater place-value position.

____

____

____

2. **Describe** the pattern you see when you move from a greater place-value position to the next lesser place-value position.

____

____

____

Make Connections

You can use your understanding of place-value patterns and a place-value chart to write numbers that are 10 times as much as or $\frac{1}{10}$ of any given number.

Hundred Thousands	Ten Thousands	One Thousands	Hundreds	Tens	Ones
		?	300	?	

10 times as much as

$\frac{1}{10}$ of

__________ is 10 times as much as 300.

__________ is $\frac{1}{10}$ of 300.

Use the steps below to complete the table.

STEP 1 Write the given number in a place-value chart.

STEP 2 Use the place-value chart to write a number that is 10 times as much as the given number.

STEP 3 Use the place-value chart to write a number that is $\frac{1}{10}$ of the given number.

Number	10 times as much as	$\frac{1}{10}$ of
10		
70		
9,000		

Name ____________________

Share and Show

Complete the sentence.

1. 500 is 10 times as much as ____________.

2. 20,000 is $\frac{1}{10}$ of ____________.

3. 900 is $\frac{1}{10}$ of ____________.

4. 600 is 10 times as much as ____________.

Use place-value patterns to complete the table.

Number	10 times as much as	$\frac{1}{10}$ of
5. 10		
6. 3,000		
7. 800		
8. 50		

Number	10 times as much as	$\frac{1}{10}$ of
9. 400		
10. 90		
11. 6,000		
12. 200		

H.O.T. **Complete the sentence with 100 or 1,000.**

13. 200 is ____________ times as much as 2.

14. 4,000 is ____________ times as much as 4.

15. 700,000 is ____________ times as much as 700.

16. 600 is ____________ times as much as 6.

17. 50,000 is ____________ times as much as 500.

18. 30,000 is ____________ times as much as 30.

19. Write Math **Explain** how you can use place-value patterns to describe how 50 and 5,000 compare.

____

____

Problem Solving

H.O.T. Sense or Nonsense?

20. Mark and Robyn used base-ten blocks to show that 300 is 100 times as much as 3. Whose model makes sense? Whose model is nonsense? **Explain** your reasoning.

Mark's Work

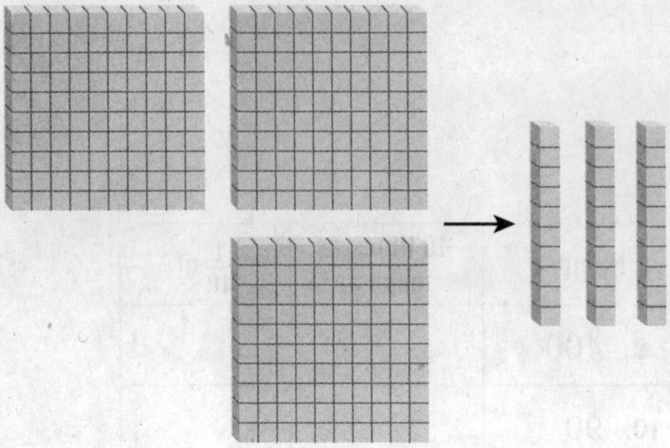

300

Robyn's Work

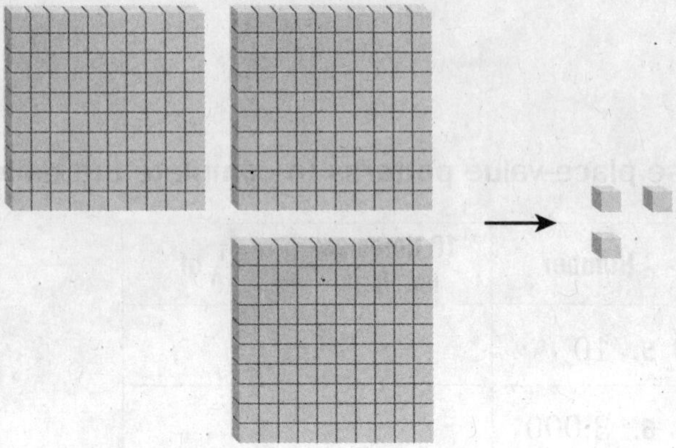

300

- **Explain** how you would help Mark understand why he should have used small cubes instead of longs.

Name ______________________________

Thousandths

Essential Question How can you describe the relationship between two decimal place-value positions?

COMMON CORE STANDARD **CC.5.NBT.1**
Understand the place value system.

Investigate

Materials ■ color pencils ■ straightedge

Thousandths are smaller parts than hundredths. If one hundredth is divided into ten equal parts, each part is one **thousandth**.

Use the model at the right to show tenths, hundredths, and thousandths.

A. Divide the larger square into 10 equal columns or rectangles. Shade one rectangle. What part of the whole is the shaded rectangle? Write that part as a decimal and a fraction.

____

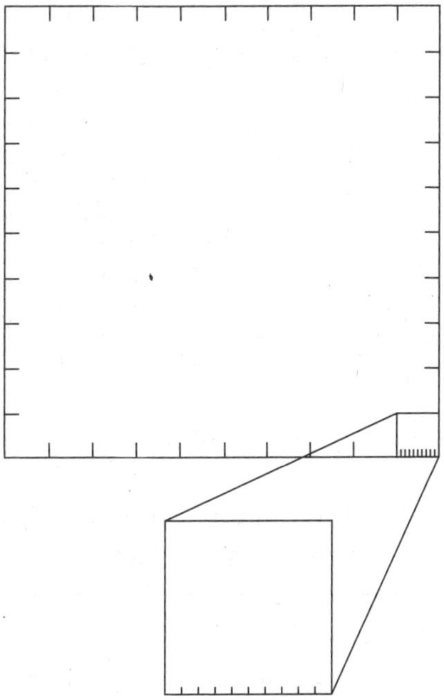

B. Divide each rectangle into 10 equal squares. Use a second color to shade in one of the squares. What part of the whole is the shaded square? Write that part as a decimal and a fraction.

____

C. Divide the enlarged hundredths square into 10 equal columns or rectangles. If each hundredths square is divided into ten equal rectangles, how many parts will the model have?

____

Use a third color to shade one rectangle of the enlarged hundredths square. What part of the whole is the shaded rectangle? Write that part as a decimal and a fraction.

____

Math Talk MATHEMATICAL PRACTICES
There are 10 times as many hundredths as there are tenths. **Explain** how the model shows this.

Draw Conclusions

1. **Explain** what each shaded part of your model in the Investigate section shows. What fraction can you write that relates each shaded part to the next greater shaded part? ____________________

____

2. **Identify** and describe a part of your model that shows one thousandth. **Explain** how you know.

____

____

____

Make Connections

The relationship of a digit in different place-value positions is the same with decimals as it is with whole numbers. You can use your understanding of place-value patterns and a place-value chart to write decimals that are 10 times as much as or $\frac{1}{10}$ of any given decimal.

Ones	• Tenths	Hundredths	Thousandths
	?	0.04	?

10 times as much $\frac{1}{10}$ of

__________ is 10 times as much as 0.04.

__________ is $\frac{1}{10}$ of 0.04.

Use the steps below to complete the table.

STEP 1 Write the given decimal in a place-value chart.

STEP 2 Use the place-value chart to write a decimal that is 10 times as much as the given decimal.

STEP 3 Use the place-value chart to write a decimal that is $\frac{1}{10}$ of the given decimal.

Decimal	10 times as much as	$\frac{1}{10}$ of
0.03		
0.1		
0.07		

MATHEMATICAL PRACTICES

Math Talk Describe the pattern you see when you move one decimal place value to the right and one decimal place value to the left.

Name ________________________________

Share and Show

Write the decimal shown by the shaded parts of each model.

1. 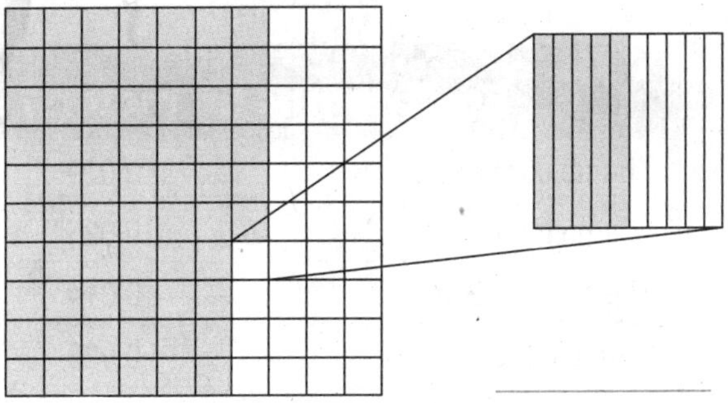 ________

2. 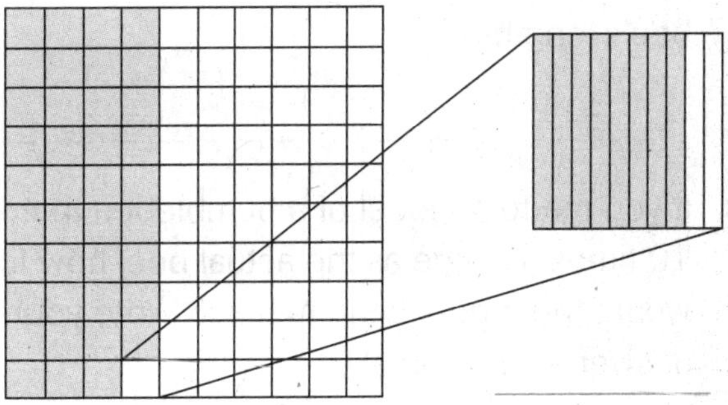 ________

3. 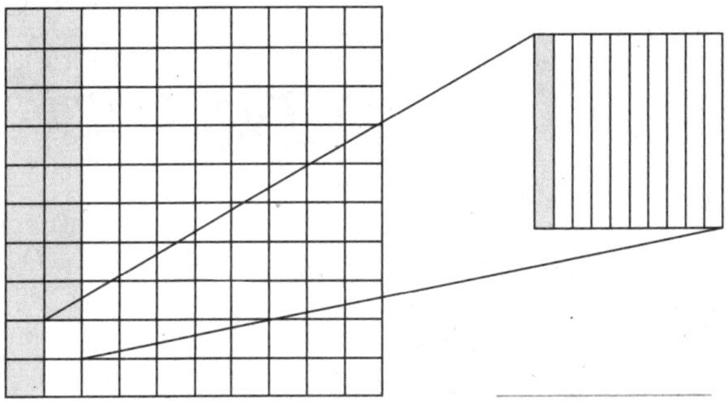 ________

4. 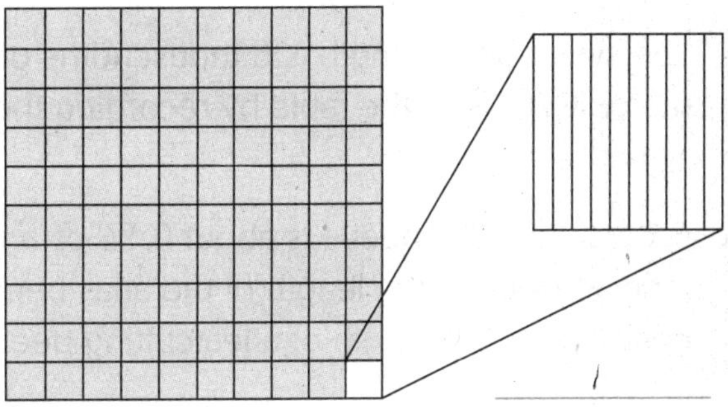 ________

Complete the sentence.

5. 0.6 is 10 times as much as ________.

6. 0.007 is $\frac{1}{10}$ of ________.

7. 0.008 is $\frac{1}{10}$ of ________.

8. 0.5 is 10 times as much as ________.

Use place-value patterns to complete the table.

	Decimal	10 times as much as	$\frac{1}{10}$ of
9.	0.2		
10.	0.07		
11.	0.05		
12.	0.4		

	Decimal	10 times as much as	$\frac{1}{10}$ of
13.	0.06		
14.	0.9		
15.	0.3		
16.	0.08		

Problem Solving REAL WORLD

Use the table for 17–20.

Bee Lengths (in meters)	
Bumblebee	0.019
Carpenter Bee	0.025
Leafcutting Bee	0.014
Orchid Bee	0.028
Sweat Bee	

17. What is the value of the digit 2 in the carpenter bee's length?

____

18. If you made a model of a bumblebee that was 10 times as large as the actual bee, how long would the model be in meters? Write your answer as a decimal.

____

19. The sweat bee's length is 6 thousandths of a meter. Complete the table by recording the sweat bee's length.

20. H.O.T. An atlas beetle is about 0.14 of a meter long. How does the length of the atlas beetle compare to the length of a leafcutting bee?

____

____

____

21. Write Math **Explain** how you can use place value to describe how 0.05 and 0.005 compare.

____

____

____

____

22. Test Practice What is the relationship between 1.0 and 0.1?

Ⓐ 0.1 is 10 times as much as 1.0

Ⓑ 1.0 is $\frac{1}{10}$ of 0.1

Ⓒ 0.1 is $\frac{1}{10}$ of 1.0

Ⓓ 1.0 is equal to 0.1

SHOW YOUR WORK

Name ______________________________

Powers of 10 and Exponents

Essential Question How can you use an exponent to show powers of 10?

COMMON CORE STANDARD CC.5.NBT.2
Understand the place value system.

UNLOCK the Problem

Expressions with repeated factors, such as $10 \times 10 \times 10$, can be written by using a base with an exponent. The **base** is the number that is used as the repeated factor. The **exponent** is the number that tells how many times the base is used as a factor.

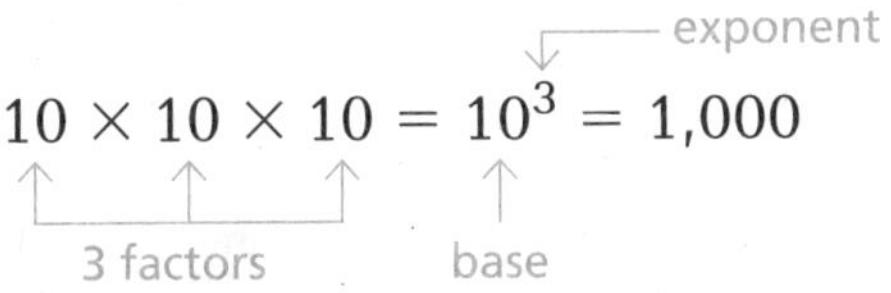

$$10 \times 10 \times 10 = 10^3 = 1{,}000$$

Word form: the third power of ten

Exponent form: 10^3

Activity Use base-ten blocks.

Materials ■ base-ten blocks

What is $10 \times 1{,}000$ written with an exponent?

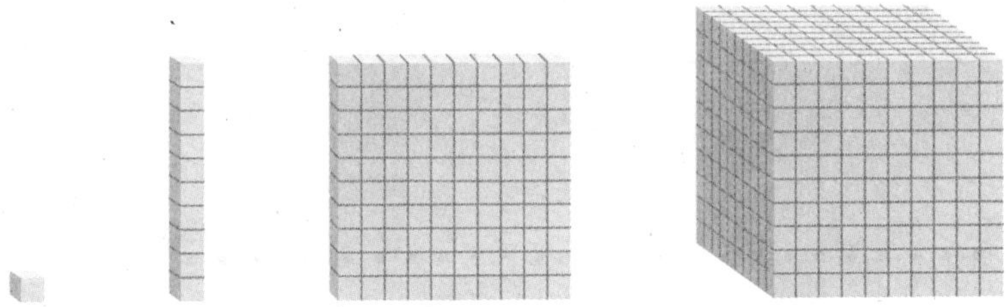

1 one	10 ones	100 ones	1,000 ones
1	1×10	$1 \times 10 \times 10$	$1 \times 10 \times 10 \times 10$
10^0	10^1	10^2	10^3

- How many ones are in 1? ______
- How many ones are in 10? ______
- How many tens are in 100? ______
  Think: 10 groups of 10 or 10×10
- How many hundreds are in 1,000? ______
  Think: 10 groups of 100 or $10 \times (10 \times 10)$
- How many thousands are in 10,000? ______

In the box at the right, draw a quick picture to show 10,000.

Use [T] for 1,000.

10,000 ones
$1 \times 10 \times 10 \times 10 \times 10$

10

So, $10 \times 1{,}000$ is 10 .

Example Multiply a whole number by a power of ten.

Hummingbirds beat their wings very fast. The smaller the hummingbird is, the faster its wings beat. The average hummingbird beats its wings about 3×10^3 times a minute. How many times a minute is that, written as a whole number?

Multiply 3 by powers of ten. Look for a pattern.

$3 \times 10^0 = 3 \times 1 =$ ____________

$3 \times 10^1 = 3 \times 10 =$ ____________

$3 \times 10^2 = 3 \times 10 \times 10 =$ ____________

$3 \times 10^3 = 3 \times 10 \times 10 \times 10 =$ ____________

So, the average hummingbird beats its wings about ____________ times a minute.

MATHEMATICAL PRACTICES

Math Talk Explain how using an exponent simplifies an expression.

- What pattern do you see?

____

____

Share and Show

Write in exponent form and word form.

1. 10×10

Exponent form: ____________

Word form: ____________

2. $10 \times 10 \times 10 \times 10$

Exponent form: ____________

Word form: ____________

Find the value.

3. 10^2 ____________

4. 4×10^2 ____________

5. 7×10^3 ____________

Name ______________________

On Your Own

Write in exponent form and word form.

6. $10 \times 10 \times 10$

exponent form: ______________

word form: ______________

____

7. $10 \times 10 \times 10 \times 10 \times 10$

exponent form: ______________

word form: ______________

____

Find the value.

8. 10^4

____

9. 2×10^3

____

10. 6×10^4

____

Complete the pattern.

11. $7 \times 10^0 = 7 \times 1 =$ ______________

$7 \times 10^1 = 7 \times 10 =$ ______________

$7 \times 10^2 = 7 \times 100 =$ ______________

$7 \times 10^3 = 7 \times 1{,}000 =$ ______________

$7 \times 10^4 = 7 \times 10{,}000 =$ ______________

12. $9 \times 10^0 =$ ______________ $= 9$

$9 \times 10^1 =$ ______________ $= 90$

$9 \times 10^2 =$ ______________ $= 900$

$9 \times 10^3 =$ ______________ $= 9{,}000$

$9 \times 10^4 =$ ______________ $= 90{,}000$

13. $12 \times 10^0 = 12 \times 1 =$ ______________

$12 \times 10^1 = 12 \times 10 =$ ______________

$12 \times 10^2 = 12 \times 100 =$ ______________

$12 \times 10^3 = 12 \times 1{,}000 =$ ______________

$12 \times 10^4 = 12 \times 10{,}000 =$ ______________

14. H.O.T. $10^3 = 10 \times 10^n$ What is the value of n?

Think: $10^3 = 10 \times$ ________ $\times$ ________,

or $10 \times$ ______________

The value of n is ______________.

15. Write Math ▶ **Explain** how to write 50,000 using exponents.

____

____

UNLOCK the Problem REAL WORLD

TEST PRACTICE

16. Lake Superior is the largest of the Great Lakes. It covers a surface area of about 30,000 square miles. How can you show the estimated area of Lake Superior as a whole number multiplied by a power of ten?

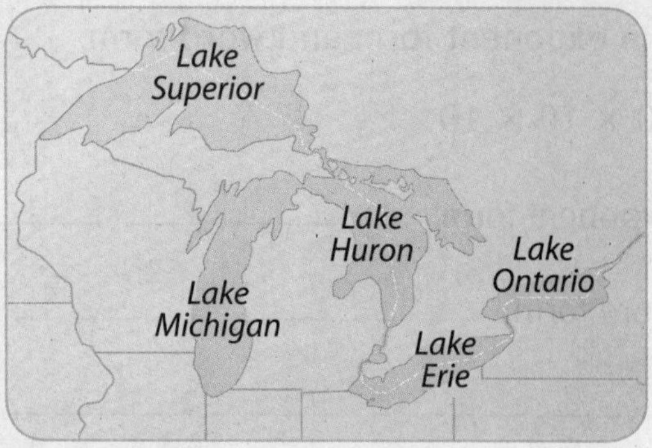

Ⓐ 3×10^2 sq mi
Ⓑ 3×10^3 sq mi
Ⓒ 3×10^4 sq mi
Ⓓ 3×10^5 sq mi

a. What are you asked to find?

____

b. How can you use a pattern to find the answer?

____

c. Write a pattern using the whole number 3 and powers of ten.

$3 \times 10^0 = 3 \times 1 =$ ________

$3 \times 10^1 = 3 \times 10 =$ ________

$3 \times 10^2 =$ ________ $=$ ________

$3 \times 10^3 =$ ________ $=$ ________

$3 \times 10^4 =$ ________ $=$ ________

d. Fill in the correct answer choice above.

17. The Earth's diameter through the equator is about 8,000 miles. What is the Earth's estimated diameter written as a whole number multiplied by a power of ten?

Ⓐ 8×10^1 miles
Ⓑ 8×10^2 miles
Ⓒ 8×10^3 miles
Ⓓ 8×10^4 miles

18. The Earth's circumference around the equator is about 25×10^3 miles. What is the Earth's estimated circumference written as a whole number?

Ⓐ 250,000 miles
Ⓑ 25,000 miles
Ⓒ 2,500 miles
Ⓓ 250 miles

FOR MORE PRACTICE:
Standards Practice Book

Name ______________________________

Multiplication Patterns

Essential Question How can you use a basic fact and a pattern to multiply by a 2-digit number?

COMMON CORE STANDARD **CC.5.NBT.2**
Understand the place value system.

UNLOCK the Problem REAL WORLD

How close have you been to a bumblebee?

The actual length of a queen bumblebee is about 20 millimeters. The photograph shows part of a bee under a microscope, at 10 times its actual size. What would the length of the bee appear to be at a magnification of 300 times its actual size?

Use a basic fact and a pattern.

Multiply. 300×20

$3 \times 2 = 6$ ← basic fact

$30 \times 2 = (3 \times 2) \times 10^1 = 60$

$300 \times 2 = (3 \times 2) \times 10^2 =$ __________

$300 \times 20 = (3 \times 2) \times (100 \times 10) = 6 \times 10^3 =$ __________

So, the length of the bee would appear to be

about __________ millimeters.

MATHEMATICAL PRACTICES

Math Talk What pattern do you see in the number sentences and the exponents?

- What would the length of the bee shown in the photograph appear to be if the microscope shows it at 10 times its actual size?

____

Example Use mental math and a pattern.

Multiply. $50 \times 8{,}000$

$5 \times 8 = 40$ ← basic fact

$5 \times 80 = (5 \times 8) \times 10^1 = 400$

$5 \times 800 = (5 \times 8) \times 10^2 =$ __________

$50 \times 800 = (5 \times 8) \times (10 \times 100) = 40 \times 10^3 =$ __________

$50 \times 8{,}000 = (5 \times 8) \times (10 \times 1{,}000) = 40 \times 10^4 =$ __________

Share and Show

Use mental math and a pattern to find the product.

1. $30 \times 4{,}000 =$ ______

- What basic fact can you use to help you find $30 \times 4{,}000$? ______

Use mental math to complete the pattern.

2. $1 \times 1 = 1$

$1 \times 10^1 =$ ______

$1 \times 10^2 =$ ______

$1 \times 10^3 =$ ______

3. $7 \times 8 = 56$

$(7 \times 8) \times 10^1 =$ ______

$(7 \times 8) \times 10^2 =$ ______

$(7 \times 8) \times 10^3 =$ ______

4. $6 \times 5 =$ ______

$(6 \times 5) \times$ ______ $= 300$

$(6 \times 5) \times$ ______ $= 3{,}000$

$(6 \times 5) \times$ ______ $= 30{,}000$

MATHEMATICAL PRACTICES

Math Talk Explain how to find $50 \times 9{,}000$ by using a basic fact and pattern.

On Your Own

Use mental math to complete the pattern.

5. $9 \times 5 = 45$

$(9 \times 5) \times 10^1 =$ ______

$(9 \times 5) \times 10^2 =$ ______

$(9 \times 5) \times 10^3 =$ ______

6. $3 \times 7 = 21$

$(3 \times 7) \times 10^1 =$ ______

$(3 \times 7) \times 10^2 =$ ______

$(3 \times 7) \times 10^3 =$ ______

7. $5 \times 4 =$ ______

$(5 \times 4) \times$ ______ $= 200$

$(5 \times 4) \times$ ______ $= 2{,}000$

$(5 \times 4) \times$ ______ $= 20{,}000$

8. $5 \times 7 =$ ______

$(5 \times 7) \times$ ______ $= 350$

$(5 \times 7) \times$ ______ $= 3{,}500$

$(5 \times 7) \times$ ______ $= 35{,}000$

9. $4 \times 2 = 8$

$(4 \times 2) \times 10^2 =$ ______

$(4 \times 2) \times 10^3 =$ ______

$(4 \times 2) \times 10^4 =$ ______

10. $6 \times 7 = 42$

$(6 \times 7) \times 10^2 =$ ______

$(6 \times 7) \times 10^3 =$ ______

$(6 \times 7) \times 10^4 =$ ______

Use mental math and a pattern to find the product.

11. $(6 \times 6) \times 10^1 =$ ______

12. $(7 \times 4) \times 10^3 =$ ______

13. $(9 \times 8) \times 10^2 =$ ______

14. $(4 \times 3) \times 10^2 =$ ______

15. $(2 \times 5) \times 10^3 =$ ______

16. $(2 \times 8) \times 10^2 =$ ______

17. $(6 \times 5) \times 10^3 =$ ______

18. $(8 \times 8) \times 10^4 =$ ______

19. $(7 \times 8) \times 10^4 =$ ______

Name ______________________

Use mental math to complete the table.

20. 1 roll = 50 dimes **Think:** 50 dimes per roll × 20 rolls = (5 × 2) × (10 × 10)

Rolls	20	30	40	50	60	70	80	90	100
Dimes	10×10^2								

21. 1 roll = 40 quarters **Think:** 40 quarters per roll × 20 rolls = (4 × 2) × (10 × 10)

Rolls	20	30	40	50	60	70	80	90	100
Quarters	8×10^2								

	×	**6**	**70**	**800**	**9,000**
22.	**80**			64×10^3	
23.	**90**				81×10^4

Problem Solving REAL WORLD

Use the table for 24–26.

Arthropod Lengths

Arthropod	Length (in millimeters)
Cluster Fly	9
Crab Spider	5
Fire Ant	4
Tree Hopper	6

24. **What if** you magnified the image of a cluster fly by 9×10^3? What would the length appear to be?

____

25. If you magnified the image of a fire ant by 4×10^3 and a tree hopper by 3×10^3, which insect would appear longer? How much longer?

____

26. H.O.T. John wants to magnify the image of a fire ant and a crab spider so they appear to be the same length. How many times their actual sizes would he need to magnify each image?

____

____

SHOW YOUR WORK

27. H.O.T. What does the product of any whole-number factor multiplied by 100 always have? **Explain.**

28. Test Practice How many zeros are in the product $(5 \times 4) \times 10^4$?

Ⓐ 3

Ⓑ 4

Ⓒ 5

Ⓓ 6

Connect to Health

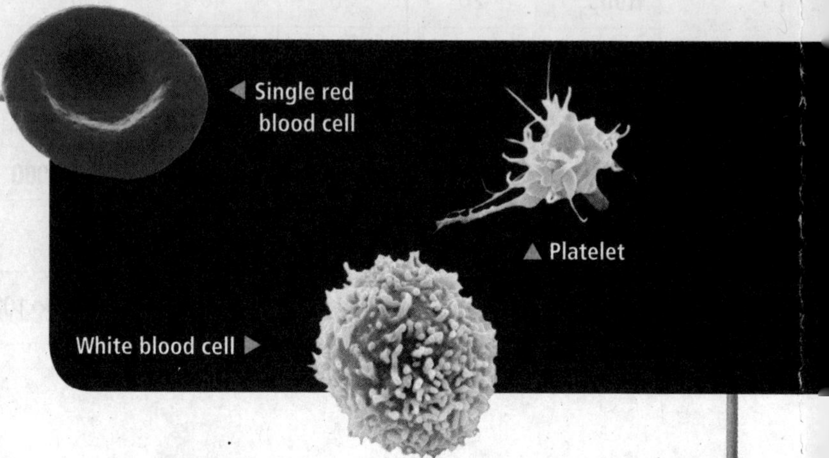

Blood Cells

Blood is necessary for all human life. It contains red blood cells and white blood cells that nourish and cleanse the body, and platelets that stop bleeding. The average adult has about 5 liters of blood.

Use patterns and mental math to solve.

29. A human body has about 30 times as many platelets as white blood cells. A small sample of blood has 8×10^3 white blood cells. About how many platelets are in the sample?

30. Basophils and monocytes are types of white blood cells. A blood sample has about 5 times as many monocytes as basophils. If there are 60 basophils in the sample, about how many monocytes are there?

31. Lymphocytes and eosinophils are types of white blood cells. A blood sample has about 10 times as many lymphocytes as eosinophils. If there are 2×10^2 eosinophils in the sample, about how many lymphocytes are there?

32. H.O.T. An average person has 6×10^2 times as many red bloods cells as white blood cells. A small sample of blood has 7×10^3 white blood cells. About how many red blood cells are in the sample?

Name ______________________________

Multiplication Patterns with Decimals

Essential Question How can patterns help you place the decimal point in a product?

COMMON CORE STANDARD CC.5.NBT.2
Understand the place value system.

UNLOCK the Problem REAL WORLD

Cindy is combining equal-sized rectangles from different fabric patterns to make a postage-stamp quilt. Each rectangle has an area of 0.75 of a square inch. If she uses 1,000 rectangles to make the quilt, what will be the area of the quilt?

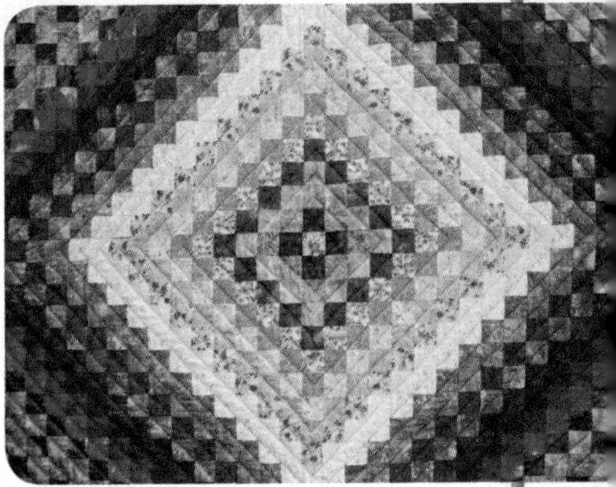

Use the pattern to find the product.

$1 \times 0.75 = 0.75$

$10 \times 0.75 = 7.5$

$100 \times 0.75 = 75.$

$1{,}000 \times 0.75 = 750.$

The quilt will have an area of ____________ square inches.

1. As you multiply by increasing powers of 10, how does the position of the decimal point change in the product? ______________________________

____

Place value patterns can be used to find the product of a number and the decimals 0.1 and 0.01.

Example 1

Jorge is making a scale model of the Willis Tower in Chicago for a theater set. The height of the tower is 1,353 feet. If the model is $\frac{1}{100}$ of the actual size of the building, how tall is the model?

$1 \times 1{,}353 = 1{,}353$

$0.1 \times 1{,}353 = 135.3$

$0.01 \times 1{,}353 =$ ____ ← $\frac{1}{100}$ of 1,353

Jorge's model of the Willis Tower is ____________ feet tall.

- What fraction of the actual size of the building is the model?

____

- Write the fraction a decimal.

____

2. As you multiply by decreasing powers of 10, how does the position of the decimal point change in the product?

____

____

Example 2

Three friends are selling items at an arts and crafts fair. Josey makes \$45.75 selling jewelry. Mark makes 100 times as much as Josey makes by selling his custom furniture. Chance makes a tenth of the money Mark makes by selling paintings. How much money does each friend make?

Josey: \$45.75

Mark: ______ × \$45.75

Think: 1 × \$45.75 = ______

10 × \$45.75 = ______

100 × \$45.75 = ______

Chance: ______ × ______

Think: 1 × ______ = ______

______ × ______ = ______

So, Josey makes \$45.75, Mark makes ______,

and Chance makes ______.

Try This! Complete the pattern.

A $10^0 \times 4.78 =$ ______

$10^1 \times 4.78 =$ ______

$10^2 \times 4.78 =$ ______

$10^3 \times 4.78 =$ ______

B $38 \times 1 =$ ______

$38 \times 0.1 =$ ______

$38 \times 0.01 =$ ______

Share and Show

Complete the pattern.

1. $10^0 \times 17.04 = 17.04$

$10^1 \times 17.04 = 170.4$

$10^2 \times 17.04 = 1{,}704$

$10^3 \times 17.04 =$ ______

Think: The decimal point moves one place to the ______ for each increasing power of 10.

Name ______________________

Complete the pattern.

2. $1 \times 3.19 =$ ______

$10 \times 3.19 =$ ______

$100 \times 3.19 =$ ______

$1{,}000 \times 3.19 =$ ______

3. $45.6 \times 10^0 =$ ______

$45.6 \times 10^1 =$ ______

$45.6 \times 10^2 =$ ______

$45.6 \times 10^3 =$ ______

4. $1 \times 6{,}391 =$ ______

$0.1 \times 6{,}391 =$ ______

$0.01 \times 6{,}391 =$ ______

MATHEMATICAL PRACTICES

Math Talk Explain how you know that when you multiply the product of 10 × 34.1 by 0.1, the result will be 34.1.

On Your Own

Complete the pattern.

5. $1.06 \times 1 =$ ______

$1.06 \times 10 =$ ______

$1.06 \times 100 =$ ______

$1.06 \times 1{,}000 =$ ______

6. $1 \times 90 =$ ______

$0.1 \times 90 =$ ______

$0.01 \times 90 =$ ______

7. $10^0 \times \$0.19 =$ ______

$10^1 \times \$0.19 =$ ______

$10^2 \times \$0.19 =$ ______

$10^3 \times \$0.19 =$ ______

8. $580 \times 1 =$ ______

$580 \times 0.1 =$ ______

$580 \times 0.01 =$ ______

9. $10^0 \times 80.72 =$ ______

$10^1 \times 80.72 =$ ______

$10^2 \times 80.72 =$ ______

$10^3 \times 80.72 =$ ______

10. $1 \times 7{,}230 =$ ______

$0.1 \times 7{,}230 =$ ______

$0.01 \times 7{,}230 =$ ______

H.O.T. **Algebra** **Find the value of *n*.**

11. $n \times \$3.25 = \$325.00$

$n =$ ______

12. $0.1 \times n = 89.5$

$n =$ ______

13. $10^3 \times n = 630$

$n =$ ______

Problem Solving REAL WORLD

H.O.T. What's the Error?

14. Kirsten is making lanyards for a convention. She needs to make 1,000 lanyards and knows that 1 lanyard uses 1.75 feet of cord. How much cord will Kirsten need?

Kirsten's work is shown below.

$1 \times 1.75 = 1.75$

$10 \times 1.75 = 10.75$

$100 \times 1.75 = 100.75$

$1{,}000 \times 1.75 = 1{,}000.75$

Find and describe Kirsten's error.

Solve the problem using the correct pattern.

So, Kirsten needs ____________ feet of cord to make 1,000 lanyards.

- **Describe** how Kirsten could have solved the problem without writing out the pattern needed.

Name ______________________

Division Patterns with Decimals

Essential Question How can patterns help you place the decimal point in a quotient?

COMMON CORE STANDARD CC.5.NBT.2
Understand the place value system.

UNLOCK the Problem REAL WORLD

The Healthy Wheat Bakery uses 560 pounds of flour to make 1,000 loaves of bread. Each loaf contains the same amount of flour. How many pounds of flour are used in each loaf of bread?

- Underline the sentence that tells you what you are trying to find.
- Circle the numbers you need to use.

You can use powers of ten to help you find quotients. Dividing by a power of 10 is the same as multiplying by 0.1, 0.01, or 0.001.

One Way Use place-value patterns.

Divide. $560 \div 1{,}000$

Look for a pattern in these products and quotients.

$560 \times 1 = 560$	$560 \div 1 = 560$
$560 \times 0.1 = 56.0$	$560 \div 10 = 56.0$
$560 \times 0.01 = 5.60$	$560 \div 100 = 5.60$
$560 \times 0.001 = 0.560$	$560 \div 1{,}000 = 0.560$

So, _______ pound of flour is used in each loaf of bread.

1. As you divide by increasing powers of 10, how does the position of the decimal point change in the quotients?

____

Another Way Use exponents.

Divide. $560 \div 10^3$

Look for a pattern.

$560 \div 10^0 = 560$

$560 \div 10^1 = 56.0$

$560 \div 10^2 = 5.60$

$560 \div 10^3 =$ _______

Remember

The zero power of 10 equals 1.

$10^0 = 1$

The first power of 10 equals 10.

$10^1 = 10$

2. Each divisor, or power of 10, is 10 times the divisor before it. How do the quotients compare?

____

CONNECT Dividing by 10 is the same as multiplying by 0.1 or finding $\frac{1}{10}$ of a number.

Example

Liang used 25.5 pounds of tomatoes to make a large batch of salsa. He used one-tenth as many pounds of onions as pounds of tomatoes. He used one-hundredth as many pounds of green peppers as pounds of tomatoes. How many pounds of each ingredient did Liang use?

Tomatoes: 25.5 pounds

Onions: 25.5 pounds ÷ ______

Think: $25.5 \div 1 =$ ______

$25.5 \div 10 =$ ______

Green Peppers: 25.5 pounds ÷ ______

Think: ______ $\div 1 =$ ______

______ $\div 10 =$ ______

______ $\div 100 =$ ______

So, Liang used 25.5 pounds of tomatoes, ______ pounds of onions,

and ______ pound of green peppers.

Try This! Complete the pattern.

A $32.6 \div 1 =$ ______

$32.6 \div 10 =$ ______

$32.6 \div 100 =$ ______

B $50.2 \div 10^0 =$ ______

$50.2 \div 10^1 =$ ______

$50.2 \div 10^2 =$ ______

MATHEMATICAL PRACTICES

Math Talk Explain how you can determine where to place the decimal point in the quotient $47.3 \div 10^2$.

Share and Show

Complete the pattern.

1. $456 \div 10^0 = 456$

$456 \div 10^1 = 45.6$

$456 \div 10^2 = 4.56$

$456 \div 10^3 =$ ______

Think: The dividend is being divided by an increasing power of 10, so the decimal point will move to the ______ one place for each increasing power of 10.

Name ______________________

Complete the pattern.

2. $225 \div 10^0 =$ ______

$225 \div 10^1 =$ ______

$225 \div 10^2 =$ ______

$225 \div 10^3 =$ ______

3. $605 \div 10^0 =$ ______

$605 \div 10^1 =$ ______

$605 \div 10^2 =$ ______

$605 \div 10^3 =$ ______

4. $74.3 \div 1 =$ ______

$74.3 \div 10 =$ ______

$74.3 \div 100 =$ ______

MATHEMATICAL PRACTICES

Math Talk **Explain** what happens to the value of a number when you divide by 10, 100, or 1,000.

On Your Own

Complete the pattern.

5. $156 \div 1 =$ ______

$156 \div 10 =$ ______

$156 \div 100 =$ ______

$156 \div 1{,}000 =$ ______

6. $32 \div 1 =$ ______

$32 \div 10 =$ ______

$32 \div 100 =$ ______

$32 \div 1{,}000 =$ ______

7. $16 \div 10^0 =$ ______

$16 \div 10^1 =$ ______

$16 \div 10^2 =$ ______

$16 \div 10^3 =$ ______

8. $12.7 \div 1 =$ ______

$12.7 \div 10 =$ ______

$12.7 \div 100 =$ ______

9. $92.5 \div 10^0 =$ ______

$92.5 \div 10^1 =$ ______

$92.5 \div 10^2 =$ ______

10. $86.3 \div 10^0 =$ ______

$86.3 \div 10^1 =$ ______

$86.3 \div 10^2 =$ ______

H.O.T. **Algebra** **Find the value of *n*.**

11. $268 \div n = 0.268$

$n =$ ______________

12. $n \div 10^2 = 0.123$

$n =$ ______________

13. $n \div 10^1 = 4.6$

$n =$ ______________

Problem Solving REAL WORLD

Use the table to solve 14–16.

Dry Ingredients for 1,000 Corn Muffins	
Ingredient	**Number of Kilograms**
Cornmeal	150
Flour	110
Sugar	66.7
Baking powder	10
Salt	4.17

14. If each muffin contains the same amount of cornmeal, how many kilograms of cornmeal are in each corn muffin?

____

15. H.O.T. If each muffin contains the same amount of sugar, how many kilograms of sugar, to the nearest thousandth, are in each corn muffin?

____

16. H.O.T. The bakery decides to make only 100 corn muffins on Tuesday. How many kilograms of sugar will be needed?

____

SHOW YOUR WORK

17. Write Math **Explain** how you know that the quotient $47.3 \div 10^1$ is equal to the product 47.3×0.1.

____

____

____

____

____

18. Test Practice Ella used 37.2 pounds of apples to make applesauce. She used one-tenth as many pounds of sugar as pounds of apples. How many pounds of sugar did Ella use?

Ⓐ 372 pounds

Ⓑ 3.72 pounds

Ⓒ 0.372 pound

Ⓓ 0.0372 pound

 FOR MORE PRACTICE: Standards Practice Book

Name ______________________________

Place Value of Decimals

Essential Question How do you read, write, and represent decimals through thousandths?

COMMON CORE STANDARD CC.5.NBT.3a
Understand the place value system.

UNLOCK the Problem REAL WORLD

The Brooklyn Battery Tunnel in New York City is 1.726 miles long. It is the longest underwater tunnel for vehicles in the United States. To understand this distance, you need to understand the place value of each digit in 1.726.

▲ The Brooklyn Battery Tunnel passes under the East River.

You can use a place-value chart to understand decimals. Whole numbers are to the left of the decimal point. Decimals are to the right of the decimal point. The thousandths place is to the right of the hundredths place.

Tens	Ones	Tenths	Hundredths	Thousandths	
	1 •	7	2	6	
1	1×1	$7 \times \frac{1}{10}$	$2 \times \frac{1}{100}$	$6 \times \frac{1}{1,000}$	Value
	1.0	0.7	0.02	0.006	

The place value of the digit 6 in 1.726 is thousandths. The value of 6 in 1.726 is $6 \times \frac{1}{1,000}$, or 0.006.

Standard Form: 1.726

Word Form: one and seven hundred twenty-six thousandths

Expanded Form: $1 \times 1 + 7 \times \left(\frac{1}{10}\right) + 2 \times \left(\frac{1}{100}\right) + 6 \times \left(\frac{1}{1,000}\right)$

Math Talk MATHEMATICAL PRACTICES Explain how the value of the last digit in a decimal can help you read a decimal.

Try This! Use place value to read and write decimals.

A **Standard Form:** 2.35
Word Form: two and ______________________

Expanded Form: $2 \times 1 +$ ______________________

B **Standard Form:** ____________
Word Form: three and six hundred fourteen thousandths

Expanded Form: ____________ $+ 6 \times \left(\frac{1}{10}\right) +$ ____________ $+$ ____________

Example Use a place-value chart.

The silk spun by a common garden spider is about 0.003 millimeter thick. A commonly used sewing thread is about 0.3 millimeter thick. How does the thickness of the spider silk and the thread compare?

STEP 1 Write the numbers in a place-value chart.

Ones	Tenths	Hundredths	Thousandths
.			
.			

STEP 2

Count the number of decimal place-value positions to the digit 3 in 0.3 and 0.003.

0.3 has ______ fewer decimal places than 0.003

2 fewer decimal places: $10 \times 10 =$ ______

0.3 is ______ times as much as 0.003

0.003 is ______ of 0.3

So, the thread is ______ times as thick as the garden spider's silk. The thickness of the garden spider's silk is ______ that of the thread.

You can use place-value patterns to rename a decimal.

Try This! Use place-value patterns.

Rename 0.3 using other place values.

0.300	3 tenths	$3 \times \frac{1}{10}$
0.300	______ hundredths	______ $\times \frac{1}{100}$
0.300	______	______

Name ______________________________

Share and Show

1. Complete the place-value chart to find the value of each digit.

Ones	Tenths	Hundredths	Thousandths
3 •	5	2	4

3×1		$2 \times \frac{1}{100}$		Value
	0.5			

Write the value of the underlined digit.

2. $0.5\underline{4}3$ ______

3. $6.\underline{2}34$ ______

4. $3.95\underline{4}$ ______

Write the number in two other forms.

5. 0.253

______
______
______

6. 7.632

______
______
______

On Your Own

Write the value of the underlined digit.

7. $0.4\underline{9}6$ ______

8. $2.\underline{7}26$ ______

9. $1.06\underline{6}$ ______

10. $6.\underline{3}99$ ______

11. $0.00\underline{2}$ ______

12. $14.37\underline{1}$ ______

Write the number in two other forms.

13. 0.489

______
______
______

14. 5.916

______
______
______

Problem Solving REAL WORLD

Use the table for 15–17.

Average Annual Rainfall (in meters)	
California	0.564
New Mexico	0.372
New York	1.041
Wisconsin	0.820
Maine	

15. What is the value of the digit 7 in New Mexico's average annual rainfall?

16. The average annual rainfall in Maine is one and seventy-four thousandths of a meter per year. Complete the table by writing that amount in standard form.

17. Which of the states has an average annual rainfall with the least number in the thousandths place?

SHOW YOUR WORK

18. H.O.T. **What's the Error?** Damian wrote the number four and twenty-three thousandths as 4.23. **Describe** and correct his error.

19. Write Math **Explain** how you know that the digit 6 in the numbers 3.675 and 3.756 does not have the same value.

20. **Test Practice** In 24.736, which digit is in the thousandths place?

Ⓐ 3 Ⓒ 6

Ⓑ 4 Ⓓ 7

 FOR MORE PRACTICE: Standards Practice Book

Name ______________________________

Multiply by 1-Digit Numbers

Essential Question How do you multiply by 1-digit numbers?

COMMON CORE STANDARD **CC.5.NBT.5**
Perform operations with multi–digit whole numbers and with decimals to hundredths.

UNLOCK the Problem REAL WORLD

Each day an airline flies 9 commercial jets from New York to London, England. Each plane holds 293 passengers. If every seat is taken on all flights, how many people fly on this airline from New York to London in 1 day?

▲ **The Queen's Guard protects Britain's Royal Family and their residences.**

Use place value and regrouping.

STEP 1 Estimate: 293 × 9

Think: 300 × 9 = ______________

STEP 2 Multiply the ones.

$$\begin{array}{r} {}^{2} \\ 293 \\ \times \quad 9 \\ \hline 7 \end{array}$$

9 × 3 ones = ________ ones

Write the ones and the regrouped tens.

STEP 3 Multiply the tens.

$$\begin{array}{r} {}^{82} \\ 293 \\ \times \quad 9 \\ \hline 37 \end{array}$$

9 × 9 tens = ________ tens

Add the regrouped tens.

________ tens + 2 tens = ________ tens

Write the tens and the regrouped hundreds.

STEP 4 Multiply the hundreds.

$$\begin{array}{r} {}^{82} \\ 293 \\ \times \quad 9 \\ \hline 2{,}637 \end{array}$$

9 × 2 hundreds = ________ hundreds

Add the regrouped hundreds.

________ hundreds + 8 hundreds = ________ hundreds

Write the hundreds.

So, in 1 day, ______________ passengers fly from New York to London.

MATHEMATICAL PRACTICES

Math Talk Explain how you record the 27 ones when you multiply 3 by 9 in Step 2.

- How can you tell if your answer is reasonable? ______________________________

____

Example

A commercial airline makes several flights each week from New York to Paris, France. If the airline serves 1,978 meals on its flights each day, how many meals are served for the entire week?

▲ **The Eiffel Tower in Paris, France, built for the 1889 World's Fair, was the world's tallest man-made structure for 40 years.**

To multiply a greater number by a 1-digit number, repeat the process of multiplying and regrouping until every place value is multiplied.

STEP 1 Estimate. 1,978 × 7

Think: 2,000 × 7 = ________

STEP 2 Multiply the ones.

$$\begin{array}{r} {}^{5} \\ 1{,}978 \\ \times\ \ \ 7 \\ \hline 6 \end{array}$$

7 × 8 ones = ______ ones

Write the ones and the regrouped tens.

STEP 3 Multiply the tens.

$$\begin{array}{r} {}^{55} \\ 1{,}978 \\ \times\ \ \ 7 \\ \hline 46 \end{array}$$

7 × 7 tens = ______ tens

Add the regrouped tens.

______ tens + 5 tens = ______ tens

Write the tens and the regrouped hundreds.

STEP 4 Multiply the hundreds.

$$\begin{array}{r} {}^{6\,55} \\ 1{,}978 \\ \times\ \ \ 7 \\ \hline 846 \end{array}$$

7 × 9 hundreds = ______ hundreds

Add the regrouped hundreds.

______ hundreds + 5 hundreds = ______ hundreds

Write the hundreds and the regrouped thousands.

STEP 5 Multiply the thousands.

$$\begin{array}{r} {}^{6\,55} \\ 1{,}978 \\ \times\ \ \ 7 \\ \hline 13{,}846 \end{array}$$

7 × 1 thousand = ______ thousands

Add the regrouped thousands.

______ thousands + 6 thousands = ______ thousands

Write the thousands. Compare your answer to the estimate to see if it is reasonable.

So, in 1 week, ____________ meals are served on flights from New York to Paris.

Name ______________________________

Share and Show

Complete to find the product.

1. 6×796 **Estimate:** $6 \times$ ________ = ________

$$\begin{array}{r} 796 \\ \times \quad 6 \\ \hline \end{array}$$

Multiply the ones and regroup.

$$\begin{array}{r} {}^{3} \\ 796 \\ \times \quad 6 \\ \hline 6 \end{array}$$

Multiply the tens and add the regrouped tens. Regroup.

$$\begin{array}{r} {}^{53} \\ 796 \\ \times \quad 6 \\ \hline 76 \end{array}$$

Multiply the hundreds and add the regrouped hundreds.

Estimate. Then find the product.

2. Estimate: ________

$$\begin{array}{r} 608 \\ \times \quad 8 \\ \hline \end{array}$$

3. Estimate: ________

$$\begin{array}{r} 556 \\ \times \quad 4 \\ \hline \end{array}$$

4. Estimate: ________

$$\begin{array}{r} 1,925 \\ \times \quad 7 \\ \hline \end{array}$$

On Your Own

Estimate. Then find the product.

5. Estimate: ________

$$\begin{array}{r} 794 \\ \times \quad 3 \\ \hline \end{array}$$

6. Estimate: ________

$$\begin{array}{r} 822 \\ \times \quad 6 \\ \hline \end{array}$$

7. Estimate: ________

$$\begin{array}{r} 3,102 \\ \times \quad 5 \\ \hline \end{array}$$

H.O.T. Algebra Solve for the unknown number.

8.

$$\begin{array}{r} 396 \\ \times \quad 6 \\ \hline 2,3\square 6 \end{array}$$

9.

$$\begin{array}{r} 5,12\square \\ \times \quad 8 \\ \hline \square\square 16 \end{array}$$

10.

$$\begin{array}{r} 8,5\square 6 \\ \times \quad 7 \\ \hline 60,03\square \end{array}$$

Practice: Copy and Solve Estimate. Then find the product.

11. 116×3 **12.** 338×4 **13.** 6×219 **14.** 7×456

15. $5 \times 1,012$ **16.** $2,921 \times 3$ **17.** $8,813 \times 4$ **18.** $9 \times 3,033$

Problem Solving REAL WORLD

H.O.T. What's the Error?

19. The Plattsville Glee Club is sending 8 of its members to a singing contest in Cincinnati, Ohio. The cost will be $588 per person. How much will it cost for the entire group of 8 students to attend?

Both Brian and Jermaine solve the problem. Brian says the answer is $40,074. Jermaine's answer is $4,604.

Estimate the cost. A reasonable estimate is __________.

Although Jermaine's answer seems reasonable, neither Brian nor Jermaine solved the problem correctly. Find the errors in Brian's and Jermaine's work. Then, solve the problem correctly.

Brian

```
        6
    $ 5 8 8
    ×     8
$ 4 0, 7 0 4
```

Jermaine

```
      6 6
  $ 5 8 8
  ×     8
$ 4, 6 0 4
```

Correct Answer

(blank grid)

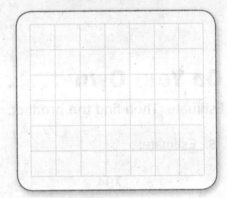

- What error did Brian make? **Explain.** ____________________

____

____

- What error did Jermaine make? **Explain.** ____________________

____

- How could you predict that Jermaine's answer might be incorrect using your estimate? ____________________

____

____

Name ______________________________

Multiply by 2-Digit Numbers

Essential Question How do you multiply by 2-digit numbers?

COMMON CORE STANDARD CC.5.NBT.5
Perform operations with multi-digit whole numbers and with decimals to hundredths.

UNLOCK the Problem REAL WORLD

A tiger can eat as much as 40 pounds of food at a time but it may go for several days without eating anything. Suppose a Siberian tiger in the wild eats an average of 18 pounds of food per day. How much food will the tiger eat in 28 days if he eats that amount each day?

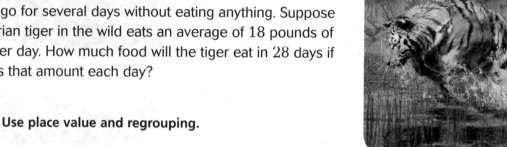

Use place value and regrouping.

STEP 1 Estimate: 28×18

Think: $30 \times 20 =$ ________

STEP 2 Multiply by the ones.

$$\begin{array}{r} 28 \\ \times\ 18 \\ \hline \end{array}$$

28×8 ones = ______ ones

STEP 3 Multiply by the tens.

$$\begin{array}{r} 28 \\ \times\ 18 \\ \hline \end{array}$$

28×1 ten = ______ tens, or ______ ones

STEP 4 Add the partial products.

$$\begin{array}{r} 28 \\ \times\ 18 \\ \hline \\ + \qquad \\ \hline \end{array}$$

← 28×8

← 28×10

So, on average, a Siberian tiger may eat __________ pounds of food in 28 days.

Remember

Use patterns of zeros to find the product of multiples of 10.

$3 \times 4 = 12$

$3 \times 40 = 120$ $\quad$ $30 \times 40 = 1{,}200$

$3 \times 400 = 1{,}200$ $\quad$ $300 \times 40 = 12{,}000$

Example

A Siberian tiger sleeps as much as 18 hours a day, or 126 hours per week. About how many hours does a tiger sleep in a year? There are 52 weeks in one year.

STEP 1 **Estimate:** 126 × 52

Think: 100 × 50 = ______

STEP 2 Multiply by the ones.

$$\begin{array}{r} 126 \\ \times\ 52 \\ \hline \end{array}$$

126 × 2 ones = ______ ones

STEP 3 Multiply by the tens.

$$\begin{array}{r} 126 \\ \times\ 52 \\ \hline \end{array}$$

126 × 5 tens = ______ tens, or ______ ones

STEP 4 Add the partial products.

$$\begin{array}{r} 126 \\ \times\ 52 \\ \hline \end{array}$$

← 126 × 2

+ ← 126 × 50

So, a Siberian tiger sleeps about ______ hours in one year.

MATHEMATICAL PRACTICES

Math Talk Are there different numbers you could have used in Step 1 to find an estimate that is closer to the actual answer? **Explain.**

- When you multiply 126 and 5 tens in Step 3, why does its product have a zero in the ones place? **Explain.** ______

Name ________________________________

Share and Show

Complete to find the product.

1.

$$\begin{array}{r} 64 \\ \times\ 43 \\ \hline \end{array}$$

← 64 × ______

+ ← 64 × ______

2.

$$\begin{array}{r} 571 \\ \times\ 38 \\ \hline \end{array}$$

← 571 × ______

+ ← 571 × ______

Estimate. Then find the product.

3. Estimate: ______________

$$\begin{array}{r} 24 \\ \times\ 15 \\ \hline \end{array}$$

✓ 4. Estimate: ______________

$$\begin{array}{r} 37 \\ \times\ 63 \\ \hline \end{array}$$

✓ 5. Estimate: ______________

$$\begin{array}{r} 384 \\ \times\ 45 \\ \hline \end{array}$$

On Your Own

Estimate. Then find the product.

6. Estimate: ______________

$$\begin{array}{r} 28 \\ \times\ 22 \\ \hline \end{array}$$

7. Estimate: ______________

$$\begin{array}{r} 93 \\ \times\ 76 \\ \hline \end{array}$$

8. Estimate: ______________

$$\begin{array}{r} 295 \\ \times\ 51 \\ \hline \end{array}$$

Practice: Copy and Solve **Estimate. Then find the product.**

9. 54 × 31
10. 42 × 26
11. 38 × 64
12. 63 × 16
13. 204 × 41
14. 534 × 25
15. 722 × 39
16. 957 × 43

Problem Solving REAL WORLD

Use the table for 17–20.

17. How much sleep does a jaguar get in 1 year?

18. In 1 year, how many more hours of sleep does a giant armadillo get than a platypus?

19. H.O.T. Owl monkeys sleep during the day, waking about 15 minutes after sundown to find food. At midnight, they rest for an hour or two, then continue to feed until sunrise. They live about 27 years. How many hours of sleep does an owl monkey that lives 27 years get in its lifetime?

20. Three-toed sloths move very slowly, using as little energy as possible. They sleep, eat, and even give birth upside down. A baby sloth may cling to its mother for as much as 36 weeks after being born. How much of that time is the sloth asleep?

21. Test Practice A sloth's maximum speed on the ground is 15 feet in 1 minute. Even though it would be unlikely for a sloth to stay in motion for more than a few moments, how far would a sloth travel in 45 minutes at that speed?

Ⓐ 60 feet
Ⓑ 270 feet
Ⓒ 675 feet
Ⓓ 6,750 feet

Animal Sleep Amounts

Animal	Amount (usual hours per week)
Jaguar	77
Giant Armadillo	127
Owl Monkey	119
Platypus	98
Three-Toed Sloth	101

SHOW YOUR WORK

Name ______________________________

Relate Multiplication to Division

Essential Question How is multiplication used to solve a division problem?

COMMON CORE STANDARD CC.5.NBT.6
Perform operations with multi-digit whole numbers and with decimals to hundredths.

You can use the relationship between multiplication and division to solve a division problem. Using the same numbers, multiplication and division are opposite, or **inverse operations.**

3	×	8	=	24		24	÷	3	=	8
↑		↑		↑		↑		↑		↑
factor		factor		product		dividend		divisor		quotient

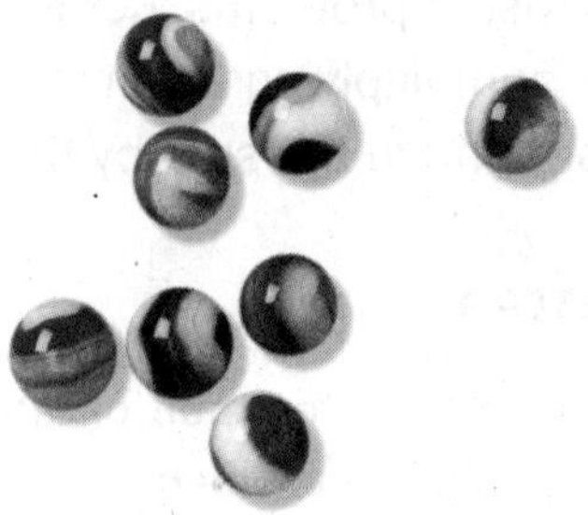

UNLOCK the Problem REAL WORLD

Joel and 5 friends collected 126 marbles. They shared the marbles equally. How many marbles will each person get?

- Underline the dividend.
- What is the divisor? ______

One Way Make an array.

- Outline a rectangular array on the grid to model 126 squares arranged in 6 rows of the same length. Shade each row a different color.

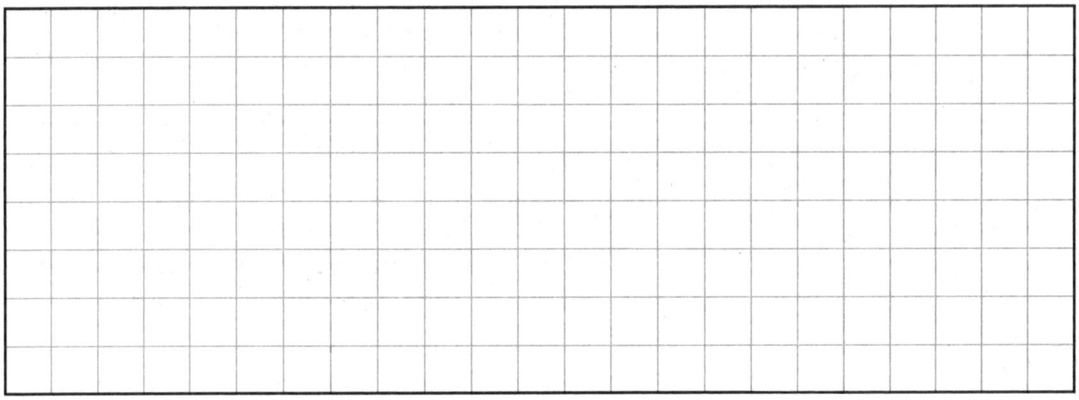

- How many squares are shaded in each row? ______
- Use the array to complete the multiplication sentence. Then, use the multiplication sentence to complete the division sentence.

6 × ______ = 126 126 ÷ 6 = ______

So, each of the 6 friends will get ______ marbles.

Another Way Use the Distributive Property.

Divide. 52 ÷ 4

You can use the Distributive Property and an area model to solve division problems. Remember that the Distributive Property states that multiplying a sum by a number is the same as multiplying each addend in the sum by the number and then adding the products.

STEP 1

Write a related multiplication sentence for the division problem.

Think: Use the divisor as a factor and the dividend as the product. The quotient will be the unknown factor.

52 ÷ 4 = ■

4 × ■ = 52

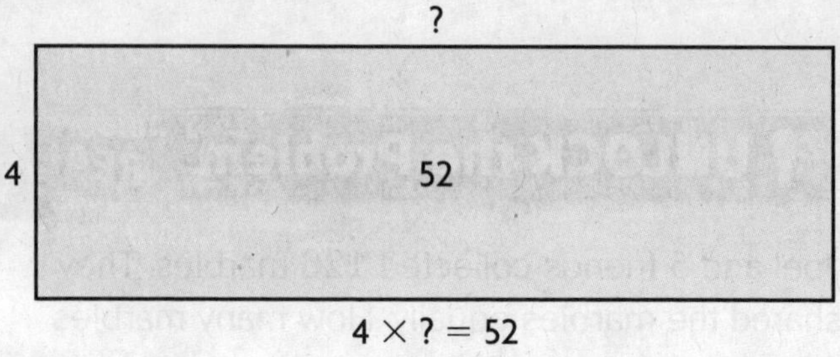

STEP 2

Use the Distributive Property to break apart the large area into smaller areas for partial products that you know.

(40 + 12) = 52

(4 × ____) + (4 × ____) = 52

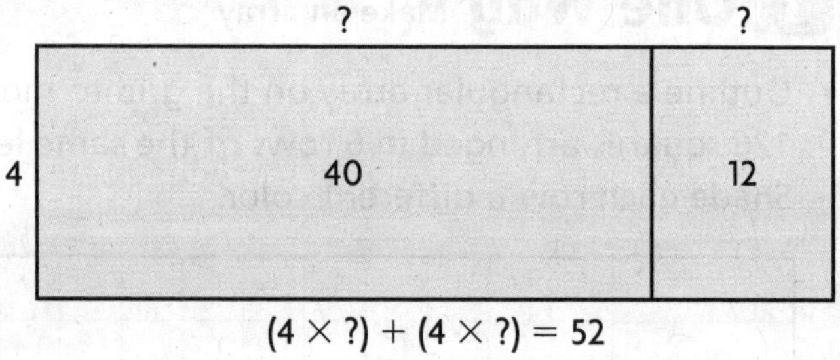

STEP 3

Find the sum of the unknown factors of the smaller areas.

____ + ____ = ____

STEP 4

Write the multiplication sentence with the unknown factor that you found. Then, use the multiplication sentence to find the quotient.

4 × ____ = 52

52 ÷ 4 = ____

- **Explain** how you can use the Distributive Property to find the quotient of 96 ÷ 8.

____

____

____

Name ________________________________

Share and Show

1. Brad has 72 toy cars that he puts into 4 equal groups. How many cars does Brad have in each group? Use the array to show your answer.

$4 \times$ _____ $= 72$ $72 \div 4 =$ _____

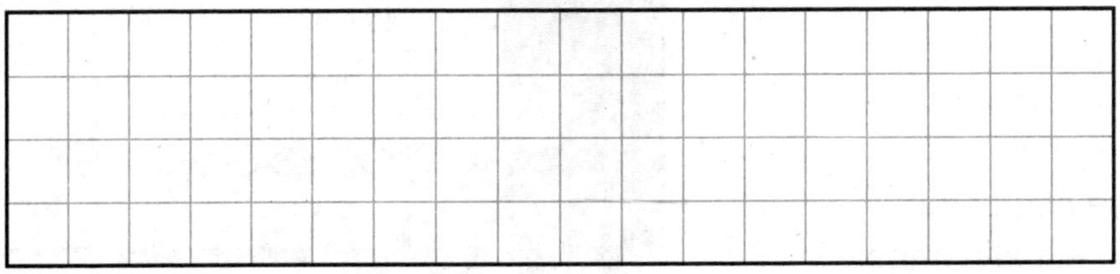

Use multiplication and the Distributive Property to find the quotient.

2. $108 \div 6 =$ _____

3. $84 \div 6 =$ _____

4. $184 \div 8 =$ _____

MATHEMATICAL PRACTICES

Math Talk Explain how using multiplication as the inverse operation helps you solve a division problem.

On Your Own

Use multiplication and the Distributive Property to find the quotient.

5. $60 \div 4 =$ _____

6. $144 \div 6 =$ _____

7. $252 \div 9 =$ _____

H.O.T. **Find each quotient. Then compare. Write <, >, or =.**

8. $51 \div 3$ ◯ $68 \div 4$

9. $252 \div 6$ ◯ $135 \div 3$

10. $110 \div 5$ ◯ $133 \div 7$

Problem Solving

Use the table to solve 11–13.

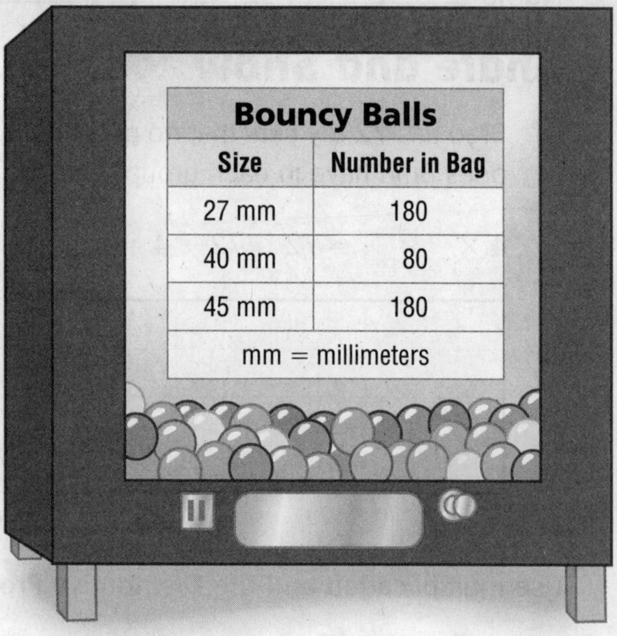

Bouncy Balls	
Size	**Number in Bag**
27 mm	180
40 mm	80
45 mm	180
mm = millimeters	

11. A group of 6 friends share a bag of the 45-millimeter bouncy balls equally among them. How many does each friend get?

____

12. H.O.T. Mr. Henderson has 2 bouncy-ball vending machines. He buys one bag of the 27-millimeter balls and one bag of the 40-millimeter balls. He puts an equal number of each in the 2 machines. How many bouncy balls does he put in each machine?

____

13. Lindsey buys a bag of each size of bouncy ball. She wants to put the same number of each size of bouncy ball into 5 party-favor bags. How many of each size of bouncy ball will she put in a bag?

____

14. **What's the Error?** Sandy writes $(4 \times 30) + (4 \times 2)$ and says the quotient for $128 \div 4$ is 8. Is she correct? **Explain.**

____

____

____

____

15. **Test Practice** Which of the following can be used to find $150 \div 6$?

Ⓐ $(6 \times 20) + (6 \times 5)$

Ⓑ $(6 \times 10) + (6 \times 5)$

Ⓒ $(2 \times 75) + (2 \times 3)$

Ⓓ $(6 \times 15) + (6 \times 5)$

SHOW YOUR WORK

Name ______________________________

Problem Solving • Multiplication and Division

Essential Question How can you use the strategy *solve a simpler problem* to help you solve a division problem?

COMMON CORE STANDARD CC.5.NBT.6
Perform operations with multi-digit whole numbers and with decimals to hundredths.

UNLOCK the Problem REAL WORLD

Mark works at an animal shelter. To feed 9 dogs, Mark empties eight 18-ounce cans of dog food into a large bowl. If he divides the food equally among the dogs, how many ounces of food will each dog get?

Use the graphic organizer below to help you solve the problem.

Read the Problem

What do I need to find?

I need to find ______________________________
______________________________.

What information do I need to use?

I need to use the number of ______________, the number of ______________ in each can, and the number of dogs that need to be fed.

How will I use the information?

I can ______________ to find the total number of ounces. Then I can solve a simpler problem to ______________ that total by 9.

Solve the Problem

- First, multiply to find the total number of ounces of dog food.

  $8 \times 18 =$ ______

- To find the number of ounces each dog gets, I'll need to divide.

  $144 \div$ ______ $=$ ■

- To find the quotient, I break 144 into two simpler numbers that are easier to divide.

$144 \div 9 =$ ■

$(90 +$ ______ $) \div 9 =$ ■

$($ ______ $\div 9) + ($ ______ $\div 9) =$ ■

______ $+ 6 =$ ______

So, each dog gets ______ ounces of food.

Try Another Problem

Michelle is building shelves for her room. She has a plank 137 inches long that she wants to cut into 7 shelves of equal length. The plank has jagged ends, so she will start by cutting 2 inches off each end. How long will each shelf be?

137 inches

Read the Problem	Solve the Problem
What do I need to find?	
What information do I need to use?	
How will I use the information?	

So, each shelf will be _____ inches long.

Math Talk MATHEMATICAL PRACTICES **Explain** how the strategy you used helped you solve the problem.

Name ______________________________

Tips

UNLOCK the Problem

✓ Underline what you need to find.

✓ Circle the numbers you need to use.

Share and Show

1. To make concrete mix, Monica pours 34 pounds of cement, 68 pounds of sand, 14 pounds of small pebbles, and 19 pounds of large pebbles into a large wheelbarrow. If she pours the mixture into 9 equal-size bags, how much will each bag weigh?

First, find the total weight of the mixture.

____

Then, divide the total by the number of bags. Break the total into two simpler numbers to make the division easier, if necessary.

Finally, find the quotient and solve the problem.

So, each bag will weigh ______ pounds.

2. **What if** Monica pours the mixture into 5 equal-size bags? How much will each bag weigh?

____

3. Taylor is building doghouses to sell. Each doghouse requires 3 full sheets of plywood which Taylor cuts into new shapes. The plywood is shipped in bundles of 14 full sheets. How many doghouses can Taylor make from 12 bundles of plywood?

____

4. Eileen is planting a garden. She has seeds for 60 tomato plants, 55 sweet corn plants, and 21 cucumber plants. She plants them in 8 rows, with the same number of plants in each row. How many seeds are planted in each row?

____

SHOW YOUR WORK

On Your Own

Choose a STRATEGY

- Act It Out
- Draw a Diagram
- Make a Table
- Solve a Simpler Problem
- Work Backward
- Guess, Check, and Revise

5. Starting on day 1 with 1 jumping jack, Keith doubles the number of jumping jacks he does every day. How many jumping jacks will Keith do on day 10?

____

6. **H.O.T.** Starting in the blue square, in how many different ways can you draw a line that passes through every square without picking up your pencil or crossing a line you've already drawn? Show the ways.

____

7. On April 11, Millie bought a lawn mower with a 50-day guarantee. If the guarantee begins on the date of purchase, what is the first day on which the mower will no longer be guaranteed?

____

8. **H.O.T.** A classroom bulletin board is 7 feet by 4 feet. If there is a picture of a student every 6 inches along the edge, including one in each corner, how many pictures are on the bulletin board?

____

9. Dave wants to make a stone walkway. The rectangular walkway is 4 feet wide and 12 feet long. Each 2 foot by 2 foot stone covers an area of 4 square feet. How many stones will Dave need to make his walkway?

____

10. **Test Practice** Dee has 112 minutes of recording time. How many 4-minute songs can she record?

Ⓐ 28 Ⓒ 18

Ⓑ 27 Ⓓ 17

Name ______________________________

Place the First Digit

Essential Question How can you tell where to place the first digit of a quotient without dividing?

COMMON CORE STANDARD CC.5.NBT.6
Perform operations with multi-digit whole numbers and with decimals to hundredths.

UNLOCK the Problem REAL WORLD

Tania has 8 purple daisies. In all, she counts 128 petals on her flowers. If each flower has the same number of petals, how many petals are on one flower?

- Underline the sentence that tells you what you are trying to find.
- Circle the numbers you need to use.
- How will you use these numbers to solve the problem?

____

Divide. 128 ÷ 8

STEP 1 Use an estimate to place the first digit in the quotient.

Estimate. 160 ÷ _____ = _____

The first digit of the quotient will be in

the __________ place.

STEP 2 Divide the tens.

```
   1
8)128
 -
 ____
```

Divide. 12 tens ÷ 8
Multiply. 8 × 1 ten

Subtract. 12 tens − _______ tens

Check. _______ tens cannot be shared among 8 groups without regrouping.

STEP 3 Regroup any tens left as ones. Then, divide the ones.

```
  16
8)128
 -8↓
 ____

 -
 ____
```

Divide. 48 ones ÷ 8
Multiply. 8 × 6 ones

Subtract. 48 ones − _______ ones

Check. _______ ones cannot be shared among 8 groups.

Since 16 is close to the estimate of _____, the answer is reasonable.

So, there are 16 petals on one flower.

MATHEMATICAL PRACTICES

Math Talk Explain how estimating the quotient helps you at both the beginning and the end of a division problem.

Example

Divide. Use place value to place the first digit. 4,236 ÷ 5

STEP 1 Use place value to place the first digit.

5)4,236

Look at the thousands.

4 thousands cannot be shared among 5 groups without regrouping.

Look at the hundreds.

_____ hundreds can be shared among 5 groups.

The first digit is in the _____ place.

STEP 2 Divide the hundreds.

```
   8
5)4,236
–
```

Divide. _____ hundreds ÷ _____

Multiply. _____ × _____ hundreds

Subtract. _____ hundreds – _____ hundreds

Check. _____ hundreds cannot be shared among 5 groups without regrouping.

STEP 3 Divide the tens.

```
   84
5)4,236
 –40↓
   23
  –20
    3
```

Divide. _____

Multiply. _____

Subtract. _____

Check. _____

_____

STEP 4 Divide the ones.

```
  847
5)4,236
 –40
   23
  –20↓
    36
   –35
     1
```

Divide. _____

Multiply. _____

Subtract. _____

Check. _____

_____

So, 4,236 ÷ 5 is _____ r_____.

Remember

Remember to estimate the quotient first.

Estimate: 4,000 ÷ 5 = _____

MATHEMATICAL PRACTICES

Math Talk Explain how you know if your answer is reasonable.

Name ____________________

Share and Show

Divide.

1. $3\overline{)579}$

2. $5\overline{)1,035}$

3. $8\overline{)1,766}$

MATHEMATICAL PRACTICES

Math Talk As you divide, **explain** how you know when to place a zero in the quotient.

On Your Own

Divide.

4. $8\overline{)275}$

5. $3\overline{)468}$

6. $4\overline{)3,220}$

7. $6\overline{)618}$

8. $4\overline{)716}$

9. $9\overline{)1,157}$

10. $6\overline{)6,827}$

11. $7\overline{)8,523}$

Practice: Copy and Solve Divide.

12. $645 \div 8$
13. $942 \div 6$
14. $723 \div 7$
15. $3,478 \div 9$
16. $3,214 \div 5$
17. $492 \div 4$
18. $2,403 \div 9$
19. $2,205 \div 6$
20. $2,426 \div 3$
21. $1,592 \div 8$
22. $926 \div 4$
23. $6,033 \div 5$

UNLOCK the Problem REAL WORLD

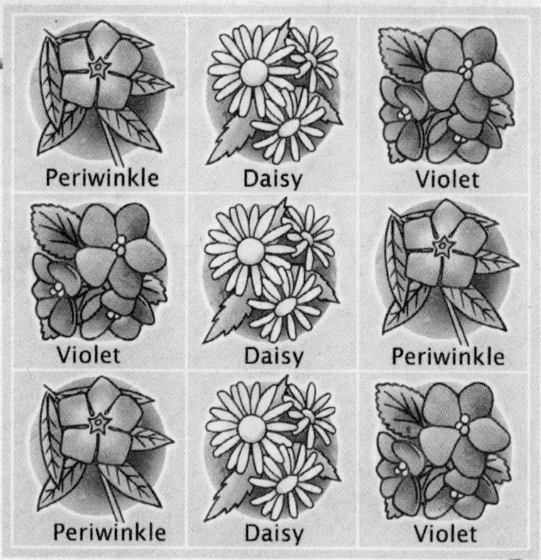

24. Rosa has a garden divided into sections. She has 125 daisy plants. If she plants an equal number of the daisy plants in each section of daisies, will she have any left over? If so, how many daisy plants will be left over?

a. What information will you use to solve the problem? ________________________

____

b. How will you use division to find the number of daisy plants left over? ____________

____

____

c. Show the steps you use to solve the problem. Estimate: $120 \div 3 =$ ______

d. Complete the sentences:

Rosa has ______ daisy plants.
She puts an equal number in each of ______ sections.

Each section has ______ plants.

Rosa has ______ daisy plants left over.

25. H.O.T. One case can hold 3 boxes. Each box can hold 3 binders. How many cases are needed to hold 126 binders?

____

26. ★ **Test Practice** In which place is the first digit in the quotient $1{,}497 \div 5$?

(A) thousands

(B) hundreds

(C) tens

(D) ones

Name ______________________________

Divide by 1-Digit Divisors

Essential Question How do you solve and check division problems?

COMMON CORE STANDARD CC.5.NBT.6
Perform operations with multi-digit whole numbers and with decimals to hundredths.

UNLOCK the Problem REAL WORLD

Jenna's family is planning a trip to Oceanside, California. They will begin their trip in Scranton, Pennsylvania, and will travel 2,754 miles over 9 days. If the family travels an equal number of miles every day, how far will they travel each day?

- Underline the sentence that tells you what you are trying to find.
- Circle the numbers you need to use.

Divide. 2,754 ÷ 9

STEP 1

Use an estimate to place the first digit in the quotient.

Estimate. 2,700 ÷ 9 = ________

The first digit of the quotient is in

the ________ place.

STEP 2

Divide the hundreds.

STEP 3

Divide the tens.

STEP 4

Divide the ones.

$9\overline{)2,754}$

−

−

−

Since ________ is close to the estimate of ________, the answer is reasonable.

So, Jenna's family will travel ________ miles each day.

MATHEMATICAL PRACTICES

Math Talk **Explain** how you know the quotient is 306 and not 36.

CONNECT Division and multiplication are inverse operations. Inverse operations are opposite operations that undo each other. You can use multiplication to check your answer to a division problem.

Example Divide. Check your answer.

To check your answer to a division problem, multiply the quotient by the divisor. If there is a remainder, add it to the product. The result should equal the dividend.

$$\begin{array}{r} 102\text{ r}2 \\ 6\overline{)614} \\ \underline{-6} \\ 01 \\ \underline{-0} \\ 14 \\ \underline{-12} \\ 2 \end{array}$$

102	← quotient
× 6	← divisor
+ 2	← remainder
	← dividend

Since the result of the check is equal to the dividend, the division is correct.

So, 614 ÷ 6 is ________.

You can use what you know about checking division to find an unknown value.

Try This! Find the unknown number by finding the value of *n* in the related equation.

A

$$\begin{array}{r} 63 \\ 7\overline{)} \end{array}$$

$n = 7 \times 63$

↑ dividend ↑ divisor ↑ quotient

Multiply the divisor and the quotient.

$n =$ ________

B

$$\begin{array}{r} 125\text{ r} \\ 6\overline{)752} \end{array}$$

$752 = 6 \times 125 + n$

↑ dividend ↑ divisor ↑ quotient ↑ remainder

Multiply the divisor and the quotient.

$752 = 750 + n$

Think: What number added to 750 equals 752?

$n =$ ________

Name ______________________________

Share and Show

Divide. Check your answer.

1. $8\overline{)624}$ Check.

2. $4\overline{)3,220}$ Check.

3. $4\overline{)1,027}$ Check.

MATHEMATICAL PRACTICES

Math Talk Explain how multiplication can help you check a quotient.

On Your Own

Divide.

4. $6\overline{)938}$

5. $4\overline{)762}$

6. $3\overline{)5,654}$

7. $8\overline{)475}$

Practice: Copy and Solve Divide.

8. $4\overline{)671}$

9. $9\overline{)2,023}$

10. $3\overline{)4,685}$

11. $8\overline{)948}$

12. $1,326 \div 4$

13. $5,868 \div 6$

14. $566 \div 3$

15. $3,283 \div 9$

Algebra Find the value of *n* in each equation. Write what *n* represents in the related division problem.

16. $n = 4 \times 58$

$n =$ ______________

17. $589 = 7 \times 84 + n$

$n =$ ______________

18. $n = 5 \times 67 + 3$

$n =$ ______________

Problem Solving REAL WORLD

Use the table to solve 19–20.

Large Gold Nuggets Found

Name	Weight	Location
Welcome Stranger	2,284 troy ounces	Australia
Welcome	2,217 troy ounces	Australia
Willard	788 troy ounces	California

19. If the Welcome gold nugget were turned into 3 equal-sized gold bricks, how many troy ounces would each brick weigh?

____

20. **Pose a Problem** Look back at Problem 19. Write a similar problem by changing the nugget and the number of bricks. Then solve the problem.

____

____

____

____

____

21. H.O.T. There are 246 students going on a field trip to pan for gold. If they are going in vans that hold 9 students each, how many vans are needed? How many students will ride in the van that isn't full?

____

22. One crate can hold 8 cases of trading cards. How many crates are needed to hold 128 cases of trading cards?

____

23. **Test Practice** At a bake sale, a fifth-grade class sold 324 cupcakes in packages of 6. How many packages of cupcakes did the class sell?

Ⓐ 1,944 Ⓒ 64

Ⓑ 108 Ⓓ 54

SHOW YOUR WORK

Name ______________________________

Division with 2-Digit Divisors

Essential Question How can you use base-ten blocks to model and understand division of whole numbers?

COMMON CORE STANDARD CC.5.NBT.6
Perform operations with multi-digit whole numbers and with decimals to hundredths.

Investigate

Materials ■ base-ten blocks

There are 156 students in the Carville Middle School chorus. The music director wants the students to stand with 12 students in each row for the next concert. How many rows will there be?

A. Use base-ten blocks to model the dividend, 156.

B. Place 2 tens below the hundred to form a rectangle. How many groups of 12 does the rectangle show? How much of the dividend is not shown in this rectangle?

____

C. Combine the remaining tens and ones into as many groups of 12 as possible. How many groups of 12 are there?

____

D. Place these groups of 12 on the right side of the rectangle to make a larger rectangle.

E. The final rectangle shows ______ groups of 12.

So, there will be ______ rows of 12 students.

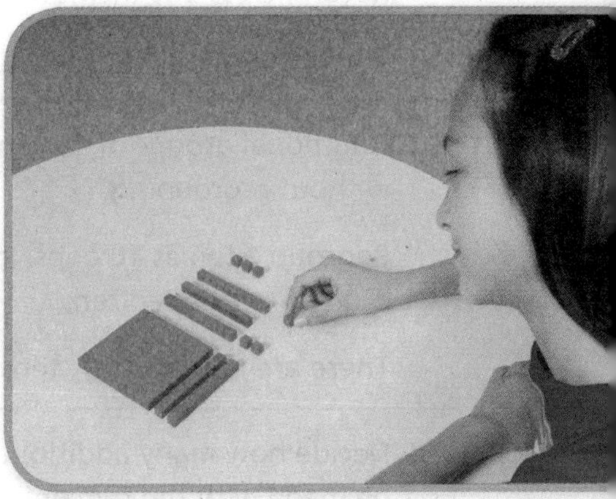

Draw Conclusions

1. **Explain** why you still need to make groups of 12 after Step B.

____

____

2. **Describe** how you can use base-ten blocks to find the quotient $176 \div 16$.

____

____

____

Make Connections

The two sets of groups of 12 that you found in the Investigate are partial quotients. First you found 10 groups of 12 and then you found 3 more groups of 12. Sometimes you may need to regroup before you can show a partial quotient.

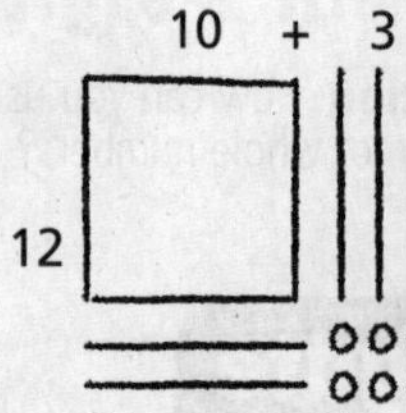

You can use a quick picture to record the partial products.

Divide. 180 ÷ 15

MODEL Use base-ten blocks.

STEP 1 Model the dividend, 180, as 1 hundred 8 tens.

Model the first partial quotient by making a rectangle with the hundred and 5 tens. In the Record, cross out the hundred and tens you use.

The rectangle shows ______ groups of 15.

STEP 2 Additional groups of 15 cannot be made without regrouping.

Regroup 1 ten as 10 ones. In the Record, cross out the regrouped ten.

There are now ______ tens and ______ ones.

STEP 3 Decide how many additional groups of 15 can be made with the remaining tens and ones. The number of groups is the second partial quotient.

Make your rectangle larger by including these groups of 15. In the Record, cross out the tens and ones you use.

There are now ______ groups of 15.

RECORD Use quick pictures.

Draw the first partial quotient.

Draw the first and second partial quotients.

So, 180 ÷ 15 is ______.

MATHEMATICAL PRACTICES

Math Talk Explain how your model shows the quotient.

Share and Show

Use the quick picture to divide.

1. 143 ÷ 13

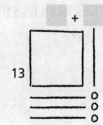

Name ___________________________

Divide. Use base-ten blocks.

2. 168 ÷ 12

3. 154 ÷ 14

4. 187 ÷ 11

Divide. Draw a quick picture.

5. 165 ÷ 11

6. 216 ÷ 18

7. 196 ÷ 14

8. 195 ÷ 15

9. 182 ÷ 13

10. 228 ÷ 12

MATHEMATICAL PRACTICES

Math Talk Explain how Exercise 10 is different from Exercises 7-9.

Connect to Social Studies

Pony Express

The Pony Express used men riding horses to deliver mail between St. Joseph, Missouri, and Sacramento, California, from April, 1860 to October, 1861. The trail between the cities was approximately 2,000 miles long. The first trip from St. Joseph to Sacramento took 9 days 23 hours. The first trip from Sacramento to St. Joseph took 11 days 12 hours.

Before the Pony Express ended in 1861, there were 100 stations, 80 riders, and 400 to 500 horses. The riders were young men about 20 years old who weighed about 120 pounds. Each rider rode 10 to 15 miles before getting a fresh horse. Riders rode a total of 75 to 100 miles each trip.

Solve.

11. Suppose two Pony Express riders rode a total of 165 miles. If they replaced each horse with a fresh horse every 11 miles, how many horses would they have used?

____

12. Suppose a Pony Express rider was paid $192 for 12 weeks of work. If he was paid the same amount each week, how much was he paid for each week of work?

____

13. Suppose three riders rode a total of 240 miles. If they used a total of 16 horses, and rode each horse the same number of miles, how many miles did they ride before replacing each horse?

____

14. H.O.T. Suppose it took 19 riders a total of 11 days 21 hours to ride from St. Joseph to Sacramento. If they all rode the same number of hours, how many hours did each rider ride?

____

 FOR MORE PRACTICE: Standards Practice Book

Name ______________________________

Divide by 2-Digit Divisors

Essential Question How can you divide by 2-digit divisors?

COMMON CORE STANDARD CC.5.NBT.6
Perform operations with multi-digit whole numbers and with decimals to hundredths.

UNLOCK the Problem REAL WORLD

Mr. Yates owns a smoothie shop. To mix a batch of his famous orange-punch smoothies, he uses 18 ounces of freshly squeezed orange juice. Each day he squeezes 560 ounces of fresh orange juice. How many batches of orange-punch smoothies can Mr. Yates make in a day?

- Underline the sentence that tells you what you are trying to find.
- Circle the numbers you need to use.

Divide. 560 ÷ 18 **Estimate.** ______________

STEP 1 Use the estimate to place the first digit in the quotient.

18)560

The first digit of the quotient will be in the ______________ place.

STEP 2 Divide the tens.

$$\begin{array}{r} 3 \\ 18\overline{)560} \\ -54 \\ \hline 2 \end{array}$$

Divide. 56 tens ÷ 18

Multiply. ______________

Subtract. ______________

Check. 2 tens cannot be shared among 18 groups without regrouping.

STEP 3 Divide the ones.

$$\begin{array}{r} 31 \text{ r}2 \\ 18\overline{)560} \\ -54\downarrow \\ \hline 20 \\ -18 \\ \hline 2 \end{array}$$

Divide. ______________

Multiply. ______________

Subtract. ______________

Check. ______________

____

MATHEMATICAL PRACTICES
Math Talk **Explain** what the remainder 2 represents.

Since 31 is close to the estimate of 30, the answer is reasonable.
So, Mr. Yates can make 31 batches of orange-punch smoothies each day.

Example

Every Wednesday, Mr. Yates orders fruit. He has set aside $1,250 to purchase Valencia oranges. Each box of Valencia oranges costs $41. How many boxes of Valencia oranges can Mr. Yates purchase?

You can use multiplication to check your answer.

Divide. 1,250 ÷ 41

DIVIDE

Estimate. ______

```
      30 r20
41)1,250
  −
  ______

  −
  ______
```

CHECK YOUR WORK

```
     30
   ×41
     30
 +1,200
 ______

   +
 ______
  1,250 ✓
```

So, Mr. Yates can buy ______ boxes of Valencia oranges.

Try This! **Divide. Check your answer.**

A 63)756

B 22)4,692

Name ______________________________

Share and Show

Divide. Check your answer.

1. $28\overline{)620}$

2. $64\overline{)842}$

3. $53\overline{)2,340}$

4. $723 \div 31$

5. $1,359 \div 45$

6. $7,925 \div 72$

MATHEMATICAL PRACTICES

Math Talk Explain why you can use multiplication to check division.

On Your Own

Divide. Check your answer.

7. $16\overline{)346}$

8. $34\overline{)421}$

9. $77\overline{)851}$

10. $21\overline{)1,098}$

11. $32\overline{)6,466}$

12. $45\overline{)9,500}$

13. $483 \div 21$

14. $2,292 \div 19$

15. $4,255 \div 30$

Practice: Copy and Solve Divide. Check your answer.

16. $775 \div 35$

17. $820 \div 41$

18. $805 \div 24$

19. $1,166 \div 53$

20. $1,989 \div 15$

21. $3,927 \div 35$

Problem Solving REAL WORLD

Use the list at the right to solve 22–24.

22. A smoothie shop receives a delivery of 980 ounces of grape juice. How many Royal Purple smoothies can be made with the grape juice?

____

23. The shop has 1,260 ounces of cranberry juice and 650 ounces of passion fruit juice. If the juices are used to make Crazy Cranberry smoothies, which juice will run out first? How much of the other juice will be left over?

____

____

24. H.O.T. In the refrigerator, there are 680 ounces of orange juice and 410 ounces of mango juice. How many Orange Tango smoothies can be made? **Explain** your reasoning.

____

____

____

____

____

____

25. ★ **Test Practice** James has 870 action figures. He decides to divide them equally among 23 boxes. How many action figures will James have left over?

Ⓐ 19   Ⓒ 31

Ⓑ 23   Ⓓ 37

Smoothie Main Ingredients

Orange Tango Smoothie
18 ounces orange juice
12 ounces mango juice

Royal Purple Smoothie
22 ounces grape juice
8 ounces apple juice

Crazy Cranberry Smoothie
20 ounces cranberry juice
10 ounces passion fruit juice

SHOW YOUR WORK

Name ______________________

PROBLEM SOLVING
Lesson CA22

Problem Solving • Division

Essential Question How can the strategy *draw a diagram* help you solve a division problem?

COMMON CORE STANDARD **CC.5.NBT.6**
Perform operations with multi-digit whole numbers and with decimals to hundredths.

UNLOCK the Problem REAL WORLD

Sean and his family chartered a fishing boat for the day. Sean caught a blue marlin and an amberjack. The weight of the blue marlin was 12 times as great as the weight of the amberjack. The combined weight of both fish was 273 pounds. How much did each fish weigh?

Read the Problem

What do I need to find?	What information do I need to use?	How will I use the information?
I need to find ______________ ______________.	I need to know that Sean caught a total of ______ pounds of fish and the weight of the blue marlin was ______ times as great as the weight of the amberjack.	I can use the strategy ______________ and then divide. I can draw and use a bar model to write the division problem that helps me find the weight of each fish.

Solve the Problem

I will draw one box to show the weight of the amberjack. Then I will draw a bar of 12 boxes of the same size to show the weight of the blue marlin. I can divide the total weight of the two fish by the total number of boxes.

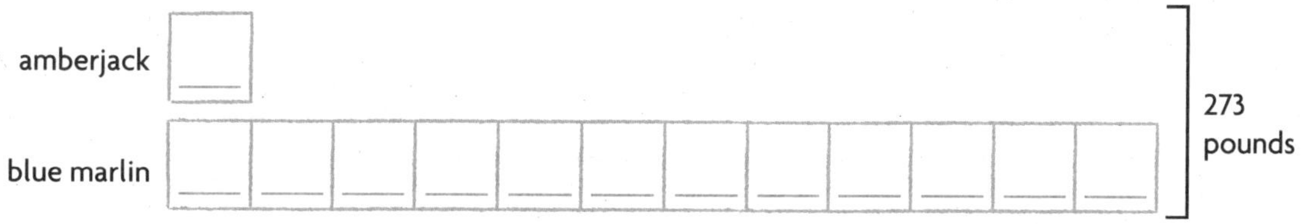

$$\begin{array}{r} 2 \\ 13\overline{)273} \\ -26 \\ \hline \\ - \\ \hline \end{array}$$

Write the quotient in each box. Multiply it by 12 to find the weight of the blue marlin.

So, the amberjack weighed __________ pounds and the blue marlin weighed __________ pounds.

Try Another Problem

Jason, Murray, and Dana went fishing. Dana caught a red snapper. Jason caught a tuna with a weight 3 times as great as the weight of the red snapper. Murray caught a sailfish with a weight 12 times as great as the weight of the red snapper. If the combined weight of the three fish was 208 pounds, how much did the tuna weigh?

Read the Problem

What do I need to find?	What information do I need to use?	How will I use the information?

Solve the Problem

So, the tuna weighed ______ pounds.

- How can you check if your answer is correct? ______

______

Math Talk MATHEMATICAL PRACTICES Explain how you could use another strategy to solve this problem.

Name ______________________________

Share and Show

Choose a STRATEGY

- Act It Out
- Draw a Diagram
- Make a Table
- Solve a Simpler Problem
- Work Backward
- Guess, Check, and Revise

1. Paula caught a tarpon with a weight that was 10 times as great as the weight of a permit fish she caught. The total weight of the two fish was 132 pounds. How much did each fish weigh?

First, draw one box to represent the weight of the permit fish and ten boxes to represent the weight of the tarpon.

Next, divide the total weight of the two fish by the total number of boxes you drew. Place the quotient in each box.

Last, find the weight of each fish.

The permit fish weighed ______ pounds.

The tarpon weighed ______ pounds.

SHOW YOUR WORK

2. **What if** the weight of the tarpon was 11 times the weight of the permit fish, and the total weight of the two fish was 132 pounds? How much would each fish weigh?

permit fish: ______ pounds

tarpon: ______ pounds

3. Jon caught four fish that weighed a total of 252 pounds. The kingfish weighed twice as much as the amberjack and the white marlin weighed twice as much as the kingfish. The weight of the tarpon was 5 times the weight of the amberjack. How much did each fish weigh?

amberjack: ______ pounds

kingfish: ______ pounds

marlin: ______ pounds

tarpon: ______ pounds

On Your Own

Use the table to solve 4–7.

Kevin's Supply List for a Saltwater Aquarium	
40-gal tank	$170
Aquarium light	$30
Filtration system	$65
Thermometer	$2
15-lb bag of gravel	$13
Large rocks	$3 per lb
Clown fish	$20 each
Damselfish	$7 each

4. Kevin is starting a saltwater aquarium with 36 fish. He wants to start with 11 times as many damselfish as clown fish. How many of each fish will Kevin buy? How much will he pay for the fish?

5. Kevin used a store coupon to buy a 40-gallon tank, an aquarium light, and a filtration system. He paid a total of $240. How much money did Kevin save by using the coupon?

6. **H.O.T.** Kevin bought 3 bags of gravel to cover the bottom of his fish tank. He has 8 pounds of gravel left over. How much gravel did Kevin use to cover the bottom of the tank?

7. **Write Math** ▶ **Pose a Problem** Look back at Problem 6. Write a similar problem by changing the number of bags of gravel and the amount of gravel left.

8. ★ **Test Practice** Captain James offers a deep-sea fishing tour. He charges $2,940 for a 14-hour trip. How much does each hour of the tour cost?

   (A) $138 (C) $210

   (B) $201 (D) $294

Name ______________________

Algebra • Properties

Essential Question How can you use properties to add and multiply decimals?

COMMON CORE STANDARD CC.5.NBT.7
Perform operations with multi-digit whole numbers and with decimals to hundredths.

You can use the properties of operations to help you evaluate numerical expressions more easily.

Properties of Addition

Commutative Property If the order of the addends changes, the sum stays the same.	$9.5 + 16.4 = 16.4 + 9.5$
Associative Property If the grouping of addends changes, the sum stays the same.	$5.14 + (4.8 + 9.8) = (5.14 + 4.8) + 9.8$
Identity Property The sum of any number and 0 is that number.	$124.5 + 0 = 124.5$

Properties of Multiplication

Commutative Property If the order of the factors changes, the product stays the same.	$3.31 \times 7.1 = 7.1 \times 3.31$
Associative Property If the grouping of factors changes, the product stays the same.	$(8.5 \times 1.4) \times 7.7 = 8.5 \times (1.4 \times 7.7)$
Identity Property The product of any number and 1 is that number.	$16.61 \times 1 = 16.61$
Zero Property The product of any number and 0 is 0.	$12.43 \times 0 = 0$

UNLOCK the Problem REAL WORLD

The table shows the number of miles that several students ran while training for a race. What is the total number of miles that Demondre, Sarah, and Tomiko ran?

Name	Miles
Sarah	1.8
Tomiko	2.6
Demondre	1.4
Greg	3.2

To find the sum of addends using mental math, you can use the Commutative and Associative Properties.

Use properties to find 1.4 + 1.8 + 2.6.

$1.4 + 1.8 + 2.6 = 1.8 +$ _______ $+ 2.6$ — Use the ______________ Property to reorder the addends.

$= 1.8 + (1.4 +$ _______ $)$ — Use the ______________ Property to group the addends.

$= 1.8 +$ _______ $=$ _______ — Add.

So, together they ran _______ miles to train for the race.

MATHEMATICAL PRACTICES

Math Talk Explain why grouping 1.4 and 2.6 makes the problem easier to solve.

Example 1 Complete the equation, and tell which property you used.

A $2.7 \times$ _______ $= 2.7$

Think: A number times 1 is equal to itself.

Property: _______________

B $17.45 \times 5.98 =$ _______ $\times 17.45$

Think: Changing the order of factors does not change the product.

Property: _______________

C $5.4 + (7.6 + 1.8) = (5.4 + 7.6) +$ _______

Think: The numbers are grouped differently.

Property: _______________

D $8.19 \times$ _______ $= 0$

Think: A number times 0 is equal to 0.

Property: _______________

Distributive Property

Multiplying a sum by a number is the same as multiplying each addend by the number and then adding the products.	$5.4 \times (4.5 + 1.1) = (5.4 \times 4.5) + (5.4 \times 1.1)$

The Distributive Property can also be used with multiplication and subtraction. For example, $2.4 \times (7.8 - 5.1) = (2.4 \times 7.8) - (2.4 \times 5.1)$.

Example 2 Use the Distributive Property to find the product.

A $6.4 \times (2.8 + 1.6)$

$6.4 \times (2.8 + 1.6) = (6.4 \times$ _______ $) + ($ _______ $\times 1.6)$ Use the Distributive Property.

$=$ _______ $+$ _______ Multiply.

$=$ _______ Add.

B $5.50 \times (7.22 - 3.84)$

$5.50 \times (7.22 - 3.84) = ($ _______ $\times 7.22) - (5.50 \times$ _______ $)$ Use the _______ Property.

$= 39.71 -$ _______ Multiply.

$=$ _______ Subtract.

Name ______________________

Share and Show

1. Use properties to find $3.2 + 5.4 + 7.8$.

$3.2 + 7.8 + 5.4$ ______________ Property of Addition

$(3.2 + \_\_\_\_\_\_) + 5.4$ ______________ Property of Addition

$\_\_\_\_\_\_ + 5.4$

______

Use properties to find the sum or product.

2. $870.4 + 114.48 + 29.6$

3. 85.16×1

4. $4.2 \times (4.4 + 1.1)$

MATHEMATICAL PRACTICES

Math Talk **Describe** how you can use properties to solve problems more easily.

On Your Own

Use properties to find the sum or product.

5. 48.74×1

6. $5.14 + 18.68 + 11.06$

7. $6.5 \times (4.0 - 2.7)$

Complete the equation, and tell which property you used.

8. $61.74 + (38.26 + 85.07) =$

$(61.74 + \_\_\_\_\_\_) + 85.07$

9. $362.15 \times 552.07 = 552.07 \times \_\_\_\_\_\_$

10. H.O.T. Show how you can use the Distributive Property to rewrite and find $(5.9 \times 7.4) + (5.9 \times 4.7)$.

Problem Solving REAL WORLD

11. Martin is setting up a salt water aquarium in his bedroom. He plans to buy 11 blue hermit crabs, 2 emerald crabs, and 2 yellow tangs. The table shows the price list for the animals. How much will Martin spend?

Price per Animal	
Blue Hermit Crab	\$7.49
Emerald Crab	\$12.50
Starfish	\$22.45
Yellow Tang	\$49.99

12. Three friends went to a restaurant. The meals they ate cost \$14.95, \$8.99, and \$11.25. Use parentheses to write two different expressions to show how much the friends spent in all. Which property does your pair of expressions demonstrate?

SHOW YOUR WORK

13. H.O.T. **Sense or Nonsense?** Ricardo wrote $(17.85 - 1.41) - 6.95 = 17.85 - (1.41 - 6.95)$. Is Ricardo's equation sense or nonsense? Does the Associative Property work for subtraction? **Explain.**

14. **Test Practice** Which property is represented by the following equation?

$65.95 + 74.85 + 88.05 = 65.95 + 88.05 + 74.85$

Ⓐ Identity Property

Ⓑ Commutative Property

Ⓒ Associative Property

Ⓓ Distributive Property

Name ______________________________

Decimal Addition

Essential Question How can you use base-ten blocks to model decimal addition?

COMMON CORE STANDARD **CC.5.NBT.7**
Perform operations with multi-digit whole numbers and with decimals to hundredths

CONNECT You can use base-ten blocks to help you find decimal sums.

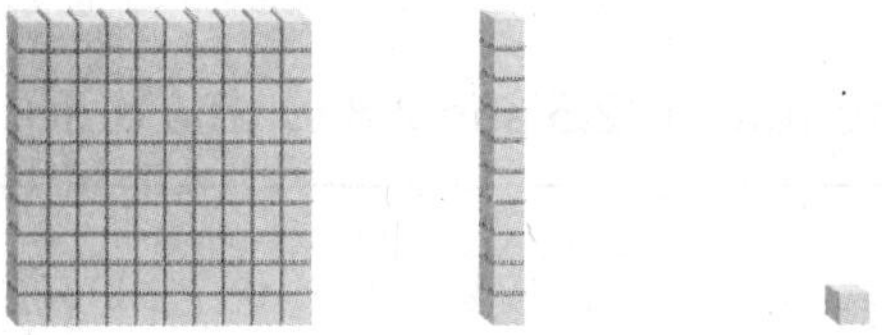

1 one | 0.1 one tenth | 0.01 one hundredth

Investigate

Materials ■ base-ten blocks

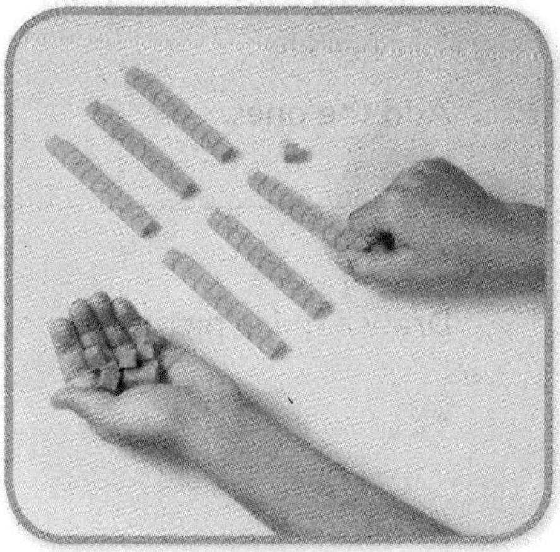

A. Use base-ten blocks to model the sum of 0.34 and 0.27.

B. Add the hundredths first by combining them.

- Do you need to regroup the hundredths? **Explain.**

____

____

____

C. Add the tenths by combining them.

- Do you need to regroup the tenths? **Explain.**

____

____

____

D. Record the sum. $0.34 + 0.27 =$ __________

Draw Conclusions

1. **What if** you combine the tenths first and then the hundredths? **Explain** how you would regroup.

____

____

2. H.O.T. **Synthesize** If you add two decimals that are each greater than 0.5, will the sum be less than or greater than 1.0? **Explain.**

____

____

Make Connections

You can use a quick picture to add decimals greater than 1.

STEP 1

Model the sum of 2.5 and 2.8 with a quick picture.

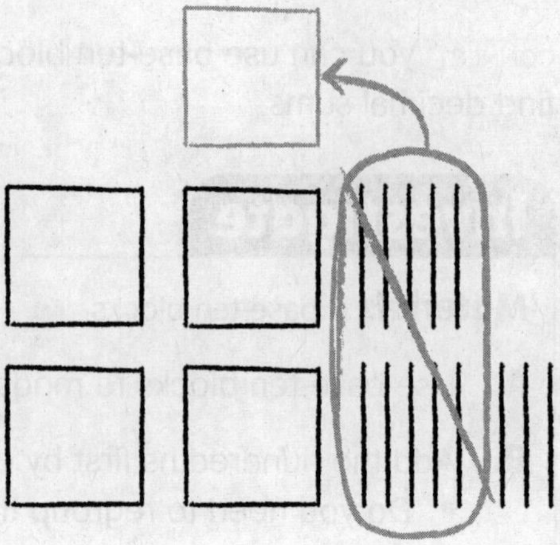

STEP 2

Add the tenths.

- Are there more than 9 tenths? ______
  If there are more than 9 tenths, regroup.

Add the ones.

STEP 3

Draw a quick picture of your answer. Then record.

2.5 + 2.8 = ______

Share and Show

Complete the quick picture to find the sum.

1. 1.37 + 1.85 = ______

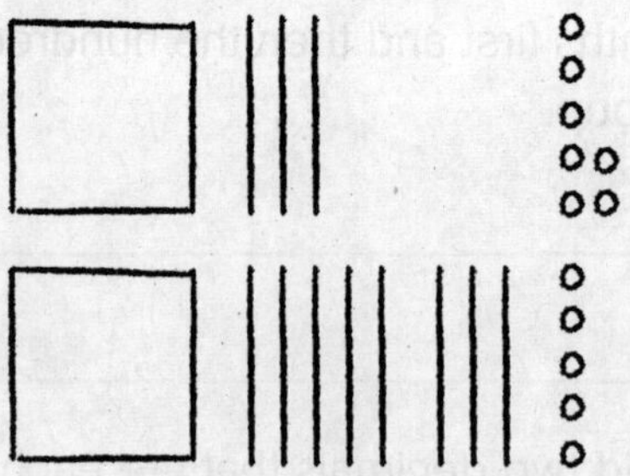

MATHEMATICAL PRACTICES

Math Talk **Explain** how you know where to write the decimal point in the sum.

Name ______________________

Add. Draw a quick picture.

2. $0.9 + 0.7 =$ ________

3. $0.65 + 0.73 =$ ________

4. $3.71 + 0.54 =$ ________

5. $1.05 + 0.78 =$ ________

6. $1.3 + 0.7 =$ ________

7. $2.72 + 0.51 =$ ________

MATHEMATICAL PRACTICES

Math Talk Explain how you solved Exercise 6.

Problem Solving

H.O.T. Sense or Nonsense?

8. Robyn and Jim used quick pictures to model 1.85 + 2.73.

Robyn's Work

1.85 + 2.73 = 3.158

Does Robyn's work make sense?
Explain your reasoning.

____

____

____

____

____

Jim's Work

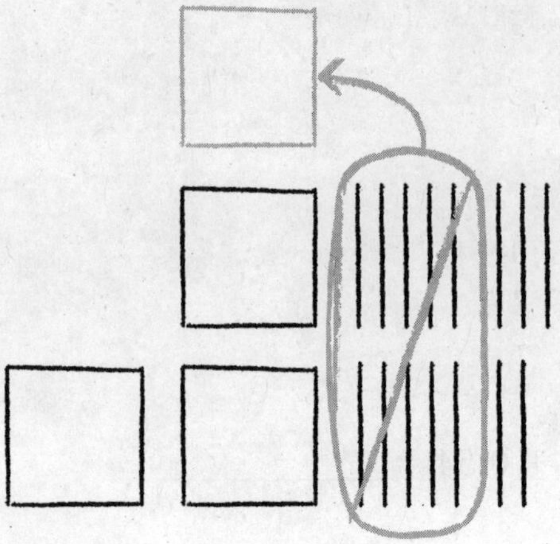

1.85 + 2.73 = 4.58

Does Jim's work make sense?
Explain your reasoning.

____

____

____

____

____

- **Explain** how you would help Robyn understand that regrouping is important when adding decimals.

____

____

____

____

Name ______________________________

Decimal Subtraction

Essential Question How can you use base-ten blocks to model decimal subtraction?

COMMON CORE STANDARD **CC.5.NBT.7**
Perform operations with multi-digit whole numbers and with decimals to hundredths

CONNECT You can use base-ten blocks to help you find the difference between two decimals.

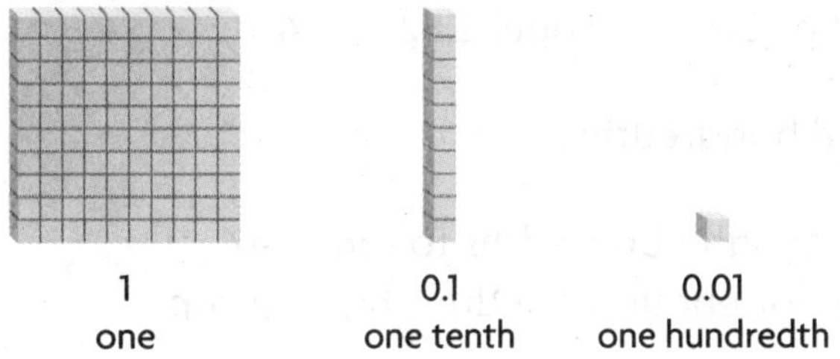

Investigate

Materials ■ base-ten blocks

A. Use base-ten blocks to find $0.84 - 0.56$. Model 0.84.

B. Subtract 0.56. Start by removing 6 hundredths.

- Do you need to regroup to subtract? **Explain**.

____

____

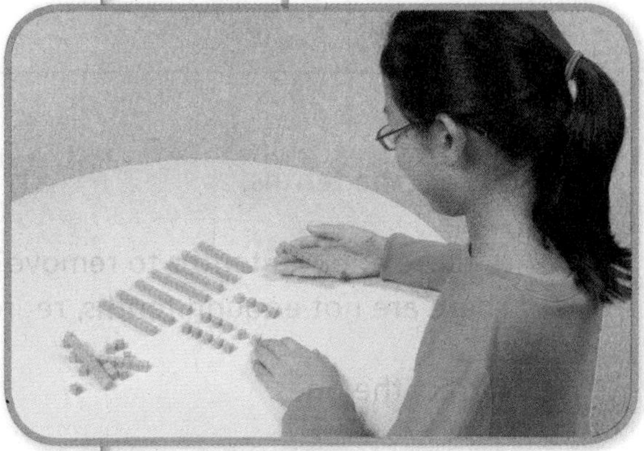

C. Subtract the tenths. Remove 5 tenths.

D. Record the difference. $0.84 - 0.56 =$ __________

Draw Conclusions

1. **What if** you remove the tenths first and then the hundredths? **Explain** how you would regroup.

____

____

2. H.O.T. **Synthesize** If two decimals are both less than 1.0, what do you know about the difference between them? **Explain**.

____

____

Make Connections

You can use quick pictures to subtract decimals that need to be regrouped.

STEP 1

- Use a quick picture to model 2.82 − 1.47.
- Subtract the hundredths.
- Are there enough hundredths to remove? ______
  If there are not enough hundredths, regroup.

STEP 2

- Subtract the tenths.
- Are there enough tenths to remove? ______
  If there are not enough tenths, regroup.
- Subtract the ones.

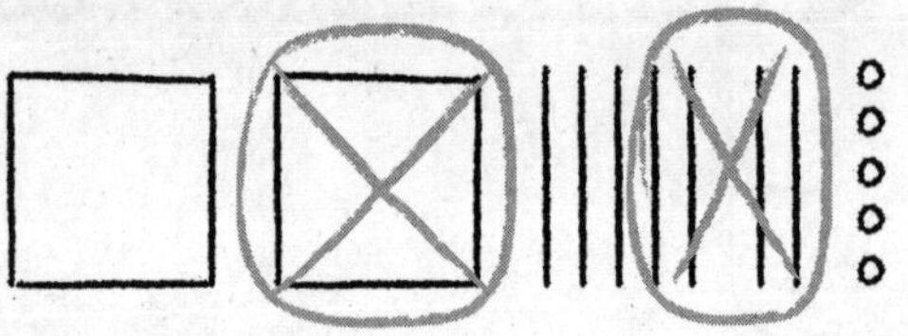

STEP 3

Draw a quick picture of your answer. Then record.

2.82 − 1.47 = ______

MATHEMATICAL PRACTICES

Math Talk Explain why you have to regroup in Step 1.

Name ___________________________

Share and Show

Complete the quick picture to find the difference.

1. $0.62 - 0.18 =$ ________

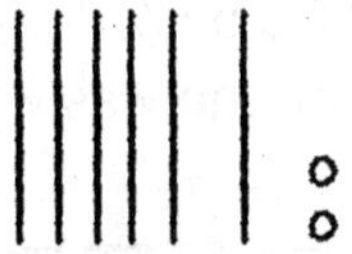

Subtract. Draw a quick picture.

2. $3.41 - 1.74 =$ ________

3. $0.84 - 0.57 =$ ________

4. $0.93 - 0.38 =$ ________

5. $2.71 - 1.34 =$ ________

6. $4.05 - 1.61 =$ ________

7. $1.37 - 0.52 =$ ________

MATHEMATICAL PRACTICES

Math Talk Explain how you can use a quick picture to find 0.81 − 0.46.

Problem Solving

H.O.T. Pose a Problem

8. Antonio left his MathBoard on his desk during lunch. The quick picture below shows the problem he was working on when he left.

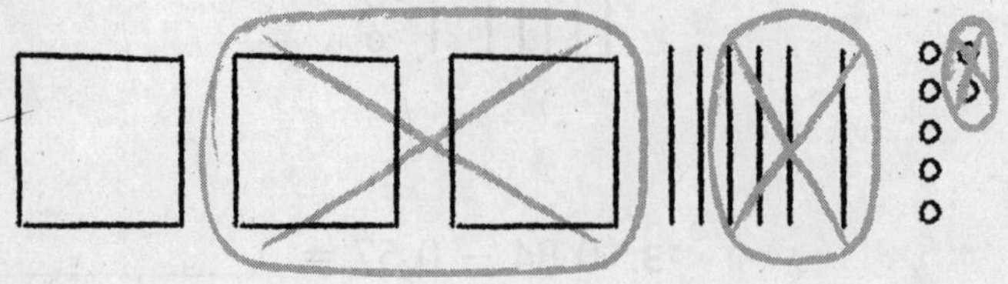

Write a problem that can be solved using the quick picture above.

Pose a problem.

Solve your problem.

- **Describe** how you can change the problem by changing the quick picture.

Name ______________________________

Subtract Decimals

Essential Question How can place value help you subtract decimals?

COMMON CORE STANDARD **CC.5.NBT.7**
Perform operations with multi-digit whole numbers and with decimals to hundredths

UNLOCK the Problem REAL WORLD

Hannah has 3.36 kilograms of apples and 2.28 kilograms of oranges. Hannah estimates she has about 1 more kilogram of apples than oranges. How many more kilograms of apples than oranges does Hannah have? How can you use this estimate to decide if your answer is reasonable?

- What operation will you use to solve the problem?

____

- Circle Hannah's estimate to check that your answer is reasonable.

Subtract. 3.36 − 2.28

- Subtract the hundredths first. If there are not enough hundredths, regroup 1 tenth as 10 hundredths.

_______ hundredths − 8 hundredths = 8 hundredths

- Then subtract the tenths and ones. Regroup as needed.

_______ tenths − 2 tenths = 0 tenths

_______ ones − 2 ones = 1 one

- Record the difference for each place value.

$$\begin{array}{r} 3.36 \\ -\ 2.28 \\ \hline \end{array}$$

Draw a quick picture to check your work.

So, Hannah has __________ more kilograms of apples than oranges.

Since __________ is close to 1, the answer is reasonable.

MATHEMATICAL PRACTICES

Math Talk **Explain** how you know when to regroup in a decimal subtraction problem.

Try This! **Use addition to check.**

Since subtraction and addition are inverse operations, you can check subtraction by adding.

STEP 1

Find the difference.

Subtract the hundredths first.

Then, subtract the tenths, ones, and tens. Regroup as needed.

		1	4	.	2		
	−		8	.	6	3	

STEP 2

Check your answer.

Add the difference to the number you subtracted. If the sum matches the number you subtracted from, your answer is correct.

$$\begin{array}{r} \underline{\quad\quad} \leftarrow \text{difference} \\ +8.63 \leftarrow \text{number subtracted} \\ \hline \underline{\quad\quad} \leftarrow \text{number subtracted from} \end{array}$$

- Is your answer correct? **Explain.**

____

____

Share and Show

Estimate. Then find the difference.

1. Estimate: ______

$$\begin{array}{r} 5.83 \\ -2.18 \\ \hline \end{array}$$

2. Estimate: ______

$$\begin{array}{r} 4.45 \\ -1.86 \\ \hline \end{array}$$

✓3. Estimate: ______

$$\begin{array}{r} 4.03 \\ -2.25 \\ \hline \end{array}$$

Find the difference. Check your answer.

4.
$$\begin{array}{r} 0.70 \\ -0.43 \\ \hline \end{array}$$

5.
$$\begin{array}{r} 13.2 \\ -8.04 \\ \hline \end{array}$$

✓6.
$$\begin{array}{r} 15.8 \\ -9.67 \\ \hline \end{array}$$

Name ______________________

On Your Own

Estimate. Then find the difference.

7. Estimate: ______

$$\begin{array}{r} 4.08 \\ -1.74 \\ \hline \end{array}$$

8. Estimate: ______

$$\begin{array}{r} 13.54 \\ -\ 6.7 \\ \hline \end{array}$$

9. Estimate: ______

$$\begin{array}{r} 19.64 \\ -\ 8.12 \\ \hline \end{array}$$

Find the difference. Check your answer.

10.
$$\begin{array}{r} 16.05 \\ -\ 1.5 \\ \hline \end{array}$$

11.
$$\begin{array}{r} 7.3 \\ -5.4 \\ \hline \end{array}$$

12.
$$\begin{array}{r} 21.4 \\ -16.97 \\ \hline \end{array}$$

H.O.T. **Find the difference.**

13. three and seventy-two hundredths subtracted from five and eighty-one hundredths

____

14. one and six hundredths subtracted from eight and thirty-two hundredths

____

H.O.T. **Algebra** **Write the unknown number for *n*.**

15. $5.28 - 3.4 = n$

$n =$ ______________

16. $n - 6.47 = 4.32$

$n =$ ______________

17. $11.57 - n = 7.51$

$n =$ ______________

Practice: Copy and Solve **Find the difference.**

18. $8.42 - 5.14$

19. $16.46 - 13.87$

20. $34.27 - 17.51$

21. $15.83 - 11.45$

22. $12.74 - 10.54$

23. $48.21 - 13.65$

UNLOCK the Problem REAL WORLD

24. In peanut butter, how many more grams of protein are there than grams of carbohydrates? Use the label at the right.

PEANUT BUTTER
Nutrition Facts
Serving Size 2 Tbsp (32.0 g)

Amount Per Serving	
Calories	190
Calories from Fat	190
	% Daily Value*
Total Fat 16g	**25%**
Saturated Fat 3g	**18%**
Polyunsaturated Fat 4.4g	
Monounsaturated Fat 7.8g	
Cholesterol 0mg	**0%**
Sodium 5mg	**0%**
Total Carbohydrates 6.2g	**2%**
Dietary Fiber 1.9g	**8%**
Sugars 2.5g	**8%**
Protein 8.1g	

*Based on a 2,000 calorie diet

a. What do you need to know? ____________

____

____

b. How will you use subtraction to find how many more grams of protein there are than grams of carbohydrates?

____

____

c. Show how you solved the problem.

d. Complete each sentence.

The peanut butter has ______ grams of protein.

The peanut butter has ______ grams of carbohydrates.

There are ______ more grams of protein than grams of carbohydrates in the peanut butter.

25. Kyle is building a block tower. Right now the tower stands 0.89 meter tall. How much higher does the tower need to be to reach a height of 1.74 meters?

____

26. ★ **Test Practice** Allie is 158.7 centimeters tall. Her younger brother is 9.53 centimeters shorter than she is. How tall is Allie's younger brother?

Ⓐ 159.27 centimeters

Ⓑ 159.23 centimeters

Ⓒ 149.27 centimeters

Ⓓ 149.17 centimeters

Name ________________________________

Choose a Method

Essential Question Which method could you choose to find decimal sums and differences?

COMMON CORE STANDARD CC.5.NBT.7
Perform operations with multi-digit whole numbers and with decimals to hundredths

UNLOCK the Problem REAL WORLD

At a track meet, Steven entered the long jump. His jumps were 2.25 meters, 1.81 meters, and 3.75 meters. What was the total distance Steven jumped?

To find decimal sums, you can use properties and mental math or you can use paper and pencil.

- Underline the sentence that tells you what you are trying to find.
- Circle the numbers you need to use.
- What operation will you use?

____

One Way Use properties and mental math.

Add. 2.25 + 1.81 + 3.75

$2.25 + 1.81 + 3.75$

$= 2.25 + 3.75 + 1.81$ Commutative Property

$= (\_\_\_\_ + \_\_\_\_) + 1.81$ Associative Property

$= \_\_\_\_ + 1.81$

$= \_\_\_\_$

Another Way Use place-value.

Add. 2.25 + 1.81 + 3.75

$$\begin{array}{r} 2.25 \\ 1.81 \\ +\ 3.75 \\ \hline \end{array}$$

So, the total distance Steven jumped was ____________ meters.

MATHEMATICAL PRACTICES

Math Talk Explain why you might choose to use the properties to solve this problem.

Try This!

In 1924, William DeHart Hubbard won a gold medal with a long jump of 7.44 meters. In 2000, Roman Schurenko won the bronze medal with a jump of 8.31 meters. How much longer was Schurenko's jump than Hubbard's?

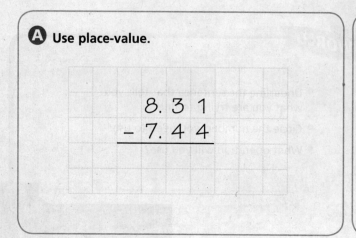

A Use place-value.

$$\begin{array}{r} 8.31 \\ -\,7.44 \\ \hline \end{array}$$

B Use a calculator.

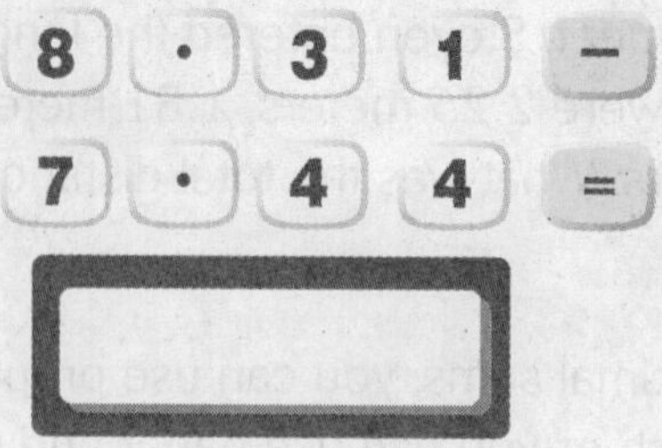

So, Schurenko's jump was ________ meter longer than Hubbard's.

- **Explain** why you cannot use the Commutative Property or the Associative Property to find the difference between two decimals.

____

____

Share and Show

Find the sum or difference.

1. 4.19 + 0.58
2. 9.99 − 4.1
3. 5.7 + 2.25 + 1.3
4. 28.6 − 9.84
5. \$15.79 + \$32.81
6. 38.44 − 25.86

Name ________________________________

On Your Own

Find the sum or difference.

7. $\begin{array}{r} \$18.39 \\ +\$\ \ 7.56 \\ \hline \end{array}$

8. $8.22 - 4.39$

9. $93.6 - 79.84$

10. $\begin{array}{r} 1.82 \\ 2.28 \\ +2.18 \\ \hline \end{array}$

11. $\begin{array}{r} 2.35 \\ -0.16 \\ \hline \end{array}$

12. $\begin{array}{r} 5.16 \\ +4.54 \\ \hline \end{array}$

13. $\begin{array}{r} 15.3 \\ -\ 6.53 \\ \hline \end{array}$

14. $\begin{array}{r} 2.64 \\ +8.41 \\ \hline \end{array}$

Practice: Copy and Solve Find the sum or difference.

15. 6.3 + 2.98 + 7.7
16. 27.96 − 16.2
17. 12.63 + 15.04
18. 9.24 − 2.68
19. \$18 − \$3.55
20. 9.73 − 2.52
21. \$54.78 + \$43.62
22. 7.25 + 0.25 + 1.5
23. 14.56 − 7.8
24. 3.35 + 1.4 + 3.65
25. \$22.50 − \$8.99
26. 9.77 + 5.54

H.O.T. Algebra Find the missing number.

27. $n - 9.02 = 3.85$

$n =$ ____________

28. $n + 31.53 = 62.4$

$n =$ ____________

29. $9.2 + n + 8.4 = 20.8$

$n =$ ____________

Problem Solving REAL WORLD

Use the table to solve 30–32.

2008 Men's Olympic Long Jump Results	
Medal	**Distance (in meters)**
Gold	8.34
Silver	8.24
Bronze	8.20

30. How much farther did the gold medal winner jump than the silver medal winner?

____

31. **Write Math** The fourth-place competitor's jump measured 8.19 meters. If his jump had been 0.10 meter greater, what medal would he have received? **Explain** how you solved the problem.

____

____

____

____

____

32. In the 2004 Olympics, the gold medalist for the men's long jump had a jump of 8.59 meters. How much farther did the 2004 gold medalist jump compared to the 2008 gold medalist?

____

33. Jake cuts a length of 1.12 meters from a 3-meter board. How long is the board now?

____

34. ★ **Test Practice** In the long jump, Danny's first attempt was 5.47 meters. His second attempt was 5.63 meters. How much farther did Danny jump on his second attempt than on his first?

Ⓐ 11.1 meters Ⓒ 5.16 meters

Ⓑ 10.1 meters Ⓓ 0.16 meter

SHOW YOUR WORK

Name ______________________________

Estimate Fraction Sums and Differences

COMMON CORE STANDARD **CC.5.NF.2**
Use equivalent fractions as a strategy to add and subtract fractions.

Essential Question How can you make reasonable estimates of fraction sums and differences?

UNLOCK the Problem REAL WORLD

Kimberly will be riding her bike to school this year. The distance from her house to the end of the street is $\frac{1}{6}$ mile. The distance from the end of the street to the school is $\frac{3}{8}$ mile. About how far is Kimberly's house from school?

You can use benchmarks to find reasonable estimates by rounding fractions to 0, $\frac{1}{2}$, or 1.

One Way Use a number line.

Estimate. $\frac{1}{6} + \frac{3}{8}$

STEP 1 Place a point at $\frac{1}{6}$ on the number line.

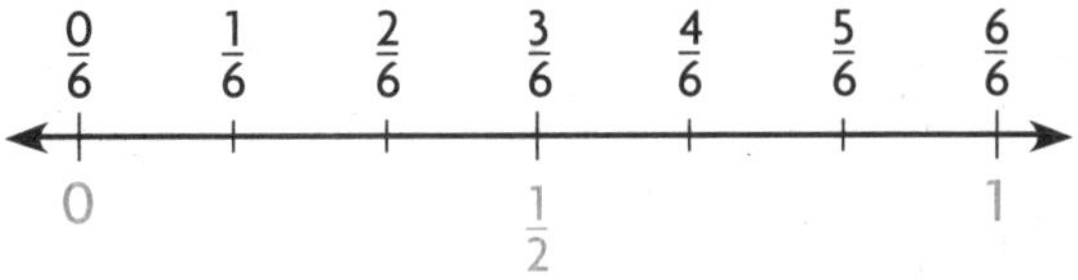

The fraction is between _______ and _______.

The fraction $\frac{1}{6}$ is closer to the benchmark _______.

Round to _______.

STEP 2 Place a point at $\frac{3}{8}$ on the number line.

The fraction is between _______ and _______.

The fraction $\frac{3}{8}$ is closer to the benchmark _______.

Round to _______.

STEP 3 Add the rounded fractions.

$\frac{1}{6} \rightarrow$ _______

$+\frac{3}{8} \rightarrow +$ _______

So, Kimberly's house is about _______ mile from the school.

Another Way Use mental math.

You can compare the numerator and the denominator to round a fraction and find a reasonable estimate.

Estimate. $\frac{9}{10} - \frac{5}{8}$

STEP 1 Round $\frac{9}{10}$. **Think:** The numerator is about the same as the denominator.

Round the fraction $\frac{9}{10}$ to ______.

STEP 2 Round $\frac{5}{8}$. **Think:** The numerator is about half the denominator.

Round the fraction $\frac{5}{8}$ to ______.

STEP 3 Subtract.

$$\frac{9}{10} \rightarrow \square$$
$$-\frac{5}{8} \rightarrow -\square$$

So, $\frac{9}{10} - \frac{5}{8}$ is about ______.

Remember

A fraction with the same numerator and denominator, such as $\frac{2}{2}$, $\frac{5}{5}$, $\frac{12}{12}$, or $\frac{96}{96}$, is equal to 1.

MATHEMATICAL PRACTICES

Math Talk Explain another way you could use benchmarks to estimate $\frac{9}{10} - \frac{5}{8}$.

Try This! Estimate.

A $2\frac{7}{8} - \frac{2}{5}$

B $1\frac{8}{9} + 4\frac{8}{10}$

Name ______________________________

Share and Show

Estimate the sum or difference.

1. $\frac{5}{6} + \frac{3}{8}$

a. Round $\frac{5}{6}$ to its closest benchmark. ______

b. Round $\frac{3}{8}$ to its closest benchmark. ______

c. Add to find the estimate. ______ + ______ = ______

2. $\frac{5}{9} - \frac{3}{8}$

3. $\frac{6}{7} + 2\frac{4}{5}$

4. $\frac{5}{6} + \frac{2}{5}$

5. $3\frac{9}{10} - 1\frac{2}{9}$

6. $\frac{4}{6} + \frac{1}{9}$

7. $\frac{9}{10} - \frac{1}{9}$

MATHEMATICAL PRACTICES

Math Talk **Explain** how you know whether your estimate for $\frac{9}{10} + 3\frac{6}{7}$ would be greater than or less than the actual sum.

On Your Own

Estimate the sum or difference.

8. $\frac{5}{8} - \frac{1}{5}$

9. $\frac{1}{6} + \frac{3}{8}$

10. $\frac{6}{7} - \frac{1}{5}$

11. $\frac{11}{12} + \frac{6}{10}$

12. $\frac{9}{10} - \frac{1}{2}$

13. $\frac{3}{6} + \frac{4}{5}$

14. $\frac{5}{6} - \frac{3}{8}$

15. $\frac{1}{7} + \frac{8}{9}$

16. $3\frac{5}{12} - 3\frac{1}{10}$

Problem Solving REAL WORLD

SHOW YOUR WORK

17. Lisa and Valerie are picnicking in Trough Creek State Park in Pennsylvania. Lisa has brought a salad that she made with $\frac{3}{4}$ cup of strawberries, $\frac{7}{8}$ cup of peaches, and $\frac{1}{6}$ cup of blueberries. About how many total cups of fruit are in the salad?

____

18. At Trace State Park in Mississippi, there is a 25-mile mountain bike trail. If Tommy rode $\frac{1}{2}$ of the trail on Saturday and $\frac{1}{5}$ of the trail on Sunday, about what fraction of the trail did he ride?

____

19. H.O.T. **Explain** how you know that $\frac{5}{8} + \frac{6}{10}$ is greater than 1.

____

____

____

____

____

20. **Write Math** Nick estimated that $\frac{5}{8} + \frac{4}{7}$ is about 2. **Explain** how you know his estimate is not reasonable.

____

____

____

21. **Test Practice** Jake added $\frac{1}{8}$ cup of sunflower seeds and $\frac{4}{5}$ cup of banana chips to his sundae. Which is the best estimate of the total amount of toppings Jake added to his sundae?

Ⓐ about $\frac{1}{2}$ cup

Ⓑ about 1 cup

Ⓒ about $1\frac{1}{2}$ cups

Ⓓ about 2 cups

Name ______________________________

Add and Subtract Fractions

Essential Question How can you use a common denominator to add and subtract fractions with unlike denominators?

COMMON CORE STANDARD **CC.5.NF.2**
Use equivalent fractions as a strategy to add and subtract fractions.

CONNECT You can use what you have learned about common denominators to add or subtract fractions with unlike denominators.

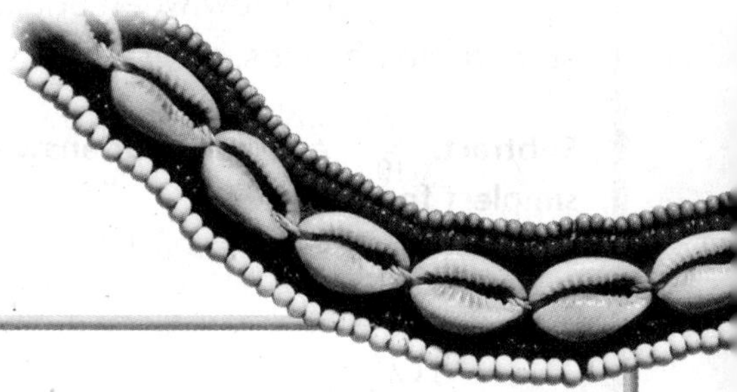

UNLOCK the Problem REAL WORLD

Malia bought shell beads and glass beads to weave into designs in her baskets. She bought $\frac{1}{4}$ pound of shell beads and $\frac{3}{8}$ pound of glass beads. How many pounds of beads did she buy?

- Underline the question you need to answer.
- Draw a circle around the information you will use.

Add. $\frac{1}{4} + \frac{3}{8}$ **Write your answer in simplest form.**

One Way

Find a common denominator by multiplying the denominators.

$4 \times 8 =$ ______ ← common denominator

Use the common denominator to write equivalent fractions with like denominators. Then add, and write your answer in simplest form.

$$\frac{1}{4} = \frac{1 \times \_\_}{4 \times \_\_} = \_\_$$

$$+\frac{3}{8} = +\frac{3 \times \_\_}{8 \times \_\_} = +\_\_$$

$$\_\_ = \_\_$$

Another Way

Find the least common denominator.

The least common denominator of $\frac{1}{4}$ and $\frac{3}{8}$ is ______.

$$\frac{1}{4} = \frac{1 \times \_\_}{4 \times \_\_} = \_\_$$

$$+\frac{3}{8} \qquad +\_\_$$

So, Malia bought ______ pound of beads.

1. **Explain** how you know whether your answer is reasonable. ______________________________

____

Example

When subtracting two fractions with unlike denominators, follow the same steps you follow when adding two fractions. However, instead of adding the fractions, subtract.

Subtract. $\frac{9}{10} - \frac{2}{5}$ **Write your answer in simplest form.**

$\frac{9}{10} =$

$-\frac{2}{5} =$

Describe the steps you took to solve the problem.

2. **Explain** how you know whether your answer is reasonable.

Share and Show

Find the sum or difference. Write your answer in simplest form.

1. $\frac{5}{12} + \frac{1}{3}$
2. $\frac{2}{5} + \frac{3}{7}$
3. $\frac{1}{6} + \frac{3}{4}$
4. $\frac{3}{4} - \frac{1}{8}$
5. $\frac{1}{4} - \frac{1}{7}$
6. $\frac{9}{10} - \frac{1}{4}$

MATHEMATICAL PRACTICES

Math Talk **Explain** why it is important to check your answer for reasonableness.

Name ______________________________

On Your Own

Find the sum or difference. Write your answer in simplest form.

7. $\frac{3}{8} + \frac{1}{4}$

8. $\frac{7}{8} + \frac{1}{10}$

9. $\frac{2}{7} + \frac{3}{10}$

10. $\frac{5}{6} + \frac{1}{8}$

11. $\frac{5}{12} + \frac{5}{18}$

12. $\frac{7}{16} - \frac{1}{4}$

13. $\frac{5}{6} - \frac{3}{8}$

14. $\frac{3}{4} - \frac{1}{2}$

15. $\frac{5}{12} - \frac{1}{4}$

Practice: Copy and Solve Find the sum or difference. Write your answer in simplest form.

16. $\frac{1}{3} + \frac{4}{18}$

17. $\frac{3}{5} + \frac{1}{3}$

18. $\frac{3}{10} + \frac{1}{6}$

19. $\frac{1}{2} + \frac{4}{9}$

20. $\frac{1}{2} - \frac{3}{8}$

21. $\frac{5}{7} - \frac{2}{3}$

22. $\frac{4}{9} - \frac{1}{6}$

23. $\frac{11}{12} - \frac{7}{15}$

H.O.T. Algebra Find the unknown number.

24. $\frac{9}{10} - ■ = \frac{1}{5}$

■ = ______

25. $\frac{5}{12} + ■ = \frac{1}{2}$

■ = ______

Problem Solving REAL WORLD

Use the picture for 26–27.

26. Sara is making a key chain using the bead design shown. What fraction of the beads in her design are either blue or red?

____

27. H.O.T. In making the key chain, Sara uses the pattern of beads 3 times. After the key chain is complete, what fraction of the beads in the key chain are either white or blue?

____

SHOW YOUR WORK

28. Write Math Jamie had $\frac{4}{5}$ of a spool of twine. He then used $\frac{1}{2}$ of a spool of twine to make friendship knots. He claims to have $\frac{3}{10}$ of the original spool of twine left over. **Explain** how you know whether Jamie's claim is reasonable.

____

____

____

____

29. **Test Practice** Which equation represents the fraction of beads that are green or yellow?

Ⓐ $\frac{1}{4} + \frac{1}{8} = \frac{3}{8}$

Ⓑ $\frac{1}{2} + \frac{1}{4} = \frac{3}{4}$

Ⓒ $\frac{1}{2} + \frac{1}{8} = \frac{5}{8}$

Ⓓ $\frac{3}{4} + \frac{2}{8} = 1$

Name ______________________

Add and Subtract Mixed Numbers

Essential Question How can you add and subtract mixed numbers with unlike denominators?

COMMON CORE STANDARD CC.5.NF.2
Use equivalent fractions as a strategy to add and subtract fractions.

UNLOCK the Problem REAL WORLD

Denise mixed $1\frac{4}{5}$ ounces of blue paint with $2\frac{1}{10}$ ounces of yellow paint. How many ounces of paint did Denise mix?

- What operation should you use to solve the problem?

  ____

- Do the fractions have the same denominator?

  ____

Add. $1\frac{4}{5} + 2\frac{1}{10}$

To find the sum of mixed numbers with unlike denominators, you can use a common denominator.

STEP 1 Estimate the sum. __________

STEP 2 Find a common denominator. Use the common denominator to write equivalent fractions with like denominators.

STEP 3 Add the fractions. Then add the whole numbers. Write the answer in simplest form.

$$1\frac{4}{5} =$$

$$+2\frac{1}{10} = +$$

So, Denise mixed ______ ounces of paint.

MATHEMATICAL PRACTICES

Math Talk Did you use the least common denominator? Explain.

1. **Explain** how you know whether your answer is reasonable. ______________________

____

____

2. What other common denominator could you have used? ______________________

____

Example

Subtract. $4\frac{5}{6} - 2\frac{3}{4}$

You can also use a common denominator to find the difference of mixed numbers with unlike denominators.

STEP 1 Estimate the difference. ______

STEP 2 Find a common denominator. Use the common denominator to write equivalent fractions with like denominators.

STEP 3 Subtract the fractions. Subtract the whole numbers. Write the answer in simplest form.

$$4\frac{5}{6} = \square$$
$$-2\frac{3}{4} = -\square$$

3. **Explain** how you know whether your answer is reasonable. ______

Share and Show

1. Use a common denominator to write equivalent fractions with like denominators and then find the sum. Write your answer in simplest form.

$$7\frac{2}{5} = \square$$
$$+4\frac{3}{4} = +\square$$

Find the sum. Write your answer in simplest form.

2. $2\frac{3}{4} + 3\frac{3}{10}$

3. $5\frac{3}{4} + 1\frac{1}{3}$

4. $3\frac{4}{5} + 2\frac{3}{10}$

Name ______________________________

Find the difference. Write your answer in simplest form.

5. $9\frac{5}{6} - 2\frac{1}{3}$

6. $10\frac{5}{9} - 9\frac{1}{6}$

7. $7\frac{2}{3} - 3\frac{1}{6}$

MATHEMATICAL PRACTICES

Math Talk Explain why you need to write equivalent fractions with common denominators to add $4\frac{5}{6}$ and $1\frac{1}{8}$.

On Your Own

Find the sum or difference. Write your answer in simplest form.

8. $1\frac{3}{10} + 2\frac{2}{5}$

9. $3\frac{4}{9} + 3\frac{1}{2}$

10. $2\frac{1}{2} + 2\frac{1}{3}$

11. $5\frac{1}{4} + 9\frac{1}{3}$

12. $8\frac{1}{6} + 7\frac{3}{8}$

13. $14\frac{7}{12} - 5\frac{1}{4}$

14. $12\frac{3}{4} - 6\frac{1}{6}$

15. $2\frac{5}{8} - 1\frac{1}{4}$

16. $10\frac{1}{2} - 2\frac{1}{5}$

Practice: Copy and Solve Find the sum or difference. Write your answer in simplest form.

17. $1\frac{5}{12} + 4\frac{1}{6}$

18. $8\frac{1}{2} + 6\frac{3}{5}$

19. $2\frac{1}{6} + 4\frac{5}{9}$

20. $3\frac{5}{8} + \frac{5}{12}$

21. $3\frac{2}{3} - 1\frac{1}{6}$

22. $5\frac{6}{7} - 1\frac{2}{3}$

23. $2\frac{7}{8} - \frac{1}{2}$

24. $4\frac{7}{12} - 1\frac{2}{9}$

Problem Solving REAL WORLD

Use the table to solve 25–28.

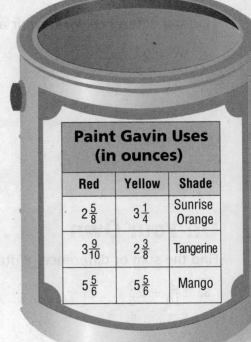

Paint Gavin Uses (in ounces)		
Red	**Yellow**	**Shade**
$2\frac{5}{8}$	$3\frac{1}{4}$	Sunrise Orange
$3\frac{9}{10}$	$2\frac{3}{8}$	Tangerine
$5\frac{5}{6}$	$5\frac{5}{6}$	Mango

25. Gavin is mixing a batch of Sunrise Orange paint for an art project. How much paint does Gavin mix?

26. Gavin plans to mix a batch of Tangerine paint. He expects to have a total of $5\frac{3}{10}$ ounces of paint after he mixes the amounts of red and yellow. **Explain** how you can tell if Gavin's expectation is reasonable.

27. H.O.T. For a special project, Gavin mixes the amount of red from one shade of paint with the amount of yellow from a different shade. He mixes the batch so he will have the greatest possible amount of paint. What amounts of red and yellow from which shades are used in the mixture for the special project? **Explain** your answer.

SHOW YOUR WORK

28. Gavin needs to make 2 batches of Mango paint. **Explain** how you could find the total amount of paint Gavin mixed.

29. **Test Practice** Yolanda walked $3\frac{6}{10}$ miles. Then she walked $4\frac{1}{2}$ more miles. How many miles did Yolanda walk?

Ⓐ $7\frac{1}{10}$ miles

Ⓑ $7\frac{7}{10}$ miles

Ⓒ $8\frac{1}{10}$ miles

Ⓓ $8\frac{7}{10}$ miles

FOR MORE PRACTICE: Standards Practice Book

Name ______________________________

Problem Solving • Practice Addition and Subtraction

Essential Question How can the strategy *work backward* help you solve a problem with fractions that involves addition and subtraction?

COMMON CORE STANDARD CC.5.NF.2
Use equivalent fractions as a strategy to add and subtract fractions.

UNLOCK the Problem REAL WORLD

The Diaz family is cross-country skiing the Big Tree trails, which have a total length of 4 miles. Yesterday, they skied the $\frac{7}{10}$ mile Oak Trail. Today, they skied the $\frac{3}{5}$ mile Pine Trail. If they plan to ski all of the Big Tree trails, how many more miles do they have left to ski?

Use the graphic organizer to help you solve the problem.

Read the Problem

What do I need to find?

I need to find the distance

______________.

What information do I need to use?

I need to use the distance

____

and the total distance

______________.

How will I use the information?

I can work backward by starting

with the ______________

and ______________ each distance they have already skied to find amount they have left.

Solve the Problem

Addition and subtraction are inverse operations. By working backward and using the same numbers, one operation undoes the other.

- Write an equation.

miles skied yesterday	+	miles skied today	+	miles they need to ski	=	total distance
↓		↓		↓		↓
______	+	______	+	m	=	4

- Then work backward to find m.

______ − ______ − ______ = m

______ = m

So, the family has ______ miles left to ski.

- **Explain** how you know your answer is reasonable. ______________________________

____

Try Another Problem

As part of their study of Native American basket weaving, Lia's class is making wicker baskets. Lia starts with a strip of wicker 36 inches long. From the strip, she first cuts one piece but does not know its length, and then cuts a piece that is $6\frac{1}{2}$ inches long. The piece left is $7\frac{3}{4}$ inches long. What is the length of the first piece she cut from the strip?

Read the Problem

What do I need to find?	What information do I need to use?	How will I use the information?

Solve the Problem

So, the length of the first piece cut was ______ inches.

Math Talk MATHEMATICAL PRACTICES What other strategy could you use to solve the problem?

Name ___

Share and Show

UNLOCK the Problem Tips

- Plan your solution by deciding on the steps you will use.
- Check your exact answer by comparing it with your estimate.
- Check your answer for reasonableness.

1. Caitlin has $4\frac{3}{4}$ pounds of clay. She uses $1\frac{1}{10}$ pounds to make a cup, and another 2 pounds to make a jar. How many pounds are left?

   First, write an equation to model the problem.

   ___

   Next, work backwards and rewrite the equation to find x.

   ___

   Solve.

   ___

   So, ___ pounds of clay remain.

2. H.O.T. **What if** Caitlin had used more than 2 pounds of clay to make a jar? Would the amount remaining have been more or less than your answer to Exercise 1?

   ___

3. A pet store donated 50 pounds of food for adult dogs, puppies, and cats to an animal shelter. $19\frac{3}{4}$ pounds was adult dog food and $18\frac{7}{8}$ pounds was puppy food. How many pounds of cat food did the pet store donate?

   ___

4. Thelma spent $\frac{1}{6}$ of her weekly allowance on dog toys, $\frac{1}{4}$ on a dog collar, and $\frac{1}{3}$ on dog food. What fraction of her weekly allowance is left?

   ___

SHOW YOUR WORK

On Your Own

Choose a STRATEGY

- Act It Out
- Draw a Diagram
- Make a Table
- Solve a Simpler Problem
- Work Backward
- Guess, Check, and Revise

5. Martin is making a model of a Native American canoe. He has $5\frac{1}{2}$ feet of wood. He uses $2\frac{3}{4}$ feet for the hull and $1\frac{1}{4}$ feet for the paddles and struts. How much wood does he have left?

______

6. H.O.T. **What if** Martin makes a hull and two sets of paddles and struts? How much wood does he have left?

______

7. Beth's summer vacation lasted 87 days. At the beginning of her vacation, she spent 3 weeks at soccer camp, 5 days at her grandmother's house, and 13 days visiting Glacier National Park with her parents. How many vacation days remained?

______

8. **Write Math** You can buy 2 DVDs for the same price you would pay for 3 CDs selling for \$13.20 apiece. **Explain** how you could find the price of 1 DVD.

______

9. **Test Practice** During the 9 hours between 8 A.M. and 5 P.M., Bret spent $5\frac{3}{4}$ hours in class and $1\frac{1}{2}$ hours at band practice. How much time did he spend on other activities?

Ⓐ $\frac{3}{4}$ hour
Ⓑ $1\frac{1}{4}$ hours
Ⓒ $1\frac{1}{2}$ hours
Ⓓ $1\frac{3}{4}$ hours

SHOW YOUR WORK

Name ____________________

Write Zeros in the Dividend

Essential Question When do you write a zero in the dividend to find a quotient?

COMMON CORE STANDARD CC.5.NF.3
Apply and extend previous understandings of multiplication and division to multiply and divide fractions.

CONNECT When decimals are divided, the dividend may not have enough digits for you to complete the division. In these cases, you can write zeros to the right of the last digit.

UNLOCK the Problem REAL WORLD

The equivalent fractions show that writing zeros to the right of a decimal does not change the value.

$$90.8 = 90\frac{8 \times 10}{10 \times 10} = 90\frac{80}{100} = 90.80$$

During a fundraising event, Adrian rode his bicycle 45.8 miles in 4 hours. Find his speed in miles per hour by dividing the distance by the time.

Divide. 45.8 ÷ 4 **Estimate.** 44 ÷ 4 = ______

STEP 1

Write the decimal point in the quotient above the decimal point in the dividend.

$4\overline{)45.8}$

STEP 2

Divide the tens, ones, and tenths.

$4\overline{)45.8}$
−___
−___
−___

STEP 3

Write a zero in the dividend and continue dividing.

$4\overline{)45.80}$
−4
05
− 4
18
−16
−___

So, Adrian's speed was ____________ miles per hour.

MATHEMATICAL PRACTICES
Math Talk Explain how you would model this problem using base-ten blocks.

CONNECT When you divide whole numbers, you can show the amount that is left over by writing a remainder or a fraction. By writing zeros in the dividend, you can also show that amount as a decimal.

Example Write zeros in the dividend.

Nancy has 372 meters of ribbon. She cuts the ribbon into 15 equal pieces. How long is each piece of ribbon?

Divide. 372 ÷ 15

- Divide until you have an amount less than the divisor left over.
- Insert a decimal point and a zero at the end of the dividend.
- Place a decimal point in the quotient above the decimal point in the dividend.
- Continue dividing.

$$
\begin{array}{r}
24.\square \\
15\overline{)372.0} \\
-30 \\
72 \\
-60 \\
\square \\
-\square \\
\hline
\end{array}
$$

So, each ribbon is ____________ meters long.

- Sarah has 78 ounces of rice. She puts an equal amount of rice in each of 12 bags. What amount of rice does she put in each bag? **Explain** how you would write the answer using a decimal.

____

____

Try This! Divide. Write a zero at the end of the dividend as needed.

Divide. 1.23 ÷ 0.06

$$
0.06\overline{)1.23} \quad \rightarrow \quad 006.\overline{)123.}
$$

$$
\begin{array}{r}
20.\square \\
6\overline{)123.0} \\
-12 \\
03 \\
-\ 0 \\
30 \\
-\square \\
\hline
\square
\end{array}
$$

Divide. 10 ÷ 8

$$
\begin{array}{r}
\square \\
8\overline{)10}
\end{array}
$$

Name ____________________

Share and Show

Write the quotient with the decimal point placed correctly.

1. $5 \div 0.8 = 625$
2. $26.1 \div 6 = 435$
3. $0.42 \div 0.35 = 12$
4. $80 \div 50 = 16$

Divide.

5. $4\overline{)32.6}$
6. $1.2\overline{)9}$
7. $15\overline{)42}$
8. $0.14\overline{)0.91}$

MATHEMATICAL PRACTICES

Math Talk Explain why you would write a zero in the dividend when dividing decimals.

On Your Own

Divide.

9. $8\overline{)84}$
10. $2.5\overline{)4}$
11. $5\overline{)16.2}$
12. $0.6\overline{)2.7}$
13. $18 \div 7.5$
14. $34.8 \div 24$
15. $5.16 \div 0.24$
16. $81 \div 18$

Practice: Copy and Solve Divide.

17. $1.6\overline{)20}$
18. $15\overline{)4.8}$
19. $0.54\overline{)2.43}$
20. $28\overline{)98}$
21. $1.8 \div 12$
22. $3.5 \div 2.5$
23. $40 \div 16$
24. $2.24 \div 0.35$

Problem Solving REAL WORLD

Solve.

25. Jerry takes trail mix on hikes. A package of dried apricots weighs 25.5 ounces. Jerry divides the apricots equally among 6 bags of trail mix. How many ounces of apricots are in each bag?

26. H.O.T. Amy has 3 pounds of raisins. She divides the raisins equally into 12 bags. How many pounds of raisins are in each bag? Tell how many zeros you had to write at the end of the dividend.

27. Write Math Find 65 ÷ 4. Write your answer using a remainder, a fraction, and a decimal. Then tell which form of the answer you prefer. **Explain** your choice.

28. **Test Practice** Todd has a piece of rope that is 1.6 meters long. He cuts the rope into 5 equal pieces. What is the length of each piece?

Ⓐ 0.8 meter

Ⓑ 0.32 meter

Ⓒ 3.2 meters

Ⓓ 8 meters

Connect to Science

Rate of Speed Formula

The formula for velocity, or rate of speed, is $r = d \div t$, where r represents rate of speed, d represents distance, and t represents time. For example, if an object travels 12 feet in 10 seconds, you can find its rate of speed by using the formula.

$r = d \div t$

$r = 12 \div 10$

$r = 1.2$ feet per second

Use division and the formula for rate of speed to solve.

29. A car travels 168 miles in 3.2 hours. Find the car's rate of speed in miles per hour.

30. A submarine travels 90 kilometers in 4 hours. Find the submarine's rate of speed in kilometers per hour.

Name ______________________________

Connect Fractions to Division

Essential Question How does a fraction represent division?

COMMON CORE STANDARD CC.5.NF.3
Apply and extend previous understandings of multiplication and division to multiply and divide fractions.

CONNECT A fraction can be written as a division problem.

$\frac{3}{4} = 3 \div 4$ $\frac{12}{2} = 12 \div 2$

UNLOCK the Problem REAL WORLD

There are 3 students in a crafts class and 2 sheets of construction paper for them to share equally. What part of the construction paper will each student get?

- Circle the dividend.
- Underline the divisor.

Use a drawing.

Divide. $2 \div 3$

STEP 1 Draw lines to divide each piece of paper into 3 equal pieces.

Each student's share of one sheet of construction paper is ______.

STEP 2 Count the number of thirds each student gets. Since there are 2 sheets of construction paper, each student will

get 2 of the ________________, or 2 × ______.

STEP 3 Complete the number sentence.

$2 \div 3 = \frac{\square}{\square}$

STEP 4 Check your answer.

Since ______ × ______ = ______, the quotient is correct.
quotient divisor dividend

So, each student will get ______ of a sheet of construction paper.

MATHEMATICAL PRACTICES

Math Talk Describe a division problem where each student gets $\frac{3}{4}$ of a sheet of construction paper.

Example

Four friends share 6 granola bars equally. How many granola bars does each friend get?

Divide. $6 \div 4$

STEP 1 Draw lines to divide each of the 6 bars into fourths.

Each friend's share of 1 granola bar is ______.

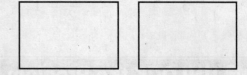

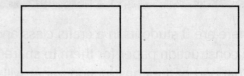

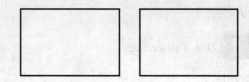

STEP 2 Count the number of fourths each friend gets. Since there are 6 granola bars, each friend will get ______ of the fourths, or $\frac{\square}{\square}$.

STEP 3 Complete the number sentence. Write the fraction as a mixed number in simplest form.

$6 \div 4 = \frac{\square}{\square}$, or $\square\frac{\square}{\square}$

STEP 4 Check your answer.

Since ______ $\times 4 =$ ______, the quotient is correct.

So, each friend will get __________ granola bars.

MATHEMATICAL PRACTICES

Math Talk Describe a different way the granola bars could have been divided into 4 equal shares.

Try This!

Ms. Ruiz has a piece of string that is 125 inches long. For a science experiment, she divides the string equally among 8 groups of students. How much string will each group get?

You can represent this problem as a division equation or a fraction.

- Divide. Write the remainder as a fraction. $125 \div 8 =$ ______
- Write $\frac{125}{8}$ as a mixed number in simplest form. $\frac{125}{8} =$ ______

So, each group will get ______ inches of string.

- **Explain** why $125 \div 8$ gives the same result as $\frac{125}{8}$.

____

____

Name ______________________________

Share and Show

Draw lines on the model to complete the number sentence.

1. Six friends share 4 pizzas equally.

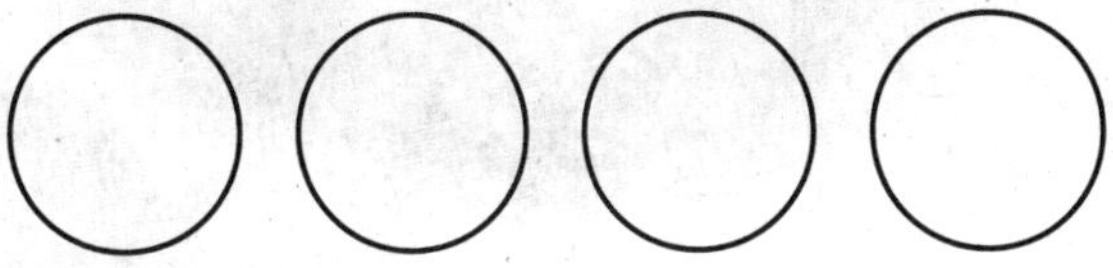

4 ÷ 6 = __________

Each friend's share is ______ of a pizza.

2. Four brothers share 5 sandwiches equally.

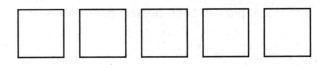

5 ÷ 4 = __________

Each brother's share is ______ sandwiches.

Complete the number sentence to solve.

3. Twelve friends share 3 pies equally. What fraction of a pie does each friend get?

3 ÷ 12 = __________

Each friend's share is ______ of a pie.

4. Three students share 8 blocks of clay equally. How much clay does each student get?

8 ÷ 3 = __________

Each student's share is ______ blocks of clay.

MATHEMATICAL PRACTICES

Math Talk Explain how you can check your answer.

On Your Own

Complete the number sentence to solve.

5. Four students share 7 oranges equally. How many oranges does each student get?

7 ÷ 4 = __________

Each student's share is ______ oranges.

6. Eight girls share 5 fruit bars equally. What fraction of a fruit bar does each girl get?

5 ÷ 8 = __________

Each girl's share is ______ of a fruit bar.

7. Nine friends share 6 pizzas equally. What fraction of a pizza does each friend get?

6 ÷ 9 = __________

Each friend's share is ______ of a pizza.

8. Two boys share 9 feet of rope equally. How many feet of rope does each boy get?

9 ÷ 2 = __________

Each boy's share is ______ feet of rope.

Problem Solving REAL WORLD

9. Shawna has 3 adults and 2 children coming over for dessert. She is going to serve 2 small apple pies. If she plans to give each person, including herself, an equal amount of pie, how much pie will each person get?

____

10. There are 36 members in the math club. Addison brought 81 brownies to share with all the members. How many brownies does each member get?

____

SHOW YOUR WORK

11. H.O.T. Eight students share 12 oatmeal muffins equally and 6 students share 15 apple muffins equally. Carmine is in both groups of students. What is the total number of muffins Carmine gets?

____

12. Write Math Nine friends order 4 large pizzas. Four of the friends share 2 pizzas equally and the other 5 friends share 2 pizzas equally. In which group does each member get a greater amount of pizza? **Explain** your reasoning.

____

____

____

____

13. Test Practice Jason baked 5 cherry pies. He wants to share them equally among 3 of his neighbors. How many pies will each neighbor get?

Ⓐ $\frac{3}{8}$ Ⓒ $1\frac{2}{3}$

Ⓑ $\frac{3}{5}$ Ⓓ $2\frac{2}{3}$

 FOR MORE PRACTICE: Standards Practice Book

Name ______________________________

Find Part of a Group

Essential Question How can you find a fractional part of a group?

COMMON CORE STANDARD CC.5.NF.4a
Apply and extend previous understandings of multiplication and division to multiply and divide fractions.

UNLOCK the Problem REAL WORLD

Maya collects stamps. She has 20 stamps in her collection. Four-fifths of her stamps have been canceled. How many of the stamps in Maya's collection have been canceled?

▲ The post office cancels stamps to keep them from being reused.

Find $\frac{4}{5}$ of 20.

- Put 20 counters on your MathBoard.

  Since you want to find $\frac{4}{5}$ of the stamps, you should arrange the 20 counters in ______ equal groups.

- Draw the counters in equal groups below. How many counters are in each group? ______

- Each group represents ______ of the stamps. Circle $\frac{4}{5}$ of the counters.

  How many groups did you circle? ______

  How many counters did you circle? ______

  $\frac{4}{5}$ of $20 =$ ______, or $\frac{4}{5} \times 20 =$ ______

So, ______ of the stamps have been canceled.

MATHEMATICAL PRACTICES
Math Talk How many groups would you circle if $\frac{3}{5}$ of the stamps were canceled? **Explain.**

Example

Max's stamp collection has stamps from different countries. He has 12 stamps from Canada. Of those twelve, $\frac{2}{3}$ of them have pictures of Queen Elizabeth II. How many stamps have the queen on them?

- Draw an array to represent the 12 stamps by drawing an ✗ for each stamp. Since you want to find $\frac{2}{3}$ of the stamps, your array should

  show ______ rows of equal size.

- Circle ______ of the 3 rows to show $\frac{2}{3}$ of 12. Then count the number of ✗s in the circle.

  There are ______ ✗s circled.

- Complete the number sentences.

  $\frac{2}{3}$ of 12 = ______, or $\frac{2}{3} \times 12$ = ______

So, there are ______ stamps with a picture of Queen Elizabeth II.

- On your MathBoard, use counters to find $\frac{4}{6}$ of 12. **Explain** why the answer is the same as when you found $\frac{2}{3}$ of 12.

____

____

Try This! Draw an array.

Susan has 16 stamps. In her collection, $\frac{3}{4}$ of the stamps are from the United States. How many of her stamps are from the United States and how many are not?

So, ______ of Susan's stamps are from the United States and ______ stamps are not.

Name ______________________________

Share and Show

1. Complete the model to solve.

   $\frac{7}{8}$ of 16, or $\frac{7}{8} \times 16$

   - How many rows of counters are there? ______
   - How many counters are in each row? ______
   - Circle ______ rows to solve the problem.
   - How many counters are circled? ______

   $\frac{7}{8}$ of 16 = ______, or $\frac{7}{8} \times 16$ = ______

Use a model to solve.

2. $\frac{2}{3} \times 18 =$ ______

3. $\frac{2}{5} \times 15 =$ ______

4. $\frac{2}{3} \times 6 =$ ______

Math Talk MATHEMATICAL PRACTICES **Explain** how you used a model to solve Exercise 4.

On Your Own

Use a model to solve.

5. $\frac{5}{8} \times 24 =$ ______

6. $\frac{3}{4} \times 24 =$ ______

7. $\frac{4}{7} \times 21 =$ ______

8. $\frac{2}{9} \times 27 =$ ______

9. $\frac{3}{5} \times 20 =$ ______

10. $\frac{7}{11} \times 22 =$ ______

Problem Solving REAL WORLD

Use the table for 11–12.

Stamps Collected	
Name	**Number of Stamps**
Zack	30
Teri	18
Paco	24

11. Four-fifths of Zack's stamps have pictures of animals. How many stamps with pictures of animals does Zack have? Use a model to solve.

____

12. H.O.T. **Write Math** Zack, Teri, and Paco combined the foreign stamps from their collections for a stamp show. Out of their collections, $\frac{3}{10}$ of Zack's stamps, $\frac{5}{6}$ of Teri's stamps, and $\frac{3}{8}$ of Paco's stamps were from foreign countries. How many stamps were in their display? **Explain** how you solved the problem.

____

____

____

____

____

SHOW YOUR WORK

13. Paula has 24 stamps in her collection. Among her stamps, $\frac{1}{3}$ have pictures of animals. Out of her stamps with pictures of animals, $\frac{3}{4}$ of those stamps have pictures of birds. How many stamps have pictures of birds on them?

____

14. **Test Practice** Barry bought 21 stamps from a hobby shop. He gave $\frac{3}{7}$ of them to his sister. How many stamps did he have left?

Ⓐ 3 stamps

Ⓑ 6 stamps

Ⓒ 9 stamps

Ⓓ 12 stamps

Name ____________________

Multiply Fractions and Whole Numbers

Essential Question How can you use a model to show the product of a fraction and a whole number?

COMMON CORE STANDARD CC.5.NF.4a
Apply and extend previous understandings of multiplication and division to multiply and divide fractions.

Investigate

Martin is planting a vegetable garden. Each row is two meters long. He wants to plant carrots along $\frac{3}{4}$ of each row. How many meters of each row will he plant with carrots?

Multiply. $\frac{3}{4} \times 2$

Materials ■ fraction strips ■ MathBoard

A. Place two 1-whole fraction strips side-by-side to represent the length of the garden.

B. Find 4 fraction strips all with the same denominator that fit exactly under the two wholes.

C. Draw a picture of your model.

1	1

D. Circle $\frac{3}{4}$ of 2 on the model you drew.

E. Complete the number sentence. $\frac{3}{4} \times 2 =$ ____________

So, Martin will plant carrots along ____________ meters of each row.

Draw Conclusions

1. **Explain** why you placed four fraction strips with the same denominator under the two 1-whole strips.

____

____

2. **Explain** how you would model $\frac{3}{10}$ of 2?

____

____

Make Connections

In the Investigate, you multiplied a whole number by a fraction. You can also use a model to multiply a fraction by a whole number.

Margo was helping clean up after a class party. There were 3 boxes remaining with pizza in them. Each box had $\frac{3}{8}$ of a pizza left. How much pizza was left in all?

Materials ■ fraction circles

STEP 1 Find $3 \times \frac{3}{8}$. Model three 1-whole fraction circles to represent the number of boxes containing pizza.

STEP 2 Place $\frac{1}{8}$ fraction circle pieces on each circle to represent the amount of pizza that was left in each box.

- Shade the fraction circles below to show your model.

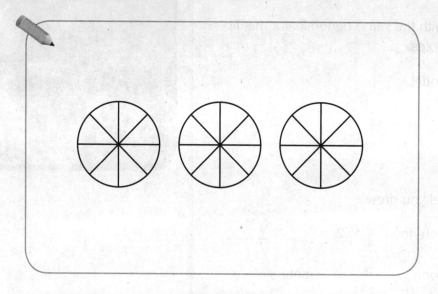

Each circle shows ______ eighths of a whole.

The 3 circles show ______ eighths of a whole.

STEP 3 Complete the number sentences.

$\frac{3}{8} + \frac{3}{8} + \frac{3}{8} =$ ____________

$3 \times \frac{3}{8} =$ ____________

So, Margo had ____________ boxes of pizza left.

MATHEMATICAL PRACTICES

Math Talk Explain how you would know there is more than one pizza left.

Name ________________________________

Share and Show

Use the model to find the product.

1. $\frac{5}{6} \times 3 =$ __________

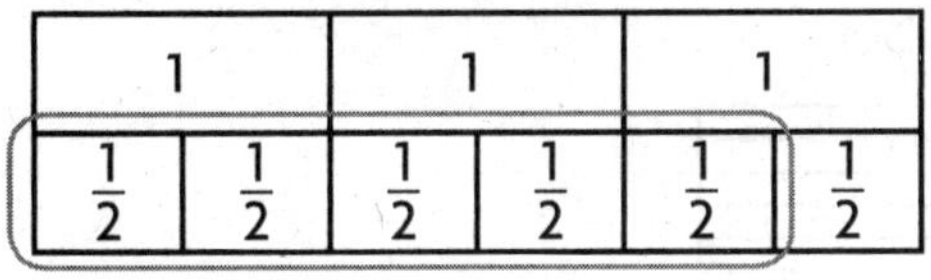

2. $2 \times \frac{5}{6} =$ __________

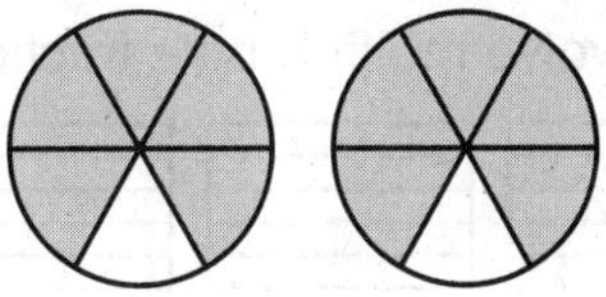

Find the product.

3. $\frac{5}{12} \times 3 =$ __________

4. $9 \times \frac{1}{3} =$ __________

5. $\frac{7}{8} \times 4 =$ __________

6. $4 \times \frac{3}{5} =$ __________

7. $\frac{7}{8} \times 2 =$ __________

8. $7 \times \frac{2}{5} =$ __________

9. $\frac{3}{8} \times 4 =$ __________

10. $11 \times \frac{3}{4} =$ __________

11. $\frac{4}{15} \times 5 =$ __________

12. **Write Math** Matt has a 5-pound bag of apples. To make a pie, he needs to use $\frac{3}{5}$ of the bag. How many pounds of apples will he use for the pie? **Explain** what a model for this problem might look like.

____

____

____

Problem Solving

H.O.T. Pose a Problem

13. Tarique drew the model below for a problem. Write 2 problems that can be solved using this model. One of your problems should involve multiplying a whole number by a fraction and the other problem should involve multiplying a fraction by a whole number.

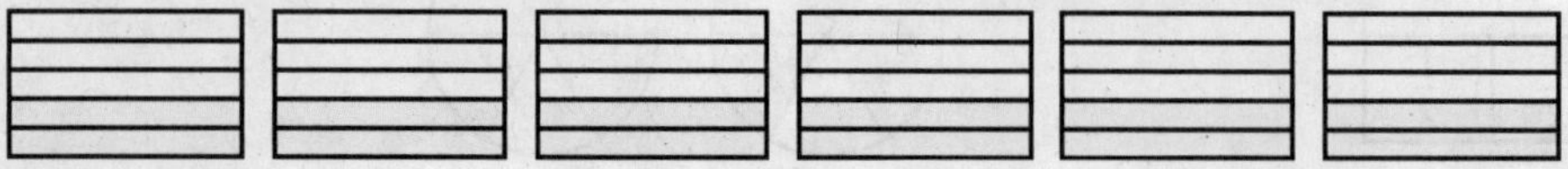

Pose problems.

Solve your problems.

- How could you change the model to give you an answer of $4\frac{4}{5}$? **Explain** and write a new equation.

Name ______________________________

Fraction and Whole Number Multiplication

Essential Question How can you find the product of a fraction and a whole number without using a model?

COMMON CORE STANDARD CC.5.NF.4a
Apply and extend previous understandings of multiplication and division to multiply and divide fractions.

UNLOCK the Problem — REAL WORLD

Charlene has five 1-pound bags of different color sands. For an art project, she will use $\frac{3}{8}$ pound of each bag of sand to create a colorful sand-art jar. How much sand will be in Charlene's sand-art jar?

- How much sand is in each bag?

____

- Will Charlene use all of the sand in each bag? Explain.

____

Multiply a fraction by a whole number.

MODEL

- Shade the model to show 5 groups of $\frac{3}{8}$.

$5 \times$ 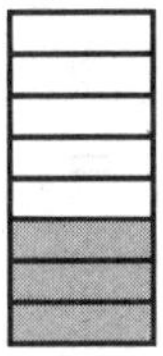 $=$

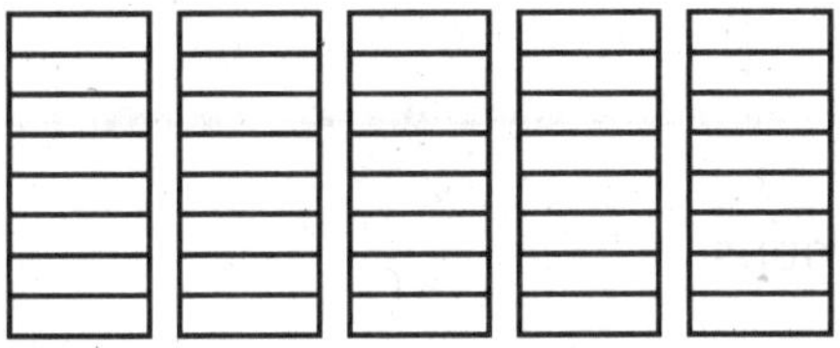

- Rearrange the shaded pieces to fill as many wholes as possible.

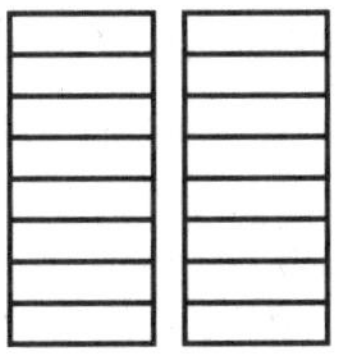 $=$

RECORD

- Write an expression to represent the problem.

$5 \times \frac{3}{8}$ **Think:** I need to find 5 groups of 3 eighth-size pieces.

- Multiply the number of eighth-size pieces in each whole by 5. Then write the answer as the total number of eighth-size pieces.

$\frac{\_\_ \times \_\_}{8} = \frac{\_\_}{\_\_}$

- Write the answer as a mixed number in simplest form.

$\frac{\_\_}{\_\_} = \_\_\frac{\_\_}{\_\_}$

So, there are _______ pounds of sand in Charlene's sand-art jar.

Math Talk MATHEMATICAL PRACTICES Explain how you can find how much sand Charlene has left.

Example Multiply a whole number by a fraction.

Kirsten brought in 4 loaves of bread to make sandwiches for the class picnic. Her classmates used $\frac{2}{3}$ of the bread. How many loaves of bread were used?

MODEL

- Shade the model to show $\frac{2}{3}$ of 4.

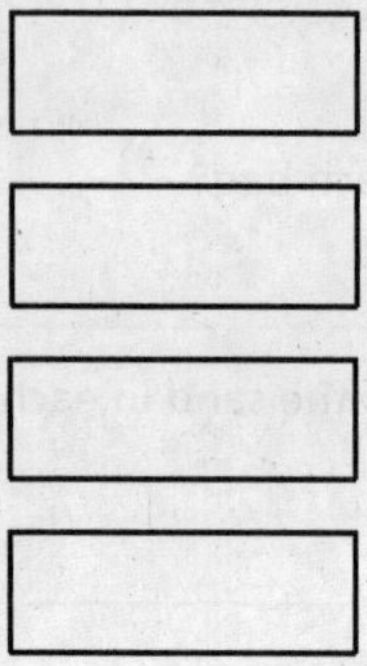

Think: I can cut the loaves into thirds and show $\frac{2}{3}$ of them being used.

- Rearrange the shaded pieces to fill as many wholes as possible.

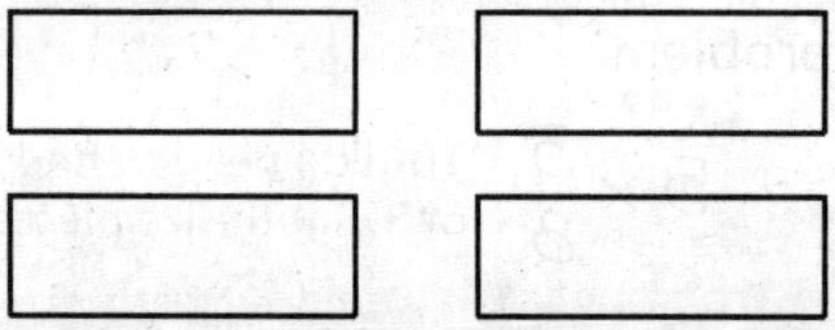

So, ______ loaves of bread were used.

RECORD

- **Write an expression to represent the problem.**

$\frac{2}{3} \times 4$

Think: I need to find $\frac{2}{3}$ of 4 wholes.

- **Multiply 4 by the number of third-size pieces in each whole. Then write the answer as the total number of third-size pieces.**

$\frac{\square \times \square}{\square} = \frac{\square}{\square}$

- **Write the answer as a mixed number.**

$\frac{\square}{\square} = \square\frac{\square}{\square}$

- Would we have the same amount of bread if we had 4 groups of $\frac{2}{3}$ of a loaf? **Explain.**

____

Try This! **Find the product. Write the product in simplest form.**

A $4 \times \frac{7}{8}$

B $\frac{5}{9} \times 12$

Name ___

Share and Show

Find the product. Write the product in simplest form.

1. $3 \times \frac{2}{5} =$ ___

- Multiply the numerator by the whole number. Write the product over the denominator.
- Write the answer as a mixed number in simplest form.

$\frac{\square \times \square}{\square} = \frac{\square}{\square}$

$\frac{\square}{\square} = \square\frac{\square}{\square}$

2. $\frac{2}{3} \times 5 =$ ___

3. $6 \times \frac{2}{3} =$ ___

4. $\frac{5}{7} \times 4 =$ ___

On Your Own

Find the product. Write the product in simplest form.

5. $5 \times \frac{2}{3} =$ ___

6. $\frac{1}{4} \times 3 =$ ___

7. $7 \times \frac{7}{8} =$ ___

8. $2 \times \frac{4}{5} =$ ___

9. $4 \times \frac{3}{4} =$ ___

10. $\frac{7}{9} \times 2 =$ ___

Practice: Copy and Solve. Find the product. Write the product in simplest form.

11. $\frac{3}{5} \times 11$

12. $3 \times \frac{3}{4}$

13. $\frac{5}{8} \times 3$

H.O.T. Algebra Find the unknown digit.

14. $\frac{\blacksquare}{2} \times 8 = 4$

$\blacksquare =$ ___

15. $\blacksquare \times \frac{5}{6} = \frac{20}{6}$, or $3\frac{1}{3}$

$\blacksquare =$ ___

16. $\frac{1}{\blacksquare} \times 18 = 3$

$\blacksquare =$ ___

UNLOCK the Problem REAL WORLD

TEST PRACTICE

17. The caterer wants to have enough turkey to feed 24 people. If he wants to provide $\frac{3}{4}$ of a pound of turkey for each person, how much turkey does he need?

Ⓐ 72 pounds Ⓒ 18 pounds

Ⓑ 24 pounds Ⓓ 6 pounds

a. What do you need to find? ______

______

b. What operation will you use? ______

c. What information are you given? ______

______

d. Solve the problem.

e. Complete the sentences.

The caterer wants to serve 24 people

______ of a pound of turkey each.

He will need ______ × ______, or

______ pounds of turkey.

f. Fill in the bubble for the correct answer choice.

18. Patty wants to run $\frac{5}{6}$ of a mile every day for 5 days. How far will she run in that time?

Ⓐ 25 miles

Ⓑ 5 miles

Ⓒ $4\frac{1}{6}$ miles

Ⓓ $1\frac{2}{3}$ miles

19. Doug has 33 feet of rope. He wants to use $\frac{2}{3}$ of it for his canoe. How many feet of rope will he use for his canoe?

Ⓐ 11 feet

Ⓑ 22 feet

Ⓒ 33 feet

Ⓓ 66 feet

Name ______________________________

Fraction Multiplication

Essential Question How do you multiply fractions?

COMMON CORE STANDARD CC.5.NF.4a
Apply and extend previous understandings of multiplication and division to multiply and divide fractions.

UNLOCK the Problem REAL WORLD

Sasha has $\frac{3}{5}$ of a scarf left to knit. If she finishes $\frac{1}{2}$ of that today, how much of the scarf will Sasha knit today?

- How much of the scarf does Sasha have left to knit?

  ____

- Of the fraction that is left, how much will she finish today?

  ____

Multiply. $\frac{1}{2} \times \frac{3}{5}$

One Way Use a model.

- Shade $\frac{3}{5}$ of the model yellow.
- Draw a horizontal line across the rectangle to show 2 equal parts.
- Shade $\frac{1}{2}$ of the yellow sections blue.
- Count the sections that are shaded twice and write a fraction for the parts of the whole that are shaded twice.

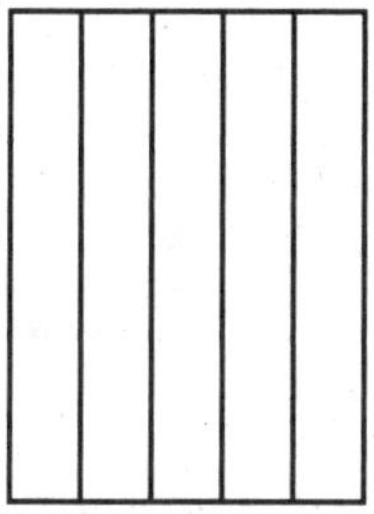

$$\frac{1}{2} \times \frac{3}{5} = \_\_\_\_$$

- Compare the numerator and denominator of the product with the numerators and denominators of the factors. **Describe** what you notice.

____

____

____

Another Way Use paper and pencil.

You can multiply fractions without using a model.

- Multiply the numerators.
- Multiply the denominators.

$$\frac{1}{2} \times \frac{3}{5} = \frac{1 \times \_\_}{2 \times \_\_}$$

$$= \frac{\_\_}{\_\_}$$

So, Sasha will knit ______ of the scarf today.

CONNECT Remember you can write a whole number as a fraction with a denominator of 1.

Example

Find $4 \times \frac{5}{12}$. Write the product in simplest form.

$$4 \times \frac{5}{12} = \frac{4}{} \times \frac{5}{12}$$

Write the whole number as a fraction.

$$= \frac{4 \times \square}{\square \times \square} = \frac{\square}{\square}$$

Multiply the numerators.
Multiply the denominators.

$$= \frac{\square \div \square}{12 \div \square} = \frac{\square}{\square}, \text{ or } \square$$

Write the product as a fraction or a mixed number in simplest form.

So, $4 \times \frac{5}{12} =$ ______, or ______.

MATHEMATICAL PRACTICES

Math Talk Is the answer reasonable? **Explain.**

Try This! **Evaluate $c \times \frac{4}{5}$ for $c = \frac{5}{8}$.**

- What number does c represent? ______
- Replace c in the expression with ______.
- Multiply the numerators.
- Multiply the denominators.
- Write the product in simplest form.

$$\frac{\square}{\square} \times \frac{4}{5}$$

$$\frac{\square \times \square}{\square \times \square} = \frac{\square}{\square}$$

$$= \frac{\square}{\square}$$

So, $c \times \frac{4}{5}$ is equal to ______ for $c = \frac{5}{8}$.

- Since $\frac{4}{5}$ is being multiplied by a number less than one, should the product be *greater than* or *less than* $\frac{4}{5}$? **Explain.** ______

Name ___________________

Share and Show

Find the product. Write the product in simplest form.

1. $6 \times \frac{3}{8}$

   $\frac{6}{1} \times \frac{3}{8} = \frac{\square}{\square}$

2. $\frac{3}{8} \times \frac{8}{9}$

3. $\frac{2}{3} \times 27$

4. $\frac{5}{12} \times \frac{3}{5}$

5. $\frac{1}{2} \times \frac{3}{5}$

6. $\frac{2}{3} \times \frac{4}{5}$

7. $\frac{1}{3} \times \frac{5}{8}$

8. $4 \times \frac{1}{5}$

MATHEMATICAL PRACTICES

Math Talk Explain how to find the product $\frac{1}{6} \times \frac{2}{3}$ in simplest form.

On Your Own

Find the product. Write the product in simplest form.

9. $2 \times \frac{1}{8}$

10. $\frac{4}{9} \times \frac{4}{5}$

11. $\frac{1}{12} \times \frac{2}{3}$

12. $\frac{1}{7} \times 30$

13. Of the pets in the pet show, $\frac{5}{6}$ are cats. $\frac{4}{5}$ of the cats are calico cats. What fraction of the pets are calico cats?

14. Five cats each ate $\frac{1}{4}$ cup of food. How much food did they eat altogether?

Algebra **Evaluate for the given value.**

15. $\frac{2}{5} \times c$ for $c = \frac{4}{7}$

16. $m \times \frac{4}{5}$ for $m = \frac{7}{8}$

17. $\frac{2}{3} \times t$ for $t = \frac{1}{8}$

18. $y \times \frac{4}{5}$ for $y = 5$

Problem Solving REAL WORLD

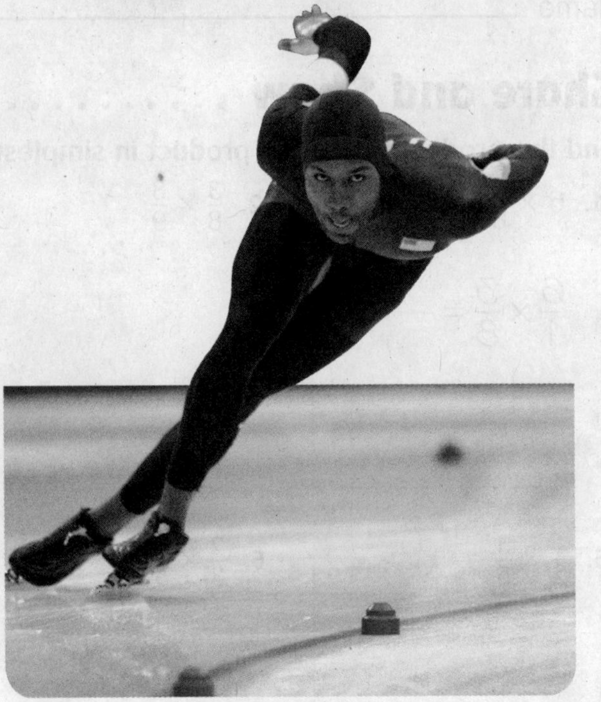

Speedskating is a popular sport in the Winter Olympics. Many young athletes in the U.S. participate in speedskating clubs and camps.

19. At a camp in Green Bay, Wisconsin, $\frac{7}{9}$ of the participants were from Wisconsin. Of that group, $\frac{3}{5}$ were 12 years old. What fraction of the group was from Wisconsin and 12 years old?

____

20. H.O.T. Maribel wants to skate $1\frac{1}{2}$ miles on Monday. If she skates $\frac{9}{10}$ mile Monday morning and $\frac{2}{3}$ of that distance Monday afternoon, will she reach her goal? **Explain.**

____

____

SHOW YOUR WORK

21. Write Math On the first day of camp, $\frac{5}{6}$ of the skaters were beginners. Of the beginners, $\frac{1}{3}$ were girls. What fraction of the skaters were girls and beginners? **Explain** why your answer is reasonable.

____

____

____

____

____

22. **Test Practice** On Wednesday, Danielle skated $\frac{2}{3}$ of the way around the track in 2 minutes. Her younger brother skated $\frac{3}{4}$ of Danielle's distance in 2 minutes. What fraction of the track did Danielle's brother finish in 2 minutes?

Ⓐ $\frac{1}{3}$

Ⓑ $\frac{1}{2}$

Ⓒ $\frac{5}{7}$

Ⓓ $\frac{3}{4}$

Name ______________________________

Area and Mixed Numbers

Essential Question How can you use a unit tile to find the area of a rectangle with fractional side lengths?

COMMON CORE STANDARD CC.5.NF.4b
Apply and extend previous understandings of multiplication and division to multiply and divide fractions.

Investigate

You can use square tiles with side lengths that are unit fractions to find the area of a rectangle.

Sonja wants to cover the rectangular floor of her closet with tile. The floor is $2\frac{1}{2}$ feet by $3\frac{1}{2}$ feet. She wants to use the fewest tiles possible and doesn't want to cut any tiles. The tiles come in three sizes: 1 foot by 1 foot, $\frac{1}{2}$ foot by $\frac{1}{2}$ foot, and $\frac{1}{4}$ foot by $\frac{1}{4}$ foot. Choose the tile that Sonja should use. What is the area of the closet floor?

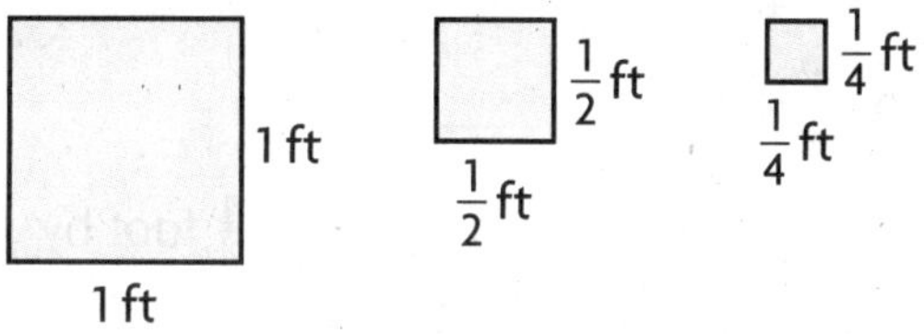

A. Choose the largest tile Sonja can use to tile the floor of the closet and avoid gaps or overlaps.

- Which square tile should Sonja choose? **Explain.** ______________________________

____

____

B. On the grid, let each square represent the dimensions of the tile you chose. Then draw a diagram of the floor.

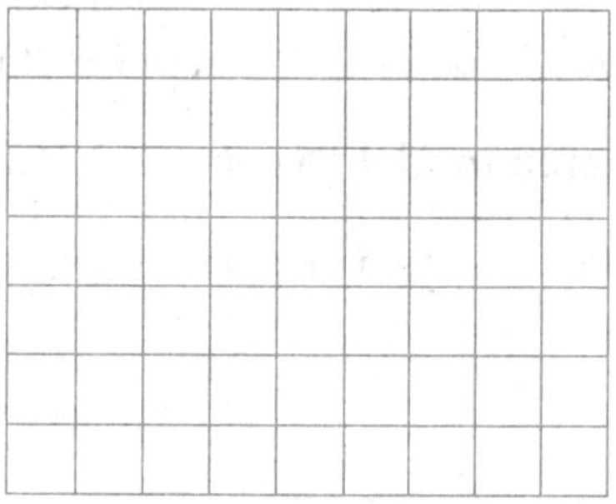

C. Count the squares in your diagram.

- How many squares cover the diagram?

  _____ × _____, or _____ squares

- What is the area of the tile you chose? ____________

- Since 1 square on your diagram represents an area of _____ square foot,

  the area represented by _____ squares is _____ × _____,

  or _____ square feet.

So, the area of the floor written as a mixed number

is _____ square feet.

MATHEMATICAL PRACTICES
Math Talk Explain how you found the area of the tile you chose.

Draw Conclusions

1. Write a number sentence for the area of the floor using fractions greater than 1. **Explain** how you knew which operation to use in your number sentence.

____

____

2. **Explain** how using fractions greater than 1 could help you multiply mixed numbers.

____

____

3. How many $\frac{1}{4}$ foot by $\frac{1}{4}$ foot tiles would Sonja need to cover one $\frac{1}{2}$ foot by $\frac{1}{2}$ foot tile? ________

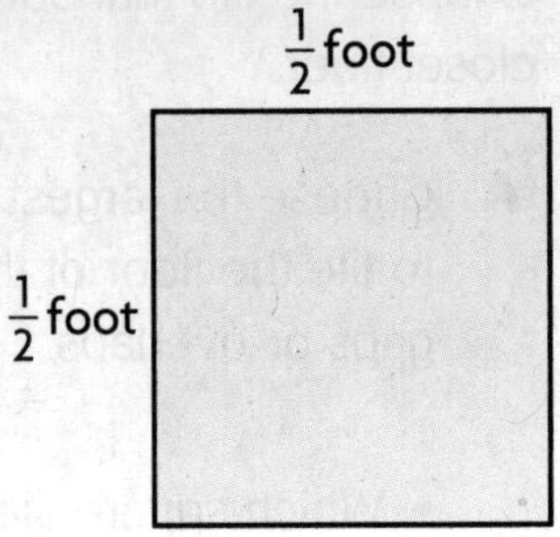

4. How could you find the number of $\frac{1}{4}$ foot by $\frac{1}{4}$ foot tiles needed to cover the same closet floor?

____

____

Make Connections

Sometimes it is easier to multiply mixed numbers if you break them apart into whole numbers and fractions.

Use an area model to solve. $1\frac{3}{5} \times 2\frac{3}{4}$

STEP 1 Rewrite each mixed number as the sum of a whole number and a fraction.

$1\frac{3}{5}$ = ____________ $2\frac{3}{4}$ = ____________

STEP 2 Draw an area model to show the original multiplication problem.

STEP 3 Draw dashed lines and label each section to show how you broke apart the mixed numbers in Step 1.

STEP 4 Find the area of each section.

STEP 5 Add the area of each section to find the total area of the rectangle.

So, the product of $1\frac{3}{5} \times 2\frac{3}{4}$ is ______.

Name ______________________

Share and Show

Use the grid to find the area. Let each square represent $\frac{1}{3}$ meter by $\frac{1}{3}$ meter.

1. $1\frac{2}{3} \times 1\frac{1}{3}$

- Draw a diagram to represent the dimensions.
- How many squares cover the diagram? ______________
- What is the area of each square? ______________
- What is the area of the diagram? ______________

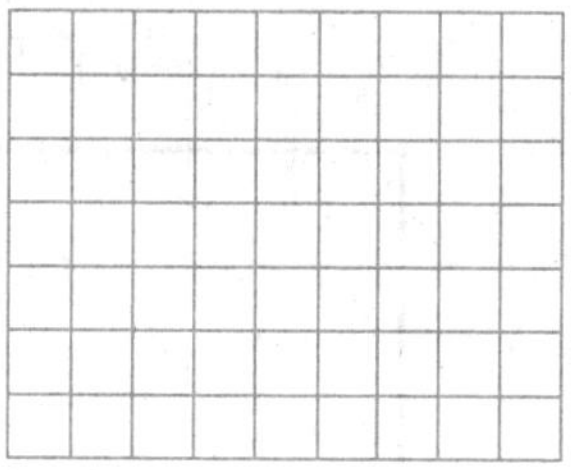

Use the grid to find the area. Let each square represent $\frac{1}{4}$ foot by $\frac{1}{4}$ foot.

2. $1\frac{3}{4} \times 1\frac{2}{4} =$ ______

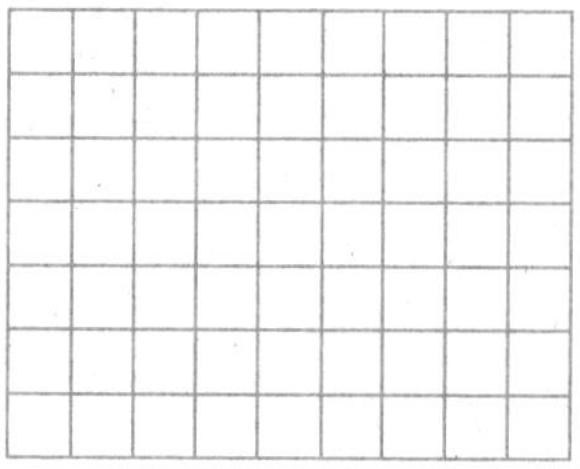

The area is ______ square feet.

3. $1\frac{1}{4} \times 1\frac{1}{2} =$ ______

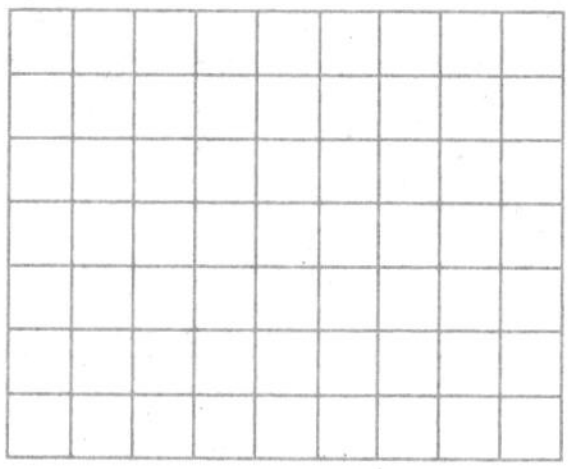

The area is ______ square feet.

Use an area model to solve.

4. $1\frac{3}{4} \times 2\frac{1}{2}$

____

5. $1\frac{3}{8} \times 2\frac{1}{2}$

____

6. $1\frac{1}{9} \times 1\frac{2}{3}$

____

7. Write Math ▸ **Explain** how finding the area of a rectangle with whole-number side lengths compares to finding the area of a rectangle with fractional side lengths.

____

____

Problem Solving REAL WORLD

H.O.T. Pose a Problem

8. Terrance is designing a garden. He drew the following diagram of his garden. Pose a problem using mixed numbers that can be solved using his diagram.

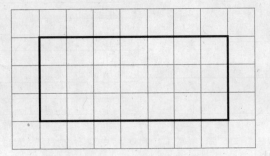

Pose a Problem.

Solve your problem.

- **Describe** how you decided on the dimensions of Terrance's garden.

Name ______________________________

Compare Fraction Factors and Products

Essential Question How does the size of the product compare to the size of one factor when multiplying fractions?

COMMON CORE STANDARDS CC.5.NF.5a; CC.5.NF.5b
Apply and extend previous understandings of multiplication and division to multiply and divide fractions.

UNLOCK the Problem REAL WORLD

Multiplication can be thought of as resizing one number by another number. For example, 2×3 will result in a product that is 2 times as great as 3.

What happens to the size of a product when a number is multiplied by a fraction rather than a whole number?

One Way Use a model.

A During the week, the Smith family ate $\frac{3}{4}$ of a box of cereal.

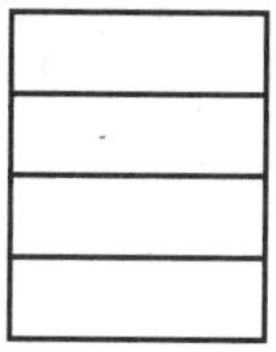

- Shade the model to show $\frac{3}{4}$ of a box of cereal.
- Write an expression for $\frac{3}{4}$ of 1 box of cereal. $\frac{3}{4} \times$ ______
- Will the product be *equal to, greater than,* or *less than* 1?

____

B The Ling family has 4 boxes of cereal. They ate $\frac{3}{4}$ of all the cereal during the week.

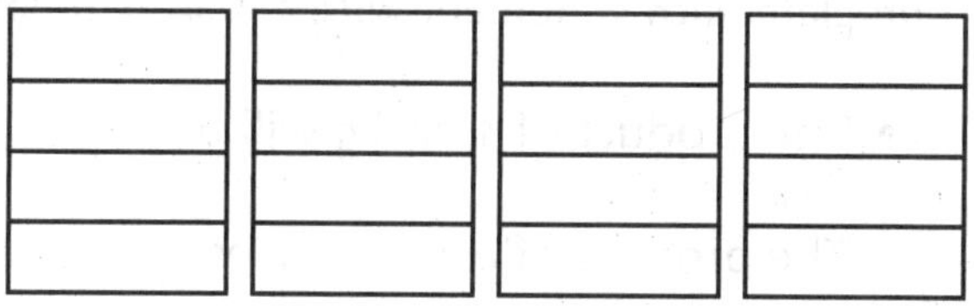

- Shade the model to show $\frac{3}{4}$ of 4 boxes of cereal.
- Write an expression for $\frac{3}{4}$ of 4 boxes of cereal. $\frac{3}{4} \times$ ______
- Will the product be *equal to, greater than,* or *less than* 4?

____

C The Carter family has only $\frac{1}{2}$ of a box of cereal at the beginning of the week. They ate $\frac{3}{4}$ of the $\frac{1}{2}$ box of cereal.

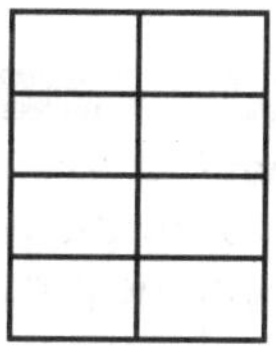

- Shade the model to show $\frac{3}{4}$ of $\frac{1}{2}$ box of cereal.
- Write an expression to show $\frac{3}{4}$ of $\frac{1}{2}$ box of cereal. $\frac{3}{4} \times$ ______
- Will the product be *equal to, greater than,* or *less than* $\frac{1}{2}$? *than* $\frac{3}{4}$?

____

Another Way Use a diagram.

You can use a diagram to show the relationship between the products when a fraction is multiplied or scaled (resized) by a number.

Graph a point to show $\frac{3}{4}$ scaled by 1, $\frac{1}{2}$, and 4.

A $1 \times \frac{3}{4}$

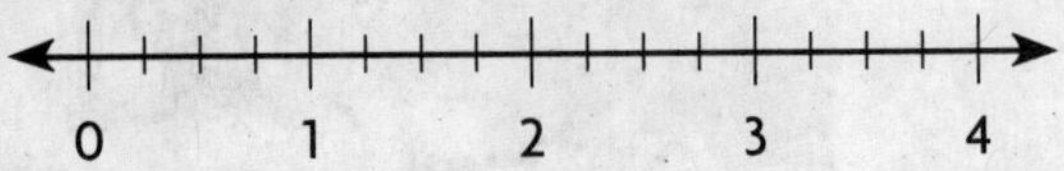

Think: Locate $\frac{3}{4}$ on the diagram and shade that distance from 0. Then graph a point to show 1 of $\frac{3}{4}$.

B $\frac{1}{2} \times \frac{3}{4}$

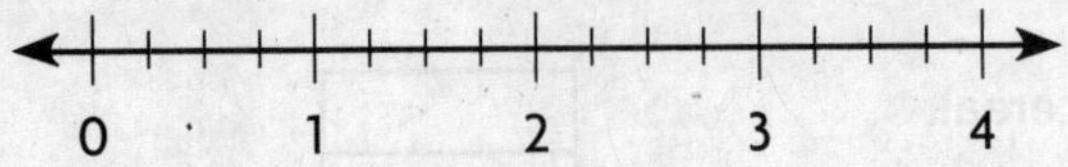

Think: Locate $\frac{3}{4}$ on the diagram and shade that distance from 0. Then graph a point to show $\frac{1}{2}$ of $\frac{3}{4}$.

C $4 \times \frac{3}{4}$

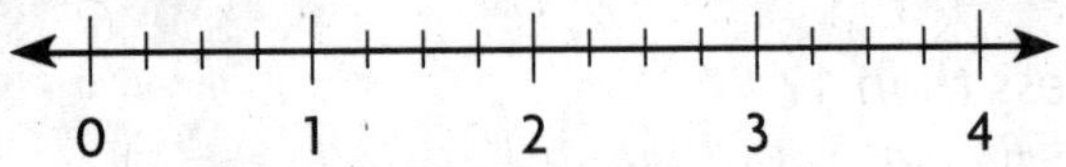

Think: Locate $\frac{3}{4}$ on the diagram and shade that distance from 0. Then graph a point to show 4 times $\frac{3}{4}$.

Complete each statement with *equal to, greater than,* or *less than*.

- The product of 1 and $\frac{3}{4}$ will be ______________ $\frac{3}{4}$.
- The product of a number less than 1 and $\frac{3}{4}$ will be ______________ $\frac{3}{4}$ and ______________ the other factor.
- The product of a number greater than 1 and $\frac{3}{4}$ will be ______________ $\frac{3}{4}$ and ______________ the other factor.

MATHEMATICAL PRACTICES

Math Talk What if $\frac{3}{5}$ was multiplied by $\frac{1}{6}$ or by the whole number 7? Would the products be equal to, greater than, or less than $\frac{3}{5}$? Explain.

Name ______________________________

Share and Show

Complete the statement with *equal to, greater than,* or *less than.*

1. $4 \times \frac{7}{8}$ will be ______________ $\frac{7}{8}$.

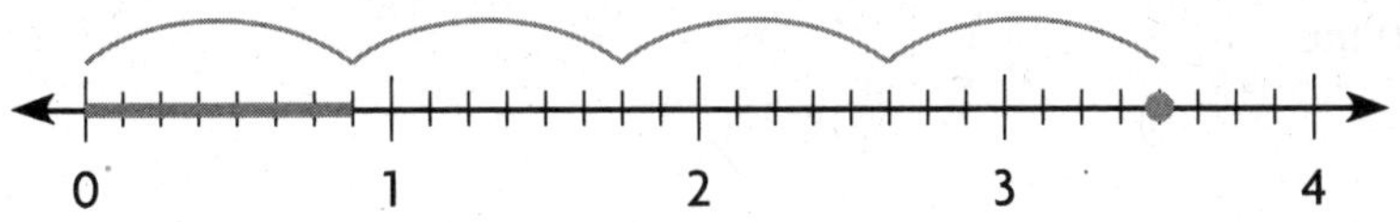

2. $\frac{3}{5} \times \frac{2}{7}$ will be ______________ $\frac{3}{5}$.

3. $\frac{5}{8} \times 6$ will be ______________ $\frac{5}{8}$.

4. $\frac{2}{3} \times \frac{5}{5}$ will be ______________ $\frac{2}{3}$.

5. $8 \times \frac{7}{8}$ will be ______________ 8.

On Your Own

Complete the statement with *equal to, greater than,* or *less than.*

6. $\frac{4}{9} \times \frac{3}{8}$ will be ______________ $\frac{3}{8}$.

7. $7 \times \frac{9}{10}$ will be ______________ $\frac{9}{10}$.

8. $5 \times \frac{1}{3}$ will be ______________ $\frac{1}{3}$.

9. $\frac{6}{11} \times 1$ will be ______________ $\frac{6}{11}$.

10. $\frac{1}{6} \times \frac{7}{7}$ will be ______________ 1.

11. $4 \times \frac{3}{5}$ will be ______________ $\frac{3}{5}$.

Problem Solving REAL WORLD

12. Lola is making cookies. She plans to multiply the recipe by 3 so she can make enough cookies for the whole class. If the recipe calls for $\frac{2}{3}$ cup of sugar, will she need more than $\frac{2}{3}$ or less than $\frac{2}{3}$ cup of sugar to make all the cookies?

____

13. Peter is planning on spending $\frac{2}{3}$ as many hours watching television this week as he did last week. Is Peter going to spend more hours or fewer hours watching television this week?

____

14. **Test Practice** Rochelle saves $\frac{1}{4}$ of her allowance. If she decides to start saving $\frac{1}{2}$ as much, which statement below is true?

Ⓐ She will be saving the same amount.

Ⓑ She will be saving more.

Ⓒ She will be saving less.

Ⓓ She will be saving twice as much.

Connect to Art

A scale model is a representation of an object with the same shape as the real object. Models can be larger or smaller than the actual object but are often smaller.

Architects often make scale models of the buildings or structures they plan to build. Models can give them an idea of how the structure will look when finished. Each measurement of the building is scaled up or down by the same factor.

Bob is building a scale model of his bike. He wants his model to be $\frac{1}{5}$ as long as his bike.

15. If Bob's bike is 60 inches long, how long will his model be? _______________

16. H.O.T. If one wheel on Bob's model is 4 inches across, how many inches across is the actual wheel on his bike? **Explain.**

____

____

Name ____________________

Compare Mixed Number Factors and Products

Essential Question How does the size of the product compare to the size of one factor when multiplying fractions greater than one?

COMMON CORE STANDARDS CC.5.NF.5a; CC.5.NF.5b
Apply and extend previous understandings of multiplication and division to multiply and divide fractions.

UNLOCK the Problem REAL WORLD

You can make generalizations about the relative size of a product when one factor is equal to 1, less than 1, or greater than 1.

One Way Use a model.

Jane has a recipe that calls for $1\frac{1}{4}$ cups of flour. She wants to know how much flour she would need if she made the recipe as written, if she made half the recipe, and if she made $1\frac{1}{2}$ times the recipe.

Shade the models to show $1\frac{1}{4}$ scaled by 1, by $\frac{1}{2}$, and by $1\frac{1}{2}$.

A $1 \times 1\frac{1}{4}$

Think: I can use what I know about the Identity Property.

- What can you say about the product when $1\frac{1}{4}$ is multiplied by 1?

____

B $\frac{1}{2} \times 1\frac{1}{4}$

Think: The product will be half of what I started with.

- What can you say about the product when $1\frac{1}{4}$ is multiplied by a fraction less than 1? ____________________

C $1\frac{1}{2} \times 1\frac{1}{4} = \left(1 \times 1\frac{1}{4}\right) + \left(\frac{1}{2} \times 1\frac{1}{4}\right)$

+

Think: The product will be what I started with and $\frac{1}{2}$ more.

- What can you say about the product when $1\frac{1}{4}$ is multiplied by a number greater than 1?

____

Math Talk MATHEMATICAL PRACTICES
Which expression has the greatest product? Which has the least product?

CONNECT You can also use a diagram to show the relationship between the products when a fraction greater than one is multiplied or scaled (resized) by a number.

Another Way Use a diagram.

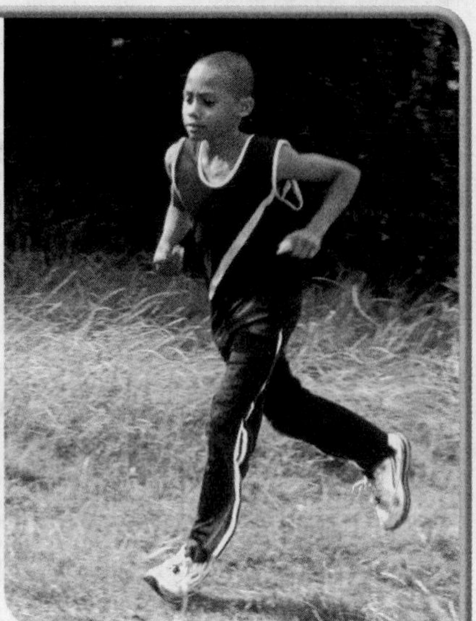

Jake wants to train for a road race. He plans to run $2\frac{1}{2}$ miles on the first day. On the second day, he plans to run $\frac{3}{5}$ of the distance he runs on the first day. On the third day, he plans to run $1\frac{2}{5}$ of the distance he runs on the first day. Which distance is greater: the distance on day 2 when he runs $\frac{3}{5}$ of $2\frac{1}{2}$ miles, or the distance on day 3 when he runs $1\frac{2}{5}$ of $2\frac{1}{2}$ miles?

Graph a point on the diagram to show the size of the product. Then complete the statement with *equal to, greater than,* or *less than.*

A $1 \times 2\frac{1}{2}$

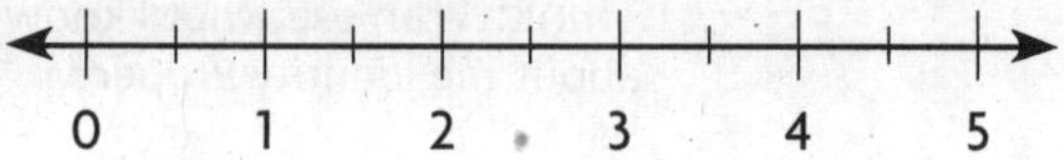

Think: Locate $2\frac{1}{2}$ on the diagram and shade that distance. Then graph a point to show 1 of $2\frac{1}{2}$.

- The product of 1 and $2\frac{1}{2}$ will be ________ $2\frac{1}{2}$.

B $\frac{3}{5} \times 2\frac{1}{2}$

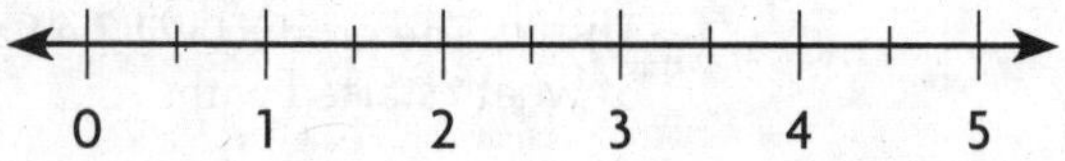

Think: Locate $2\frac{1}{2}$ on the diagram and shade that distance. Then graph a point to show $\frac{3}{5}$ of $2\frac{1}{2}$.

- The product of a number less than 1 and $2\frac{1}{2}$ is ________ $2\frac{1}{2}$.

C $1\frac{2}{5} \times 2\frac{1}{2} = \left(1 \times 2\frac{1}{2}\right) + \left(\frac{2}{5} \times 2\frac{1}{2}\right)$

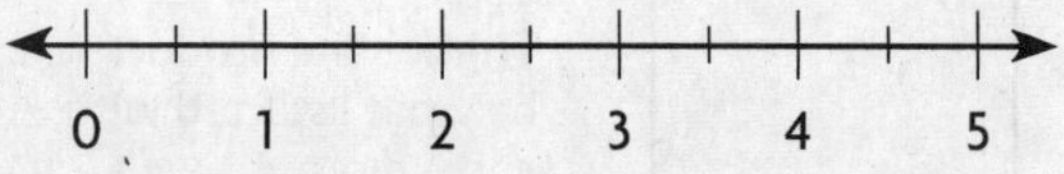

Think: Locate $2\frac{1}{2}$ on the diagram and shade that distance. Then graph a point to show 1 of $2\frac{1}{2}$ and $\frac{2}{5}$ more of $2\frac{1}{2}$.

- The product of a number greater than 1 and $2\frac{1}{2}$ will be ________ $2\frac{1}{2}$ and ________ the other factor.

So, ______ of ______ miles is a greater distance than ______ of ______ miles.

Name ______________________________

Share and Show

Complete the statement with *equal to, greater than,* or *less than.*

1. $\frac{5}{6} \times 2\frac{1}{5}$ will be ______________ $2\frac{1}{5}$.

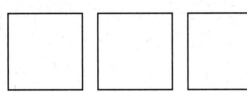

Shade the model to show $\frac{5}{6} \times 2\frac{1}{5}$.

2. $1\frac{1}{5} \times 2\frac{2}{3}$ will be ______________ $2\frac{2}{3}$.

3. $\frac{4}{5} \times 2\frac{2}{5}$ will be ______________ $2\frac{2}{5}$.

On Your Own

Complete the statement with *equal to, greater than,* or *less than.*

4. $\frac{2}{2} \times 1\frac{1}{2}$ will be ______________ $1\frac{1}{2}$.

5. $\frac{2}{3} \times 3\frac{1}{6}$ will be ______________ $3\frac{1}{6}$.

6. $2 \times 2\frac{1}{4}$ will be ______________ $2\frac{1}{4}$.

7. $4 \times 1\frac{3}{7}$ will be ______________ $1\frac{3}{7}$.

H.O.T. **Algebra** **Tell whether the unknown factor is *less than 1* or *greater than 1*.**

8. ■ $\times 1\frac{2}{3} = \frac{5}{6}$

The unknown factor is ______________ 1.

9. ■ $\times 1\frac{1}{4} = 2\frac{1}{2}$

The unknown factor is ______________ 1.

Problem Solving REAL WORLD

SHOW YOUR WORK

10. Kyle is making a scale drawing of his math book. The dimensions of his drawing will be $\frac{1}{3}$ the dimensions of his book. If the width of his book is $8\frac{1}{2}$ inches, will the width of his drawing be equal to, greater than, or less than $8\frac{1}{2}$ inches?

____

11. Write Math ➤ **Sense or Nonsense?** Penny wants to make a model of a beetle that is larger than life-size. Penny says she is going to use a scaling factor of $\frac{7}{12}$. Does this make sense or is it nonsense? **Explain.**

____

____

____

____

12. H.O.T. Shannon, Mary, and John earn a weekly allowance. Shannon earns an amount that is $\frac{2}{3}$ of what John earns. Mary earns an amount that is $1\frac{2}{3}$ of what John earns. John earns \$20 a week. Who earns the greatest allowance? Who earns the least?

____

____

13. **Test Practice** Addie's puppy weighs $1\frac{2}{3}$ times what it weighed when it was born. It weighed $1\frac{1}{3}$ pounds at birth. Which statement below is true?

Ⓐ The puppy weighs the same as it did at birth.

Ⓑ The puppy weighs less than it did at birth.

Ⓒ The puppy weighs more than it did at birth.

Ⓓ The puppy weighs twice what it did at birth.

Name ______________________________

Problem Solving • Find Unknown Lengths

Essential Question How can you use the strategy *guess, check, and revise* to solve problems with fractions?

COMMON CORE STANDARD CC.5.NF.5b
Apply and extend previous understandings of multiplication and division to multiply and divide fractions.

UNLOCK the Problem REAL WORLD

Sarah wants to design a rectangular garden with a section for flowers that attract butterflies. She wants the area of this section to be $\frac{3}{4}$ square yard. If she wants the width to be $\frac{1}{3}$ the length, what will the dimensions of the butterfly section be?

Read the Problem

What do I need to find?

I need to find ______________

____

____

____

______________.

What information do I need to use?

The part of the garden for butterflies has an area of ______ square yard and the width is ______ the length.

How will I use the information?

I will ______ the sides of the butterfly area. Then I will ______ my guess and ______ it if it is not correct.

Solve the Problem

I can try different lengths and calculate the widths by finding $\frac{1}{3}$ the length. For each length and width, I find the area and then compare. If the product is less than or greater than $\frac{3}{4}$ square yard, I need to revise the length.

Guess		Check	Revise
Length (in yards)	**Width (in yards) ($\frac{1}{3}$ of the length)**	**Area of Butterfly Garden (in square yards)**	
$\frac{3}{4}$	$\frac{1}{3} \times \frac{3}{4} = \frac{1}{4}$	$\frac{3}{4} \times \frac{1}{4} = \frac{3}{16}$ too low	Try a longer length.
$2\frac{1}{4}$, or $\frac{9}{4}$			

So, the dimensions of Sarah's butterfly garden will be ______ yard by ______ yards.

Try Another Problem

Marcus is building a rectangular box for his kitten to sleep in. He wants the area of the bottom of the box to be 360 square inches and the length of one side to be $1\frac{3}{5}$ the length of the other side. What should the dimensions of the bottom of the bed be?

Read the Problem

What do I need to find?	What information do I need to use?	How will I use the information?

Solve the Problem

So, the dimensions of the bottom of the kitten's bed will be __________ by __________.

- **What if** the longer side was still $1\frac{3}{5}$ the length of the shorter side and the shorter side was 20 inches long? What would the area of the bottom of the bed be then? ______________________________

Name ______________________________

Share and Show

1. When Pascal built a dog house, he knew he wanted the floor of the house to have an area of 24 square feet. He also wanted the width to be $\frac{2}{3}$ the length. What are the dimensions of the dog house?

First, choose two numbers that have a product of 24.

Guess: ______ feet and ______ feet

Then, check those numbers. Is the greater number $\frac{2}{3}$ of the other number?

Check: $\frac{2}{3} \times$ ______ $=$ ______

My guess is ____________.

Finally, if the guess is not correct, revise it and check again. Continue until you find the correct answer.

So, the dimensions of the dog house are ________________.

2. **What if** Pascal wanted the area of the floor to be 54 square feet and the width still to be $\frac{2}{3}$ the length? What would the dimensions of the floor be?

3. Leo wants to paint a mural that covers a wall with an area of 1,440 square feet. The height of the wall is $\frac{2}{5}$ of its length. What is the length and the height of the wall?

On Your Own

Choose a STRATEGY

- Act It Out
- Draw a Diagram
- Make a Table
- Solve a Simpler Problem
- Work Backward
- Guess, Check, and Revise

4. Barry wants to make a drawing that is $\frac{1}{4}$ the size of the original. If a tree in the original drawing is 14 inches tall, how tall will the tree in Barry's drawing be?

____

5. H.O.T. A blueprint is a scale drawing of a building. The dimensions of the blueprint for Penny's doll house are $\frac{1}{4}$ of the measurements of the actual doll house. The floor of the doll house has an area of 864 square inches. If the width of the doll house is $\frac{2}{3}$ the length, what are the dimensions of the floor on the blueprint of the doll house?

____

6. **Write Math** ▸ **Pose a Problem** Look back at Exercise 4. Write a similar problem using a different measurement and a different fraction. Then solve your problem.

____

____

____

____

____

7. ★ **Test Practice** Albert's photograph has an area of 80 square inches. The length of the photo is $1\frac{1}{4}$ the width. Which of the following could be the dimensions of the photograph?

Ⓐ 5 inches by 16 inches

Ⓑ 12 inches by 10 inches

Ⓒ 6 inches by 5 inches

Ⓓ 10 inches by 8 inches

SHOW YOUR WORK

Name ______________________________

Multiply Mixed Numbers

Essential Question How do you multiply mixed numbers?

COMMON CORE STANDARD CC.5.NF.6
Apply and extend previous understandings of multiplication and division to multiply and divide fractions.

UNLOCK the Problem REAL WORLD

One-third of a $1\frac{1}{4}$ acre park has been set aside as a dog park. Find the number of acres that are used as a dog park.

- Is the area of the dog park less than or greater than the area of the $1\frac{1}{4}$ acre park?

____

Multiply. $\frac{1}{3} \times 1\frac{1}{4}$

One Way Use a model.

STEP 1 Shade the model to represent the whole park.

Think: The whole park is _______ acres.

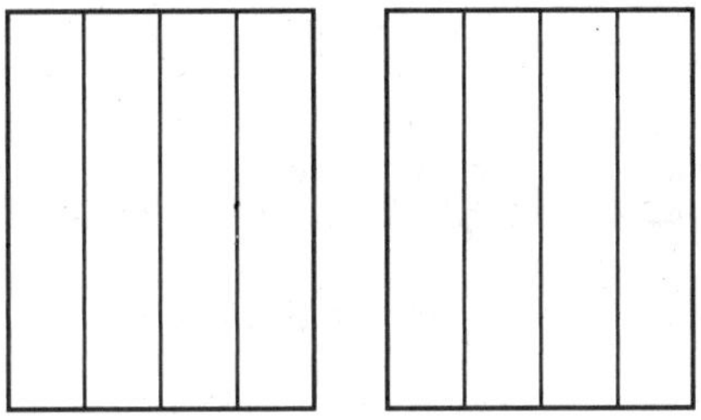

STEP 2 Double-shade the model to represent the part of the park that is a dog park.

Think: The dog park is _______ of the park.

Draw horizontal lines across each rectangle to show _____________.

- How many parts does each rectangle show? _______
- What fraction of each rectangle is shaded twice?

_______ and _______

- What fraction represents all the parts which are shaded twice?

_______ + _______ = _______

So, _______ acre has been set aside.

Another Way Rename the mixed number as a fraction.

STEP 1 Write the mixed number as a fraction greater than 1.

$$\frac{1}{3} \times 1\frac{1}{4} = \frac{1}{3} \times \frac{\quad}{4}$$

STEP 2 Multiply the fractions.

$$= \frac{1 \times \quad}{3 \times 4} = \frac{\quad}{\quad}$$

So, $\frac{1}{3} \times 1\frac{1}{4} =$ _______.

Math Talk MATHEMATICAL PRACTICES Explain why your answer is reasonable.

Example 1 Rename the whole number.

Multiply. $12 \times 2\frac{1}{6}$ **Write the product in simplest form.**

STEP 1 Determine how the product will compare to the greater factor.

$12 \times 2\frac{1}{6}$ will be ____________ 12.

STEP 2 Write the whole number and mixed number as fractions.

STEP 3 Multiply the fractions.

STEP 4 Write the product in simplest form.

$$12 \times 2\frac{1}{6} = \frac{\square}{1} \times \frac{\square}{6}$$

$$= \frac{\square}{\square} = \frac{\square}{\square}, \textit{ or } \square$$

So, $12 \times 2\frac{1}{6} =$ ______.

Example 2 Use the Distributive Property.

Multiply. $16 \times 4\frac{1}{8}$ **Write the product in simplest form.**

STEP 1 Rewrite the expression by using the Distributive Property.

STEP 2 Multiply 16 by each number.

STEP 3 Add.

$$16 \times 4\frac{1}{8} = 16 \times \left(\_\_\_\_ + \frac{1}{8}\right)$$

$$= (16 \times 4) + \left(16 \times \frac{\square}{\square}\right)$$

$$= \_\_\_\_ + 2 = \_\_\_\_$$

So, $16 \times 4\frac{1}{8} =$ ______.

MATHEMATICAL PRACTICES

Math Talk Explain how you know that your answers to both examples are reasonable.

1. **Explain** why you might choose to use the Distributive Property to solve Example 2.

____

2. When you multiply two factors greater than 1, is the product less than, between, or greater than the two factors? **Explain.**

____

____

Name ________________________________

Share and Show

Find the product. Write the product in simplest form.

1. $1\frac{2}{3} \times 3\frac{4}{5} = \frac{\square}{3} \times \frac{\square}{5}$

$= \frac{\square}{\square}$

$=$ ______

2. $\frac{1}{2} \times 1\frac{1}{3}$ ______

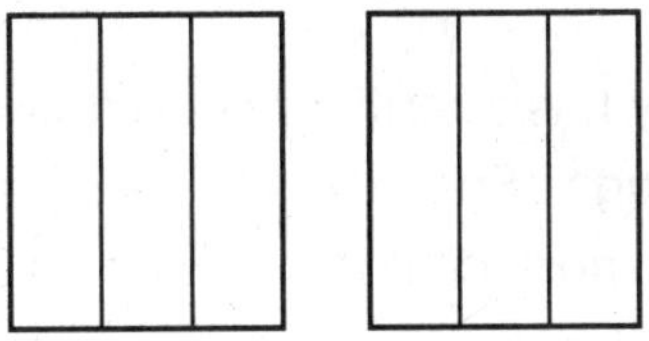

Shade the model to find the product.

3. $1\frac{1}{8} \times 2\frac{1}{3}$ ______

4. $\frac{3}{4} \times 6\frac{5}{6}$ ______

5. $1\frac{2}{7} \times 1\frac{3}{4}$ ______

6. $\frac{3}{4} \times 1\frac{1}{4}$ ______

Use the Distributive Property to find the product.

7. $16 \times 2\frac{1}{2}$ ______

8. $1\frac{4}{5} \times 15$ ______

MATHEMATICAL PRACTICES

Math Talk Explain how multiplying a mixed number by a whole number is similar to multiplying two mixed numbers.

On Your Own

Find the product. Write the product in simplest form.

9. $\frac{3}{4} \times 1\frac{1}{2}$ ______

10. $4\frac{2}{5} \times 1\frac{1}{2}$ ______

11. $5\frac{1}{3} \times \frac{3}{4}$ ______

12. $2\frac{1}{2} \times 1\frac{1}{5}$ ______

13. $12\frac{3}{4} \times 2\frac{2}{3}$ ______

14. $3 \times 4\frac{1}{2}$ ______

15. $2\frac{3}{8} \times \frac{4}{9}$ ______

16. $1\frac{1}{3} \times 1\frac{1}{4} \times 1\frac{1}{5}$ ______

Use the Distributive Property to find the product.

17. $10 \times 2\frac{3}{5}$ ______

18. $3\frac{3}{4} \times 12$ ______

Connect to Health

Changing Recipes

You can make a lot of recipes more healthful by reducing the amounts of fat, sugar, and salt.

Kelly has a muffin recipe that calls for $1\frac{1}{2}$ cups of sugar. She wants to use $\frac{1}{2}$ that amount of sugar and more cinnamon and vanilla. How much sugar will she use?

Multiply $1\frac{1}{2}$ by $\frac{1}{2}$ to find what part of the original amount of sugar to use.

Write the mixed number as a fraction greater than 1.

$$\frac{1}{2} \times 1\frac{1}{2} = \frac{1}{2} \times \frac{\square}{2}$$

Multiply.

$$= \frac{\square}{\square}$$

So, Kelly will use ______ cup of sugar.

19. Michelle has a recipe that calls for $2\frac{1}{2}$ cups of vegetable oil. She wants to use $\frac{2}{3}$ that amount of oil and use applesauce to replace the rest. How much vegetable oil will she use?

____

20. Tony's recipe for soup calls for $1\frac{1}{4}$ teaspoons of salt. He wants to use $\frac{1}{2}$ that amount. How much salt will he use?

____

21. Jeffrey's recipe for oatmeal muffins calls for $2\frac{1}{4}$ cups of oatmeal and makes one dozen muffins. If he makes $1\frac{1}{2}$ dozen muffins for a club meeting, how much oatmeal will he use?

____

22. H.O.T. Cara's muffin recipe calls for $1\frac{1}{2}$ cups of flour for the muffins and $\frac{1}{4}$ cup of flour for the topping. If she makes $\frac{1}{2}$ of the original recipe, how much flour will she use?

____

Name ______________________________

Divide Fractions and Whole Numbers

Essential Question How do you divide a whole number by a fraction and divide a fraction by a whole number?

COMMON CORE STANDARDS CC.5.NF.7a; CC.5.NF.7c
Apply and extend previous understandings of multiplication and division to multiply and divide fractions.

Investigate

Materials ■ fraction strips

A. Mia walks a 2-mile fitness trail. She stops to exercise every $\frac{1}{5}$ mile. How many times does Mia stop to exercise?

- Draw a number line from 0 to 2. Divide the number line into fifths. Label each fifth on your number line.

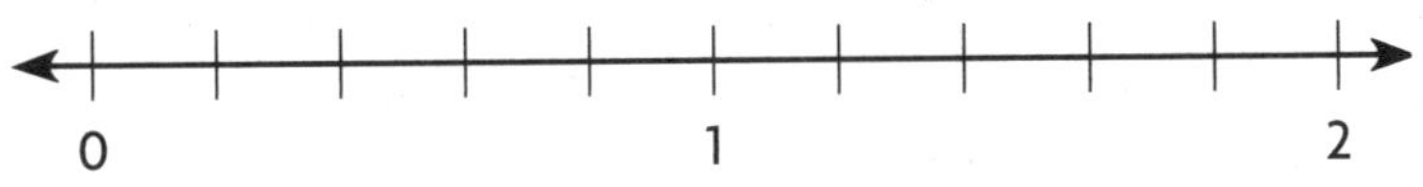

- Skip count by fifths from 0 to 2 to find $2 \div \frac{1}{5}$.

  There are ______ one-fifths in 2 wholes.

You can use the relationship between multiplication and division to explain and check your solution.

- Record and check the quotient.

  $2 \div \frac{1}{5} =$ ______ because ______ $\times \frac{1}{5} = 2$.

So, Mia stops to exercise ______ times.

B. Roger has 2 yards of string. He cuts the string into pieces that are $\frac{1}{3}$ yard long. How many pieces of string does Roger have?

- Model 2 using 2 whole fraction strips.
- Then place enough $\frac{1}{3}$ strips to fit exactly under the 2 wholes. There are ______ one-third-size pieces in 2 wholes.
- Record and check the quotient.

  $2 \div \frac{1}{3} =$ ______ because ______ $\times \frac{1}{3} = 2$.

So, Roger has ______ pieces of string.

Draw Conclusions

1. When you divide a whole number by a fraction, how does the quotient compare to the dividend? **Explain.**

____

____

2. **Explain** how knowing the number of fifths in 1 could help you find the number of fifths in 2.

____

____

3. **Describe** how you would find $4 \div \frac{1}{5}$.

____

____

Make Connections

You can use fraction strips to divide a fraction by a whole number.

Calia shares half of a package of clay equally among herself and each of 2 friends. What fraction of the whole package of clay will each friend get?

STEP 1 Place a $\frac{1}{2}$ strip under a 1-whole strip to show the $\frac{1}{2}$ package of clay.

STEP 2 Find 3 fraction strips, all with the same denominator, that fit exactly under the $\frac{1}{2}$ strip.

Each piece is ______ of the whole.

STEP 3 Record and check the quotient.

$\frac{1}{2} \div 3 =$ ______ because ______ $\times 3 = \frac{1}{2}$.

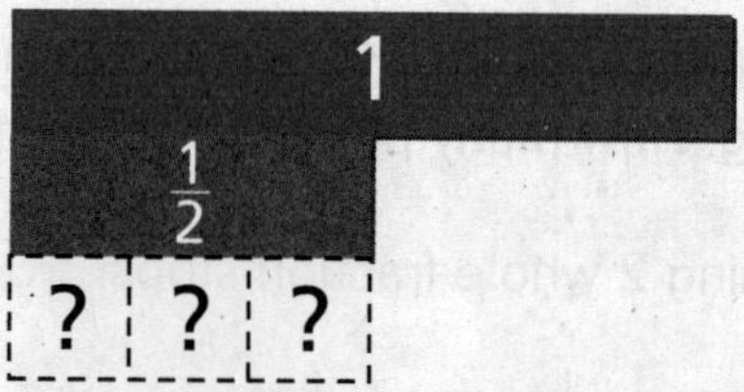

Think: How much of the whole is each piece when $\frac{1}{2}$ is divided into 3 equal pieces?

So, each friend will get ______ of the whole package of clay.

MATHEMATICAL PRACTICES

Math Talk When you divide a fraction by a whole number, how does the quotient compare to the dividend? **Explain.**

Name ______________________

Share and Show

Divide and check the quotient.

1. 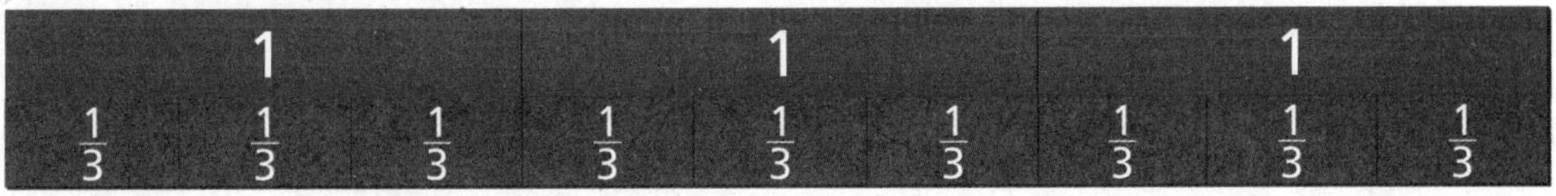

$3 \div \frac{1}{3} =$ _____ because _____ $\times \frac{1}{3} = 3.$

2. 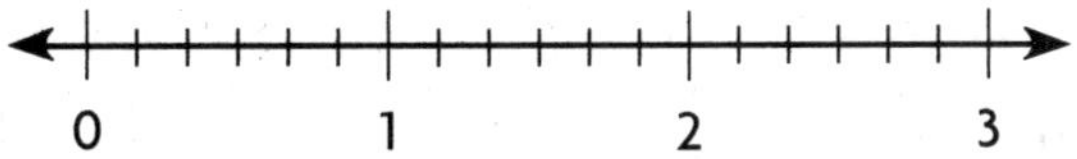

Think: What label should I write for each tick mark?

$3 \div \frac{1}{6} =$ _____ because

_____ $\times \frac{1}{6} = 3.$

3. 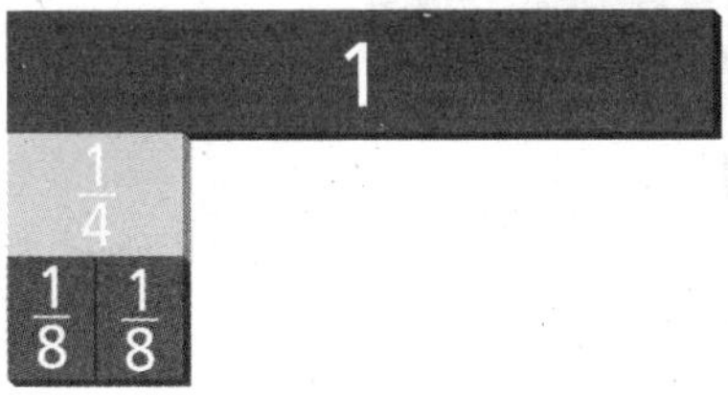

$\frac{1}{4} \div 2 =$ _____ because

_____ $\times 2 = \frac{1}{4}.$

Divide. Draw a number line or use fraction strips.

4. $1 \div \frac{1}{3} =$ _____

5. $3 \div \frac{1}{4} =$ _____

6. $\frac{1}{5} \div 2 =$ _____

7. $2 \div \frac{1}{2} =$ _____

8. $\frac{1}{4} \div 3 =$ _____

9. $5 \div \frac{1}{2} =$ _____

10. $4 \div \frac{1}{2} =$ _____

11. $\frac{1}{6} \div 2 =$ _____

12. $3 \div \frac{1}{5} =$ _____

Problem Solving

H.O.T. Sense or Nonsense?

13. Emilio and Julia used different ways to find $\frac{1}{2} \div 4$. Emilio used a model to find the quotient. Julia used a related multiplication equation to find the quotient. Whose answer makes sense? Whose answer is nonsense? **Explain** your reasoning.

Emilio's Work

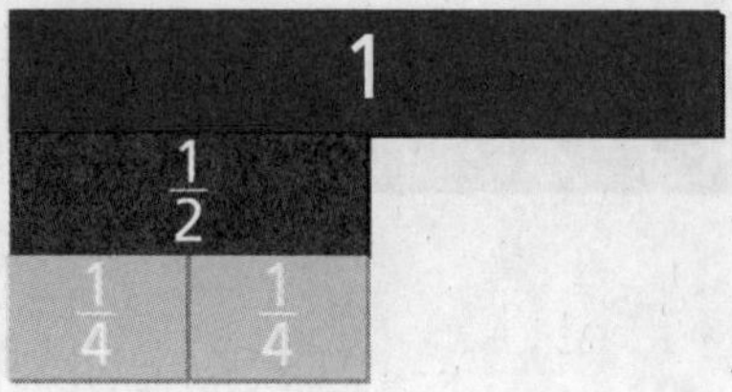

$\frac{1}{2} \div 4 = \frac{1}{4}$

Julia's Work

If $\frac{1}{2} \div 4 = \blacksquare$, then $\blacksquare \times 4 = \frac{1}{2}$.

I know that $\frac{1}{8} \times 4 = \frac{1}{2}$.

So, $\frac{1}{2} \div 4 = \frac{1}{8}$ because $\frac{1}{8} \times 4 = \frac{1}{2}$.

- For the answer that is nonsense, describe how to find the correct answer.

- If you were going to find $\frac{1}{2} \div 5$, **explain** how you would find the quotient using fraction strips.

Name ______________________

Fraction and Whole-Number Division

Essential Question How can you divide fractions by solving a related multiplication sentence?

COMMON CORE STANDARD CC.5.NF.7a; CC.5.NF.7b; CC.5.NF.7c
Apply and extend previous understandings of multiplication and division to multiply and divide fractions.

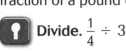

UNLOCK the Problem — REAL WORLD

Three friends share a $\frac{1}{4}$-pound block of fudge equally. What fraction of a pound of fudge does each friend get?

Divide. $\frac{1}{4} \div 3$

- Let the rectangle represent a 1-pound block of fudge. Divide the rectangle into fourths and then divide each fourth into three equal parts.

  The rectangle is now divided into ______ equal parts.

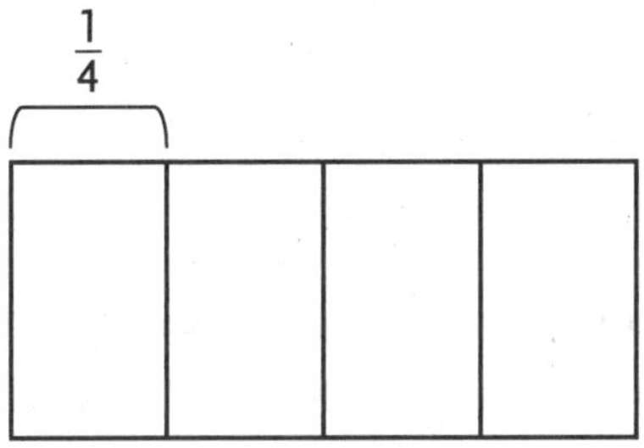

- When you divide one fourth into 3 equal parts, you are finding one of three equal parts or $\frac{1}{3}$ of $\frac{1}{4}$. Shade $\frac{1}{3}$ of $\frac{1}{4}$.

  The shaded part is ______ of the whole rectangle.

- Complete the number sentence.

$\frac{1}{4} \div 3 = \frac{1}{3} \times \frac{1}{4} =$ ______

So, each friend gets ______ of a pound of fudge.

Example

Brad has 9 pounds of ground turkey to make turkey burgers for a picnic. How many $\frac{1}{3}$-pound turkey burgers can he make?

- Will the number of turkey burgers be less than or greater than 9?

  ____

Divide. $9 \div \frac{1}{3}$

- Draw 9 rectangles to represent each pound of ground turkey. Divide each rectangle into thirds.

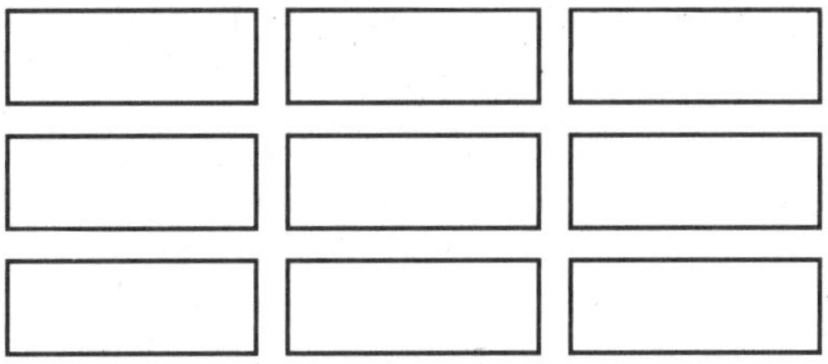

- When you divide the ______ rectangles into thirds, you are finding the number of thirds in 9 rectangles or

  finding 9 groups of ______. There are ______ thirds.

- Complete the number sentence.

$9 \div \frac{1}{3} =$ ______ $\times$ ______ $=$ ______

So, Brad can make ______ one-third-pound turkey burgers.

CONNECT You have learned how to use a model and write a multiplication sentence to solve a division problem.

Examples

A $\frac{1}{4} \div 2 = \frac{1}{8}$ $\frac{1}{2} \times \frac{1}{4} = \frac{1}{8}$

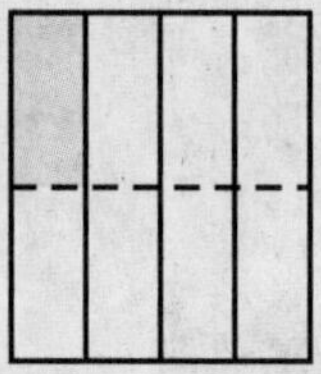

B $4 \div \frac{1}{2} = 8$ $4 \times 2 = 8$

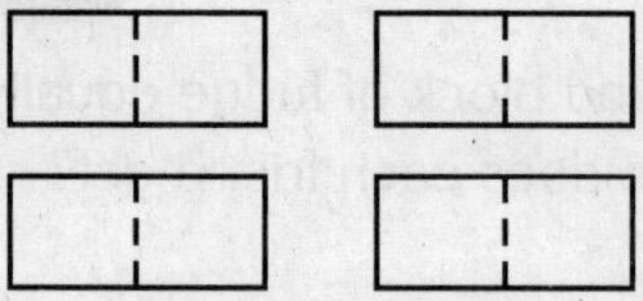

1. Look at Example A. **Describe** how the model shows that dividing by 2 is the same as multiplying by $\frac{1}{2}$.

____

____

2. Look at Example B. **Describe** how the model shows that dividing by $\frac{1}{2}$ is the same as multiplying by 2.

____

____

When you divide whole numbers, the quotient is always less than the dividend. For example, the quotient for $6 \div 2$ is less than 6 and the quotient for $2 \div 3$ is less than 2. Complete the Try This! to learn how the quotient compares to the dividend when you divide fractions and whole numbers.

Try This!

For the two expressions below, which will have a quotient that is greater than its dividend? Explain.

$\frac{1}{2} \div 3$ $3 \div \frac{1}{2}$

____

____

So, when I divide a fraction by a whole number, the quotient is ___________ the dividend. When I divide a whole number by a fraction less than 1, the quotient is ___________ the dividend.

Name ____________________

Share and Show

1. Use the model to complete the number sentence.

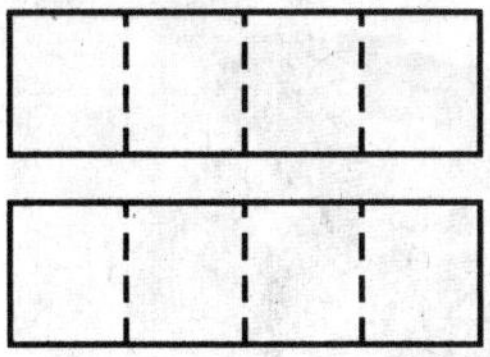

$2 \div \frac{1}{4} = 2 \times$ ______ $=$ ______

2. Use the model to complete the number sentence.

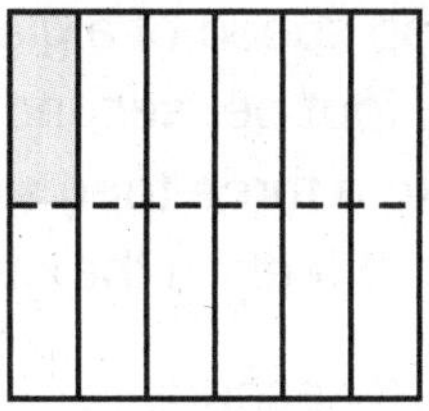

$\frac{1}{6} \div 2 =$ ______ $\times \frac{1}{6} =$ ______

Write a related multiplication sentence to solve.

3. $3 \div \frac{1}{4}$ ______

4. $\frac{1}{5} \div 4$ ______

5. $\frac{1}{9} \div 3$ ______

6. $7 \div \frac{1}{2}$ ______

On Your Own

Write a related multiplication sentence to solve.

7. $5 \div \frac{1}{3}$ ______

8. $8 \div \frac{1}{2}$ ______

9. $\frac{1}{7} \div 4$ ______

10. $\frac{1}{2} \div 9$ ______

11. $\frac{1}{3} \div 4$ ______

12. $\frac{1}{4} \div 12$ ______

13. $6 \div \frac{1}{5}$ ______

14. H.O.T. $\frac{2}{3} \div 3$ ______

UNLOCK the Problem REAL WORLD

TEST PRACTICE

15. The slowest mammal is the three-toed sloth. The top speed of a three-toed sloth on the ground is about $\frac{1}{4}$ foot per second. The top speed of a giant tortoise on the ground is about $\frac{1}{3}$ foot per second. How much longer would it take a three-toed sloth than a giant tortoise to travel 10 feet on the ground?

Ⓐ 10 seconds Ⓒ 40 seconds

Ⓑ 30 seconds Ⓓ 70 seconds

a. What do you need to find? ______________________

____

b. What operations will you use to solve the problem? ______________________

____

c. Show the steps you used to solve the problem.

d. Complete the sentences.

A three-toed sloth would travel 10 feet in

_______ seconds.

A giant tortoise would travel 10 feet in

_______ seconds.

Since _______ − _______ = _______,
it would take a three-toed sloth

_______ seconds longer to travel 10 feet.

e. Fill in the bubble for the correct answer choice.

16. Robert divides 8 cups of almonds into $\frac{1}{8}$-cup servings. How many servings does he have?

Ⓐ 1 Ⓒ 8

Ⓑ 16 Ⓓ 64

17. Tina cuts $\frac{1}{3}$ yard of fabric into 4 equal parts. What is the length of each part?

Ⓐ 12 yards Ⓒ $\frac{3}{4}$ yard

Ⓑ $1\frac{1}{3}$ yards Ⓓ $\frac{1}{12}$ yard

Name ______________________________

Interpret Division with Fractions

Essential Question How can you use diagrams, equations, and story problems to represent division?

COMMON CORE STANDARD CC.5.NF.7a; CC.5.NF.7b; CC.5.NF.7c
Apply and extend previous understandings of multiplication and division to multiply and divide fractions.

UNLOCK the Problem REAL WORLD

Elizabeth has 6 cups of raisins. She divides the raisins into $\frac{1}{4}$-cup servings. How many servings does she have?

- How many $\frac{1}{4}$-cups are in 1 cup?

  ____

- How many cups does Elizabeth have?

  ____

You can use diagrams, equations, and story problems to represent division.

Draw a diagram to solve.

- Draw 6 rectangles to represent the cups of raisins. Draw lines to divide each rectangle into fourths.

- To find $6 \div \frac{1}{4}$, count the total number of fourths in the 6 rectangles.

$6 \div$ ______ $=$ ______

So, Elizabeth has ______ servings.

Example 1 Write an equation to solve.

Four friends share $\frac{1}{4}$ of a gallon of orange juice. What fraction of a gallon of orange juice does each friend get?

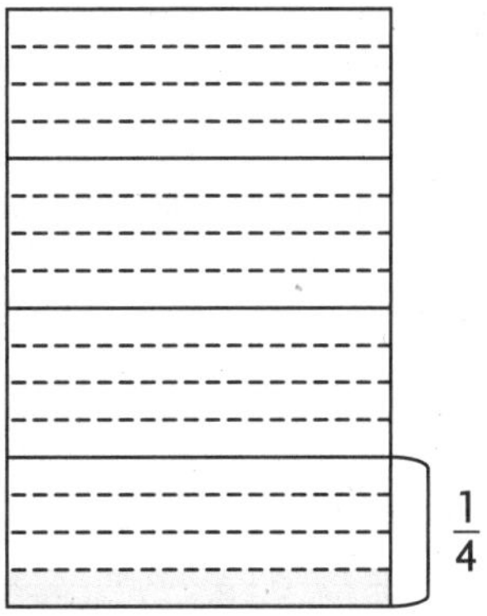

STEP 1

Write an equation.

$\frac{1}{4} \div$ ______ $= n$

STEP 2

Write a related multiplication equation. Then solve.

$\frac{1}{4} \times$ ______ $= n$

______ $= n$

So, each friend will get ______ of a gallon of orange juice.

Example 2 Write a story problem. Then draw a diagram to solve.

$4 \div \frac{1}{3}$

STEP 1 Choose the item you want to divide.

Think: Your problem should be about how many groups of $\frac{1}{3}$ are in 4 wholes.

Possible items: 4 sandwiches, 4 feet of ribbon, 4 pies

STEP 2 Write a story problem to represent $4 \div \frac{1}{3}$ using the item you chose. Describe how it is divided into thirds. Then ask how many thirds there are.

____

____

____

STEP 3 Draw a diagram to solve.

$4 \div \frac{1}{3} =$ ______

Example 3 Write a story problem. Then draw a diagram to solve.

$\frac{1}{2} \div 5$

STEP 1 Choose the item you want to divide.

Think: Your problem should describe $\frac{1}{2}$ of an item that can be divided into 5 equal parts.

Possible items: $\frac{1}{2}$ of a pizza, $\frac{1}{2}$ of a yard of rope, $\frac{1}{2}$ of a gallon of milk

STEP 2 Write a story problem to represent $\frac{1}{2} \div 5$ using the item you chose. Describe how it is divided into 5 equal parts. Then ask about the size of each part.

____

____

____

STEP 3 Draw a diagram to solve.

$\frac{1}{2} \div 5 =$ ______

MATHEMATICAL PRACTICES

Math Talk Explain how you decided what type of diagram to draw for your problem.

Name ______________________________

Share and Show

1. Complete the story problem to represent $3 \div \frac{1}{4}$.

Carmen has a roll of paper that is ______ feet long. She cuts

the paper into pieces that are each ______ foot long. How many pieces of paper does Carmen have?

2. Draw a diagram to represent the problem. Then solve.

April has 6 fruit bars. She cuts the bars into halves. How many $\frac{1}{2}$-size bar pieces does she have?

____

3. Write an equation to represent the problem. Then solve.

Two friends share $\frac{1}{4}$ of a large peach pie. What fraction of the whole pie does each friend get?

____

____

On Your Own

4. Write an equation to represent the problem. Then solve.

Benito has $\frac{1}{3}$-kilogram of grapes. He divides the grapes equally into 3 bags. What fraction of a kilogram of grapes is in each bag?

____

____

5. Draw a diagram to represent the problem. Then solve.

Sonya has 5 sandwiches. She cuts each sandwich into fourths. How many $\frac{1}{4}$-size sandwich pieces does she have?

____

6. Write a story problem to represent $2 \div \frac{1}{8}$. Then solve.

____

____

____

Problem Solving REAL WORLD

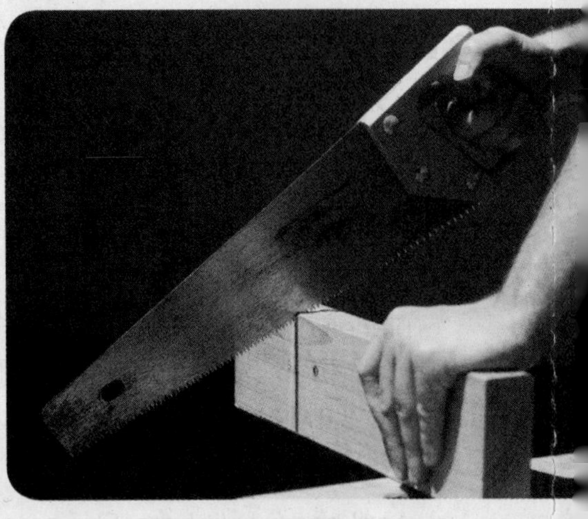

H.O.T. Pose a Problem

7. Amy wrote the following problem to represent $4 \div \frac{1}{6}$.

Jacob has a board that is 4 feet long. He cuts the board into pieces that are each $\frac{1}{6}$ foot long. How many pieces does Jacob have now?

Then Amy drew this diagram to solve her problem.

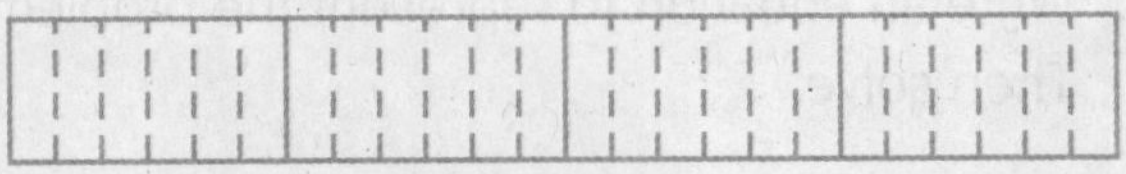

So, Jacob has 24 pieces.

Write a new problem using a different item to be divided and different fractional pieces. Then draw a diagram to solve your problem.

Pose a problem.

Draw a diagram to solve your problem.

8. ★ **Test Practice** Melvin has $\frac{1}{4}$ of a gallon of fruit punch. He shares the punch equally with each of 2 friends and himself. Which equation represents the fraction of a gallon of punch that each of the friends get?

Ⓐ $\frac{1}{4} \div \frac{1}{3} = n$

Ⓑ $\frac{1}{4} \div 3 = n$

Ⓒ $3 \div \frac{1}{4} = n$

Ⓓ $3 \div 4 = n$

Name ______________________________

Problem Solving • Use Multiplication

Essential Question How can the strategy *draw a diagram* help you solve fraction division problems by writing a multiplication sentence?

COMMON CORE STANDARD CC.5.NF.7c
Apply and extend previous understandings of multiplication and division to multiply and divide fractions.

UNLOCK the Problem REAL WORLD

Erica makes 6 submarine sandwiches and cuts each sandwich into thirds. How many $\frac{1}{3}$-size sandwich pieces does she have?

Read the Problem

What do I need to find?

I need to find ______________________________

____

______________________________.

What information do I need to use?

I need to use the size of each __________ of sandwich and the number of __________ she cuts.

How will I use the information?

I can ______________________ to organize the information from the problem. Then I can use the organized information to find

____

______________________________.

Solve the Problem

Since Erica cuts 6 submarine sandwiches, my diagram needs to show 6 rectangles to represent the sandwiches. I can divide each of the 6 rectangles into thirds.

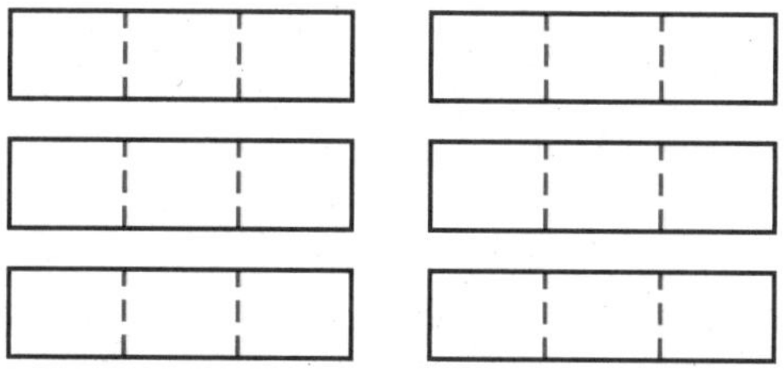

To find the total number of thirds in the 6 rectangles, I can multiply the number of thirds in each rectangle by the number of rectangles.

$6 \div \frac{1}{3} = 6 \times$ ______ $=$ ______

So, Erica has ______ one-third-size sandwich pieces.

MATHEMATICAL PRACTICES

Math Talk Explain how you can use multiplication to check your answer.

Try Another Problem

Roberto is cutting 3 blueberry pies into halves to give to his neighbors. How many neighbors will get a $\frac{1}{2}$-size pie piece?

Read the Problem	Solve the Problem
What do I need to find?	
What information do I need to use?	
How will I use the information?	

So, ______ neighbors will get a $\frac{1}{2}$-size pie piece.

- **Explain** how the diagram you drew for the division problem helps you write a multiplication sentence.

____

____

Name ______________________

Share and Show

1. A chef has 5 blocks of butter. Each block weighs 1 pound. She cuts each block into fourths. How many $\frac{1}{4}$-pound pieces of butter does the chef have?

   First, draw rectangles to represent the blocks of butter.

   Then, divide each rectangle into fourths.

   Finally, multiply the number of fourths in each block by the number of blocks.

   So, the chef has _______ one-fourth-pound pieces of butter.

2. **What if** the chef had 3 blocks of butter and cut the blocks into thirds? How many $\frac{1}{3}$-pound pieces of butter would the chef have?

   ____

3. Jason has 2 pizzas that he cuts into fourths. How many $\frac{1}{4}$-size pizza slices does he have?

   ____

4. Thomas makes 5 sandwiches that he cuts into thirds. How many $\frac{1}{3}$-size sandwich pieces does he have?

   ____

5. Holly cuts 3 pans of brownies into eighths. How many $\frac{1}{8}$-size brownie pieces does she have?

   ____

SHOW YOUR WORK

On Your Own

Choose a STRATEGY
- Act It Out
- Draw a Diagram
- Make a Table
- Solve a Simpler Problem
- Work Backward
- Guess, Check, and Revise

6. Julie wants to make a drawing that is $\frac{1}{4}$ the size of the original. If a tree in the original drawing is 8 inches tall, how tall will the tree in Julie's drawing be?

____

7. Three friends go to a book fair. Allen spends \$2.60. Maria spends 4 times as much as Allen. Akio spends \$3.45 less than Maria. How much does Akio spend?

____

SHOW YOUR WORK

8. **H.O.T.** Brianna has a sheet of paper that is 6 feet long. She cuts the length of paper into sixths and then cuts the length of each of these $\frac{1}{6}$ pieces into thirds. How many pieces does she have? How many inches long is each piece?

____

9. **Write Math** **Pose a Problem** Look back at Problem 8. Write a similar problem by changing the length of the paper and the size of the pieces.

____

____

____

____

____

____

10. **Test Practice** Adrian made 3 carrot cakes. He cut each cake into fourths. How many $\frac{1}{4}$-size cake pieces does he have?

Ⓐ 16
Ⓑ 12
Ⓒ $1\frac{1}{3}$
Ⓓ 1

Name ______________________________

Customary Length

Essential Question How can you compare and convert customary units of length?

COMMON CORE STANDARD CC.5.MD.1
Convert like measurement units within a given measurement system.

UNLOCK the Problem REAL WORLD

To build a new swing, Mr. Mattson needs 9 feet of rope for each side of the swing and 6 more feet for the monkey bar. The hardware store sells rope by the yard.

- How many feet of rope does Mr. Mattson need for the swing? ______________
- How many feet does Mr. Mattson need for the swing and the monkey bar combined? ______________

Mr. Mattson needs to find how many yards of rope he needs to buy. He will need to convert 24 feet to yards. How many groups of 3 feet are in 24 feet?

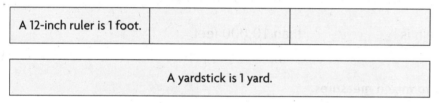

A 12-inch ruler is 1 foot.		

A yardstick is 1 yard.

______ feet = 1 yard

Use a bar model to write an equation.

MODEL

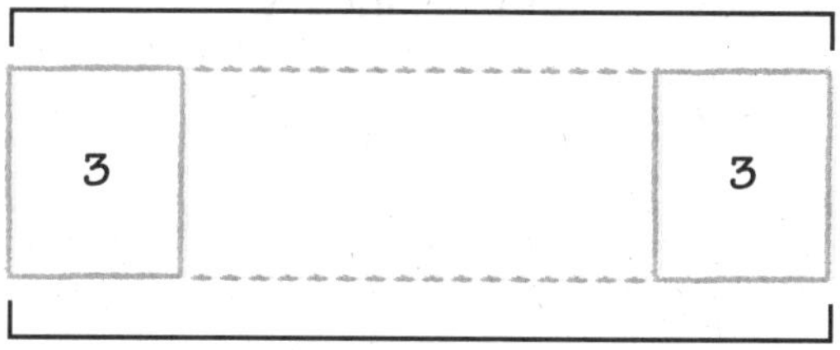

RECORD

total feet	feet in 1 yard	total yards
↓	↓	↓
24 ÷	______ =	______

So, Mr. Mattson needs to buy ______ yards of rope.

MATHEMATICAL PRACTICES
Math Talk What operation did you use when you found groups of 3 feet in 24 feet? Do you multiply or divide when you convert a smaller unit to a larger unit? **Explain.**

Example 1 Use the table to find the relationship between miles and feet.

Customary Units of Length
1 foot (ft) = 12 inches (in.)
1 yard (yd) = 3 ft
1 mile (mi) = 5,280 ft
1 mile = 1,760 yd

The distance between the new high school and the football field is 2 miles. How does this distance compare to 10,000 feet?

When you convert larger units to smaller units, you need to multiply.

STEP 1 Convert 2 miles to feet.

Think: 1 mile is equal to 5,280 feet.

I need to ____________ the total number of miles by ____________.

total miles → 2 × feet in 1 mile → ____________ = total feet → ____________

2 miles = ____________ feet

STEP 2 Compare. Write <, >, or =.

____________ feet ◯ 10,000 feet

Since ____________ is ____________ than 10,000, the distance between the new high school and the football field is ____________ than 10,000 feet.

Example 2 Convert to mixed measures.

Mixed measures use more than one unit of measurement. You can convert a single unit of measurement to mixed measures.

Convert 62 inches into feet and inches.

STEP 1 Use the table.

Think: 12 inches is equal to 1 foot

I am changing from a smaller unit to a larger unit, so I ____________.

STEP 2 Convert.

total inches → 62 ÷ inches in 1 foot → ______ is feet → ______ r inches → ______

So, 62 inches is equal to ______ feet ______ inches.

- **Explain** how to convert the mixed measures, 12 yards 2 feet, to a single unit of measurement in feet. How many feet is it?

____

Name ______________________

Share and Show

Convert.

1. 2 mi = ________ yd

2. 6 yd = ________ ft

3. 90 in. = ______ ft ______ in.

MATHEMATICAL PRACTICES

Math Talk Explain how you know when to multiply to convert a measurement.

On Your Own

Convert.

4. 57 ft = ________ yd

5. 13 ft = ________ in.

6. 240 in. = ________ ft

7. 6 mi = ________ ft

8. 96 ft = ________ yd

9. 75 in. = ______ ft ______ in.

Practice: Copy and Solve Convert.

10. 60 in. = ■ ft

11. ■ ft = 7 yd 1 ft

12. 4 mi = ■ yd

13. 125 in. = ■ ft ■ in.

14. 46 ft = ■ yd ■ ft

15. 42 yd 2 ft = ■ ft

Compare. Write <, >, or =.

16. 8 ft ◯ 3 yd

17. 2 mi ◯ 10,500 ft

18. 3 yd 2 ft ◯ 132 in.

Problem Solving REAL WORLD

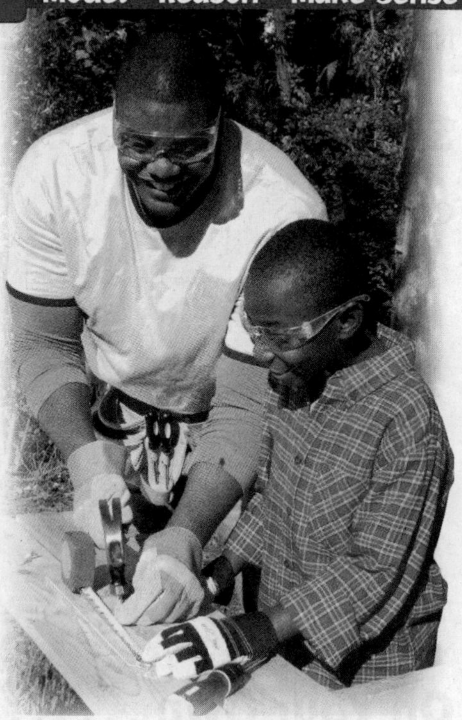

19. H.O.T. Javon is helping his dad build a tree house. He has a piece of trim that is 13 feet long. How many pieces can Javon cut that are 1 yard long? How much of a yard will he have left over?

____

20. Test Practice Katy's driveway is 120 feet long. How many yards long is Katy's driveway?

Ⓐ 60 yards
Ⓑ 40 yards
Ⓒ 20 yards
Ⓓ 10 yards

Connect to Reading

Compare and Contrast

When you compare and contrast, you tell how two or more things are alike and different. You can compare and contrast information in a table.

Complete the table below. Use the table to answer the questions.

Linear Units				
Yards	1	2	3	4
Feet	3	6	9	
Inches	36	72		

21. How are the items in the table alike? How are they different?

____

____

22. What do you notice about the relationship between the number of larger units and the number of smaller units as the length increases?

____

____

Name ______________________________

Customary Capacity

Essential Question How can you compare and convert customary units of capacity?

COMMON CORE STANDARD **CC.5.MD.1**
Convert like measurement units within a given measurement system.

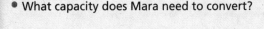

UNLOCK the Problem REAL WORLD

Mara has a can of paint with 3 cups of purple paint in it. She also has a bucket with a capacity of 26 fluid ounces. Will the bucket hold all of the paint Mara has?

- What capacity does Mara need to convert?

  ____

- After Mara converts the units, what does she need to do next?

  ____

  ____

The **capacity** of a container is the amount the container can hold.

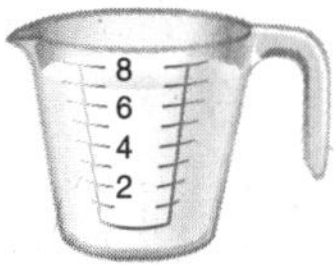

1 cup (c) = ______ fluid ounces (fl oz)

Use a bar model to write an equation.

STEP 1 Convert 3 cups to fluid ounces.

MODEL

8	8	8

RECORD

total cups	fl oz in 1 cup	total fl oz
↓	↓	↓
3 ×	______ =	______

STEP 2 Compare. Write <, >, or =.

______ fl oz ◯ 26 fl oz

Since ______ fluid ounces is ________ than 26 fluid ounces,

Mara's bucket ________ hold all of the paint.

- **What if** Mara has 7 cups of green paint and a container filled with 64 fluid ounces of yellow paint? Which color paint does Mara have more of? **Explain** your reasoning.

  ____

  ____

Example

Coral made 32 pints of fruit punch for a party. She needs to transport the punch in 1-gallon containers. How many containers does Coral need?

Customary Units of Capacity
1 cup (c) = 8 fluid ounces (fl oz)
1 pint (pt) = 2 cups
1 quart (qt) = 2 pints
1 gallon (gal) = 4 quarts

> To convert a smaller unit to a larger unit, you need to divide. Sometimes you may need to convert more than once.

Convert 32 pints to gallons.

STEP 1 Write an equation to convert pints to quarts.

total pints ↓ pints in 1 qt ↓ total quarts ↓

32 ◯ ______ ◯ ______

STEP 2 Write an equation to convert quarts to gallons.

total quarts ↓ quarts in 1 gal ↓ total gallons ↓

______ ◯ ______ ◯ ______

So, Coral needs ______ 1-gallon containers to transport the punch.

Share and Show

1. Use the picture to complete the statements and convert 3 quarts to pints.

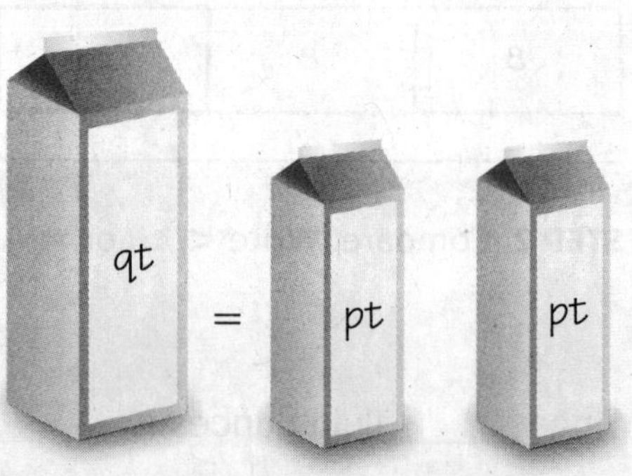

   a. 1 quart = ______ pints

   b. 1 quart is ______ than 1 pint.

   c. 3 qt ◯ ______ pt in 1 qt = ______ pt

Convert.

2. 3 gal = ______ pt

✓3. 5 qt = ______ pt

✓4. 6 qt = ______ c

MATHEMATICAL PRACTICES

Math Talk Explain how converting units of capacity is similar to converting units of length. How is it different?

Name ______________________________

On Your Own

Convert.

5. 38 c = ______ pt

6. 36 qt = ______ gal

7. 104 fl oz = ______ c

8. 4 qt = ______ c

9. 7 gal = ______ pt

10. 96 fl oz = ______ pt

Practice: Copy and Solve **Convert.**

11. 200 c = ■ qt

12. 22 pt = ■ fl oz

13. 8 gal = ■ qt

14. 72 fl oz = ■ c

15. 2 gal = ■ pt

16. 48 pt = ■ gal

Compare. Write <, >, or =.

17. 28 c ◯ 14 pt

18. 25 pt ◯ 13 qt

19. 20 qt ◯ 80 c

20. 12 gal ◯ 50 qt

21. 320 fl oz ◯ 18 pt

22. 15 qt ◯ 63 c

23. **Write Math** Which of exercises 17–22 could you solve mentally? **Explain** your answer for one exercise.

____

____

Problem Solving REAL WORLD

Show your work. For 24–26, use the table.

24. H.O.T. Complete the table, and make a graph showing the relationship between pints and quarts. Draw a line through the points to make the graph.

Pints	Quarts
0	0
2	
4	
6	
8	

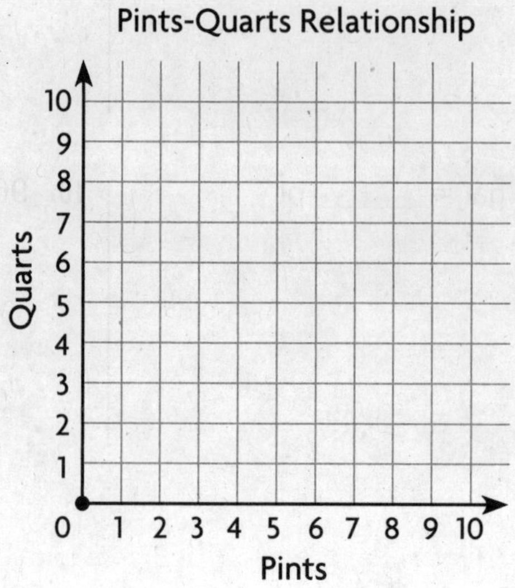

25. Describe any pattern you notice in the pairs of numbers you graphed. Write a rule to describe the pattern.

____

____

____

____

26. H.O.T. **Explain** how you can use your graph to find the number of quarts equal to 5 pints.

____

____

____

27. ★ **Test Practice** Shelby made 5 quarts of juice for a picnic. How many cups of juice did Shelby make?

Ⓐ 1 cup Ⓒ 10 cups

Ⓑ 5 cups Ⓓ 20 cups

Name ______________________________

Weight

Essential Question How can you compare and convert customary units of weight?

COMMON CORE STANDARD CC.5.MD.1
Convert like measurement units within a given measurement system.

UNLOCK the Problem REAL WORLD

Hector's school is having a model rocket competition. To qualify, each rocket must weigh 4 pounds or less. Hector's unpainted rocket weighs 62 ounces. What is the weight of the most paint he can use for his model rocket to qualify for entry?

- What weight does Hector need to convert?

  ____

- After Hector converts the weight, what does he need to do next?

  ____

1 pound = ______ ounces

Use a bar model to write an equation.

STEP 1 Convert 4 pounds to ounces.

MODEL

16	16	16	16

RECORD

total lb ↓ 4 ◯ oz in 1 lb ↓ ______ ◯ total oz ↓ ______

STEP 2 Subtract the rocket's weight from the total ounces a rocket can weigh to qualify.

______ − 62 = ______

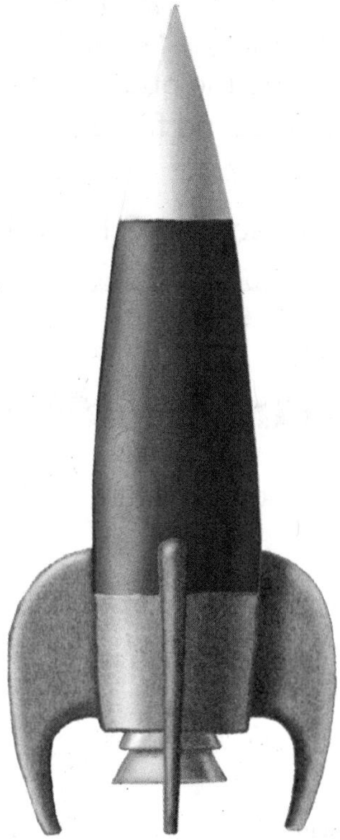

So, the weight of the paint can be at most ______ ounces for Hector's model rocket to qualify for entry.

Math Talk MATHEMATICAL PRACTICES How did you choose which operation to use to change from pounds to ounces? **Explain.**

Example

The rocket boosters for a U.S. space shuttle weigh 1,292,000 pounds each when the shuttle is launched. How many tons does each rocket booster weigh?

Use mental math to convert pounds to tons.

Units of Weight
1 pound (lb) = 16 ounces (oz)
1 ton (T) = 2,000 lb

STEP 1 Decide which operation to use.

Since pounds are smaller than tons, I need to ________ the number of pounds by ________.

STEP 2 Break 2,000 into two factors that are easy to divide by mentally.

2,000 = ________ × 2

STEP 3 Divide 1,292,000 by the first factor. Then divide the quotient by the second factor.

1,292,000 ÷ ________ = ________

________ ÷ 2 = ________

So, each rocket booster weighs ________ tons when launched.

Share and Show

1. Use the picture to complete each equation.

a. 1 pound = ______ ounces

b. 2 pounds = ______ ounces

c. 3 pounds = ______ ounces

d. 4 pounds = ______ ounces

e. 5 pounds = ______ ounces

Convert.

2. 15 lb = ______ oz

3. 3 T = ______ lb

4. 320 oz = ______ lb

MATHEMATICAL PRACTICES

Math Talk Explain how you can compare 11 pounds to 175 ounces mentally.

Name ______________________________

On Your Own

Convert.

5. 5 T = ________ lb

6. 19 T = ________ lb

7. 16,000 lb = ______ T

8. 192 oz = ______ lb

9. 416 oz = ______ lb

10. 24 lb = ______ oz

Practice: Copy and Solve Convert.

11. 23 lb = ■ oz

12. 6 T = ■ lb

13. 144 oz = ■ lb

14. 15 T = ■ lb

15. 352 oz = ■ lb

16. 18 lb = ■ oz

Compare. Write <, >, or =.

17. 130 oz ◯ 8 lb

18. 34 lb ◯ 544 oz

19. 14 lb ◯ 229 oz

20. 16 T ◯ 32,000 lb

21. 5 lb ◯ 79 oz

22. 85,000 lb ◯ 40 T

Problem Solving REAL WORLD

23. **Write Math** **Explain** how you can use mental math to compare 7 pounds to 120 ounces.

____

____

____

____

24. ★ **Test Practice** Carlos used 32 ounces of walnuts in a muffin recipe. How many pounds of walnuts did Carlos use?

Ⓐ 8 pounds

Ⓑ 4 pounds

Ⓒ 2 pounds

Ⓓ 1 pound

Problem Solving REAL WORLD

H.O.T. Pose a Problem

25. Kia wants to have 4 pounds of munchies for her party. She has 36 ounces of popcorn and wants the rest to be pretzel sticks. How many ounces of pretzel sticks does she need to buy?

4 pounds = 64 ounces

36 ounces	______ ounces

64 − 36 = ______

So, Kia needs to buy ______ ounces of pretzel sticks.

Write a new problem using different amounts of snacks. Some weights should be in pounds and others in ounces. Make sure the amount of snacks given is less than the total amount of snacks needed.

Pose a Problem

____

____

____

____

____

____

____

Draw a bar model for your problem. Then solve.

- Write an expression you could use to solve your problem. **Explain** how the expression represents the problem.

____

____

____

Name ______________________________

Multistep Measurement Problems

Essential Question How can you solve multistep problems that include measurement conversions?

COMMON CORE STANDARD **CC.5.MD.1**
Convert like measurement units within a given measurement system.

UNLOCK the Problem REAL WORLD

A leaky faucet in Jarod's house drips 2 cups of water each day. After 2 weeks of dripping, the faucet is fixed. If it dripped the same amount each day, how many quarts of water dripped from Jarod's leaky faucet in 2 weeks?

Use the steps to solve the multistep problem.

STEP 1

Record the information you are given.

The faucet drips ______ cups of water each day.

The faucet drips for ______ weeks.

STEP 2

Find the total amount of water dripped in 2 weeks.

Since you are given the amount of water dripped each day, you must convert 2 weeks into days and multiply.

Think: There are 7 days in 1 week.

cups each day ↓ days in 2 weeks ↓ total cups ↓

2 × ______ = ______

The faucet drips ______ cups in 2 weeks.

STEP 3

Convert from cups to quarts.

Think: There are 2 cups in 1 pint.

There are 2 pints in 1 quart.

______ cups = ______ pints

______ pints = ______ quarts

So, Jarod's leaky faucet drips ______ quarts of water in 2 weeks.

- **What if** the faucet dripped for 4 weeks before it was fixed? How many quarts of water would have leaked?

____

Example

A carton of large, Grade A eggs weighs about 1.5 pounds. If a carton holds a dozen eggs, how many ounces does each egg weigh?

STEP 1

In ounces, find the weight of a carton of eggs.

Think: 1 pound = _______ ounces

Weight of a carton (in ounces):

total lb ↓ oz in 1 lb ↓ total oz ↓

1.5 × _____ = _____

The carton of eggs weighs about _______ ounces.

STEP 2

In ounces, find the weight of each egg in a carton.

Think: 1 carton (dozen eggs) = _______ eggs

So, each egg weighs about _______ ounces.

Weight of each egg (in ounces):

total oz ↓ eggs in 1 carton ↓ oz of 1 egg ↓

24 ÷ _______ = _______

Share and Show

Solve.

1. After each soccer practice, Scott runs 4 sprints of 20 yards each. If he continues his routine, how many practices will it take for Scott to have sprinted a total of 2 miles combined?

   Scott sprints __________ yards each practice.

   Since there are __________ yards in 2 miles, he will need to continue his routine for

   __________ practices.

2. A worker at a mill is loading 5-lb bags of flour into boxes to deliver to a local warehouse. Each box holds 12 bags of flour. If the warehouse orders 3 Tons of flour, how many boxes are needed to fulfill the order?

   ____

3. Cory brings five 1-gallon jugs of juice to serve during parent night at his school. If the paper cups he is using for drinks can hold 8 fluid ounces, how many drinks can Cory serve for parent night?

   ____

MATHEMATICAL PRACTICES

Math Talk Explain the steps you took to solve Exercise 2.

Name ______________________________

On Your Own

Solve.

4. A science teacher needs to collect lake water for a lab she is teaching. The lab requires each student to use 4 fluid ounces of lake water. If 68 students are participating, how many pints of lake water will the teacher need to collect?

5. A string of decorative lights is 28 feet long. The first light on the string is 16 inches from the plug. If the lights on the string are spaced 4 inches apart, how many lights are there on the string?

6. When Jamie's car moves forward such that each tire makes one full rotation, the car has traveled 72 inches. How many full rotations will the tires need to make for Jamie's car to travel 10 yards?

7. A male African elephant weighs 7 Tons. If a male African lion at the local zoo weighs $\frac{1}{40}$ of the weight of the male African elephant, how many pounds does the lion weigh?

8. An office supply company is shipping a case of wooden pencils to a store. There are 64 boxes of pencils in the case. If each box of pencils weighs 2.5 ounces, what is the weight, in pounds, of the case of wooden pencils?

9. H.O.T. A gallon of unleaded gasoline weighs about 6 pounds. About how many ounces does 1 quart of unleaded gasoline weigh? HINT: 1 quart $= \frac{1}{4}$ of a gallon

UNLOCK the Problem REAL WORLD

10. At a local animal shelter there are 12 small-size dogs and 5 medium-size dogs. Every day, the small-size dogs are each given 12.5 ounces of dry food and the medium-size dogs are each given 18 ounces of the same dry food. How many pounds of dry food does the shelter serve in one day?

a. What are you asked to find? ____________

____

b. What information will you use? ____________

____

____

c. What conversion will you need to do to solve the problem?

____

____

d. Show the steps you use to solve the problem.

e. Complete the sentences. The small-size dogs eat a total of ______ ounces of dry food each day.

The medium-size dogs eat a total of ______ ounces of dry food each day.

The shelter serves ______ ounces, or ______ pounds, of dry food each day.

11. ★ **Test Practice** For a class assignment, students are asked to record the total amount of water they drink in one day. Melinda records that she drank four 8-fluid ounce glasses of water and two 1-pint bottles. How many quarts of water did Melinda drink during the day?

Ⓐ 2 quarts Ⓒ 6 quarts

Ⓑ 4 quarts Ⓓ 8 quarts

Name ______________________________

Metric Measures

Essential Question How can you compare and convert metric units?

COMMON CORE STANDARD CC.5.MD.1
Convert like measurement units within a given measurement system.

UNLOCK the Problem REAL WORLD

Using a map, Alex estimates the distance between his house and his grandparent's house to be about 15,000 meters. About how many kilometers away from his grandparent's house does Alex live?

- Underline the sentence that tells you what you are trying to find.
- Circle the measurement you need to convert.

The metric system is based on place value. Each unit is related to the next largest or next smallest unit by a power of 10.

One Way Convert 15,000 meters to kilometers.

kilo- **(k)**	hecto- **(h)**	deka- **(da)**	meter **(m)** liter **(L)** gram **(g)**	deci- **(d)**	centi- **(c)**	milli- **(m)**

Power of 10 — Power of 10 — Power of 10

STEP 1 Find the relationship between the units.

Meters are ______ powers of 10 smaller than kilometers.

There are ______ meters in 1 kilometer.

STEP 2 Determine the operation to be used.

I am converting from a __________ unit to a __________ unit, so I will __________.

STEP 3 Convert.

number of meters		meters in 1 kilometer		number of kilometers
↓		↓		↓
15,000	◯	______	=	______

So, Alex's house is ______ kilometers from his grandparent's house.

Math Talk MATHEMATICAL PRACTICES
Chose two units in the chart. **Explain** how you use powers of 10 to describe how the two units are related.

Another Way Use a diagram.

Jamie made a bracelet 1.8 decimeters long. How many millimeters long is Jamie's bracelet?

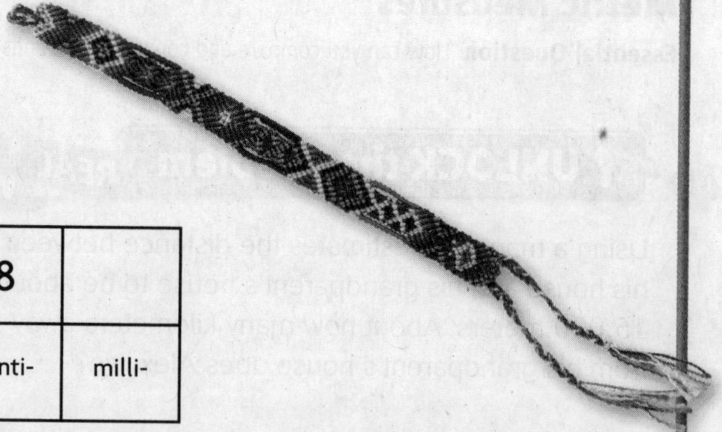

Convert 1.8 decimeters to millimeters.

				1	8	
kilo-	hecto-	deka-	meter liter gram	deci-	centi-	milli-

STEP 1 Show 1.8 decimeters.

Since the unit is decimeters, place the decimal point so that decimeters are the whole number unit.

STEP 2 Convert.

Cross out the decimal and rewrite it so that millimeters will be the whole number unit. Write zeros to the left of the decimal point as needed to complete the whole number.

STEP 3 Record the value with the new units.

1.8 dm = ________ mm

So, Jamie's bracelet is ________ millimeters long.

Try This! **Complete the equation to show the conversion.**

A Convert 247 milligrams to centigrams, decigrams, and grams.

Are the units being converted to a larger unit or a smaller unit? ________

Should you multiply or divide by powers of 10 to convert? ________

247 mg ◯ 10 = ________ cg

247 mg ◯ 100 = ________ dg

247 mg ◯ 1,000 = ________ g

B Convert 3.9 hectoliters to dekaliters, liters, and deciliters.

Are the units being converted to a larger unit or a smaller unit? ________

Should you multiply or divide by powers of 10 to convert? ________

3.9 hL ◯ 10 = ________ daL

3.9 hL ◯ 100 = ________ L

3.9 hL ◯ 1,000 = ________ dL

Name ______________________________

Share and Show

Complete the equation to show the conversion.

1. 8.47 L ◯ 10 = ______ dL

   8.47 L ◯ 100 = ______ cL

   8.47 L ◯ 1,000 = ______ mL

Think: Are the units being converted to a larger unit or a smaller unit?

2. 9,824 dg ◯ 10 = ______ g

   9,824 dg ◯ 100 = ______ dag

   9,824 dg ◯ 1,000 = ______ hg

Convert.

3. 4,250 cm = ______ m

4. 6,000 mL = ______ L

5. 4 dg = ______ cg

Math Talk MATHEMATICAL PRACTICES Explain how you can compare the lengths 4.25 dm and 4.25 cm without converting.

On Your Own

Convert.

6. 9.34 kL = ______ daL

7. 45 hg = ______ dag

8. 40 mm = ______ cm

9. 7 g = ______ mg

10. 5 km = ______ m

11. 1,521 mL = ______ dL

Compare. Write <, >, or =.

12. 32 hg ◯ 3.2 kg

13. 6 km ◯ 660 m

14. 525 mL ◯ 525 cL

Problem Solving REAL WORLD

For 15–16, use the table.

15. Kelly made one batch of peanut and pretzel snack mix. How many grams does she need to add to the snack mix to make 2 kilograms?

16. H.O.T. Kelly plans to take juice on her camping trip. Which will hold more juice, 8 cans or 2 bottles? How much more?

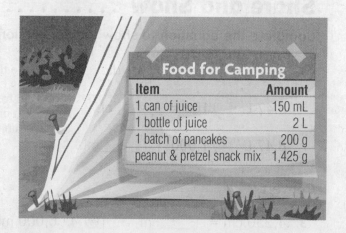

Food for Camping

Item	Amount
1 can of juice	150 mL
1 bottle of juice	2 L
1 batch of pancakes	200 g
peanut & pretzel snack mix	1,425 g

SHOW YOUR WORK

17. Erin's water bottle holds 600 milliliters of water. Dylan's water bottle holds 1 liter of water. Whose water bottle has the greater capacity? How much greater?

18. Liz and Alana each participated in the high jump at the track meet. Liz's high jump was 1 meter. Alana's high jump was 132 centimeters. Who jumped higher? How much higher?

19. H.O.T. Are there less than 1 million, exactly 1 million, or greater than 1 million milligrams in 1 kilogram? **Explain** how you know.

20. **Test Practice** Monica has 426 millimeters of fabric. How many centimeters of fabric does Monica have?

Ⓐ 4,260 centimeters
Ⓑ 42.6 centimeters
Ⓒ 4.26 centimeters
Ⓓ 0.426 centimeters

Name ______________________

Problem Solving • Customary and Metric Conversions

Essential Question How can you use the strategy *make a table* to help you solve problems about customary and metric conversions?

COMMON CORE STANDARD CC.5.MD.1
Convert like measurement units within a given measurement system.

UNLOCK the Problem REAL WORLD

Aaron is making fruit punch for a family reunion. He needs to make 120 cups of punch. If he wants to store the fruit punch in gallon containers, how many gallon containers will Aaron need?

Use the graphic organizer below to help you solve the problem.

Conversion Table

	gal	qt	pt	c
1 gal	1	4	8	16
1 qt	$\frac{1}{4}$	1	2	4
1 pt	$\frac{1}{8}$	$\frac{1}{2}$	1	2
1 c	$\frac{1}{16}$	$\frac{1}{4}$	$\frac{1}{2}$	1

Read the Problem

What do I need to find?

I need to find ____.

What information do I need to use?

I need to use ____.

How will I use the information?

I will make a table to show the relationship between the number of ____________ and the number of ____________.

Solve the Problem

There are ______ cups in 1 gallon. So, each cup is ______ of a gallon.
Complete the table below.

c	1	2	3	4	120
gal	$\frac{1}{16}$	$\frac{1}{8}$	$\frac{3}{16}$	$\frac{1}{4}$	

Multiply by ______.

So, Aaron needs ______ gallon containers to store the punch.

- Will all of the gallon containers Aaron uses be filled to capacity? **Explain.** ____

Try Another Problem

Sharon is working on a project for art class. She needs to cut strips of wood that are each 1 decimeter long to complete the project. If Sharon has 7 strips of wood that are each 1 meter long, how many 1-decimeter strips can she cut?

Conversion Table

	m	dm	cm	mm
1 m	1	10	100	1,000
1 dm	$\frac{1}{10}$	1	10	100
1 cm	$\frac{1}{100}$	$\frac{1}{10}$	1	10
1 mm	$\frac{1}{1,000}$	$\frac{1}{100}$	$\frac{1}{10}$	1

Read the Problem

What do I need to find?	What information do I need to use?	How will I use the information?

Solve the Problem

So, Sharon can cut _____ 1-decimeter lengths to complete her project.

- What relationship did the table you made show? ____________________

____

MATHEMATICAL PRACTICES

Math Talk Explain how you could use another strategy to solve this problem.

Name ______________________________

Share and Show

1. Edgardo has a drink cooler that holds 10 gallons of water. He is filling the cooler with a 1-quart container. How many times will he have to fill the quart container to fill the cooler?

   First, make a table to show the relationship between gallons and quarts. You can use a conversion table to find how many quarts are in a gallon.

gal	1	2	3	4	10
qt	4				

   Then, look for a rule to help you complete your table.

   number of gallons × ______ = number of quarts

   Finally, use the table to solve the problem.

   Edgardo will need to fill the quart container ______ times.

SHOW YOUR WORK

2. H.O.T. **What if** Edgardo only uses 32 quarts of water to fill the cooler. How can you use your table to find how many gallons that is?

____

____

____

____

3. If Edgardo uses a 1-cup container to fill the cooler, how will that affect the number of times he has to fill a container to fill the cooler? **Explain.**

____

____

____

____

On Your Own

Choose a STRATEGY

- Act It Out
- Draw a Diagram
- Make a Table
- Solve a Simpler Problem
- Work Backward
- Guess, Check, and Revise

4. Jeremy made a belt that was 6.4 decimeters long. How many centimeters long is the belt Jeremy made?

5. Dan owns 9 DVDs. His brother Mark has 3 more DVDs than Dan has. Their sister, Marsha, has more DVDs than either of her brothers. Together, the three have 35 DVDs. How many DVDs does Marsha have?

SHOW YOUR WORK

6. H.O.T. Kevin is making a picture frame. He has a piece of trim that is 4 feet long. How many 14-inch-long pieces can Kevin cut from the trim? How much of a foot will he have left over?

7. Write Math **Explain** how you could find the number of cups in five gallons of water.

8. Carla uses $2\frac{3}{4}$ cups of flour and $1\frac{3}{8}$ cups of sugar in her cookie recipe. How many cups does she use in all?

9. Tony needs 16-inch-long pieces of gold chain to make each of 3 necklaces. He has a piece of chain that is $4\frac{1}{2}$ feet long. How much chain will he have left after making the necklaces?

Ⓐ 6 inches Ⓒ 18 inches

Ⓑ 12 inches Ⓓ 24 inches

Name ____________________

Elapsed Time

Essential Question How can you solve elapsed time problems by converting units of time?

COMMON CORE STANDARD **CC.5.MD.1**
Convert like measurement units within a given measurement system.

UNLOCK the Problem REAL WORLD

A computer company claims its laptop has a battery that lasts 4 hours. The laptop actually ran for 200 minutes before the battery ran out. Did the battery last 4 hours?

1 hour = ______ minutes

Think: The minute hand moves from one number to the next in 5 minutes.

Convert 200 minutes to hours and minutes.

STEP 1 Convert minutes into hours and minutes.

200 min = ____ hr ____ min

total min		min in 1 hr		hr		min
↓		↓		↓		↓
______	◯	______	is	______	r	______

STEP 2 Compare. Write <, >, or =.

______ hr ______ min ◯ 4 hr

Since ______ hours ______ minutes is ____________ 4 hours, the battery ____________ last as long as the computer company claims.

Try This! **Convert to mixed measures.**

Jill spent much of her summer away from home. She spent 10 days with her grandparents, 9 days with her cousins, and 22 days at camp. How many weeks and days was she away from home?

STEP 1 Find the total number of days away.

10 days + 9 days + 22 days = ______ days

STEP 2 Convert the days into weeks and days.

______ ÷ 7 is ______ r ______

So, Jill was away from home ______ weeks and ______ days.

Units of Time
60 seconds (s) = 1 minute (min)
60 minutes = 1 hour (hr)
24 hours = 1 day (d)
7 days = 1 week (wk)
52 weeks = 1 year (yr)
12 months (mo) = 1 year
365 days = 1 year

One Way Use a number line to find elapsed time.

Monica spent $2\frac{1}{2}$ hours working on her computer. If she started working at 10:30 A.M., what time did Monica stop working?

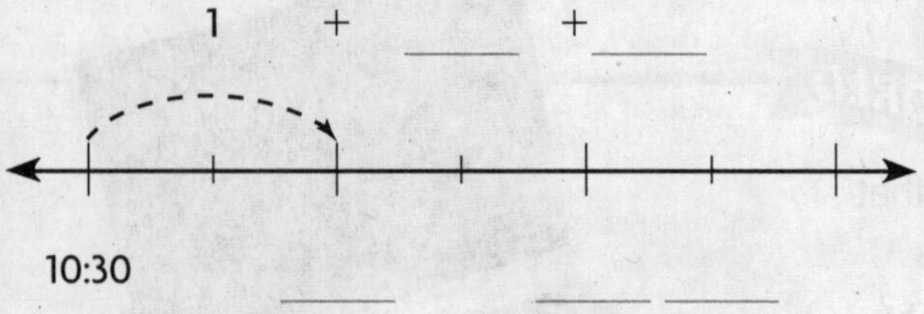

Think: $\frac{1}{2}$ hour = 30 minutes

Another Way Use a clock to find elapsed time.

Start End

So, Monica stopped working at ____________.

Try This! Find a start time.

Robert's soccer team needs to be off the soccer field by 12:15 P.M. Each game is at most $1\frac{3}{4}$ hours long. What time should the game begin to be sure that the team finishes on time?

$\frac{1}{4}$ hour = 15 minutes, so $\frac{3}{4}$ hour = ______ minutes

STEP 1 Subtract the minutes first.

45 minutes earlier is ____________.

STEP 2 Then subtract the hour.

1 hour and 45 minutes earlier is ____________.

So, the game should begin at ____________.

MATHEMATICAL PRACTICES

Math Talk Explain how you could convert 3 hours 45 minutes to minutes.

Name ____________________

Share and Show

Convert.

1. 540 min = ______ hr

2. 8 d = ______ hr

3. 110 hr = _____ d _____ hr

Find the end time.

4. Start time: 9:17 A.M.

Elapsed time: 5 hr 18 min

End time: ____________

MATHEMATICAL PRACTICES

Math Talk **Explain** how to find how long a movie lasts if it starts at 1:35 P.M. and ends at 3:40 P.M.

On Your Own

Convert.

5. 3 yr = ______ d

6. 208 wk = ______ yr

7. 350 min = _____ hr _____ min

Find the start, elapsed, or end time.

8. Start time: 11:38 A.M.

Elapsed time: 3 hr 10 min

End time: ____________

9. Start time: ____________

Elapsed time: 2 hr 37 min

End time: 1:15 P.M.

10. Start time: ____________

Elapsed time: $2\frac{1}{4}$ hr

End time: 5:30 P.M.

11. Start time: 7:41 P.M.

Elapsed time: ____________

End time: 8:50 P.M.

Problem Solving REAL WORLD

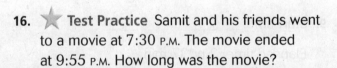

For 12–14, use the graph.

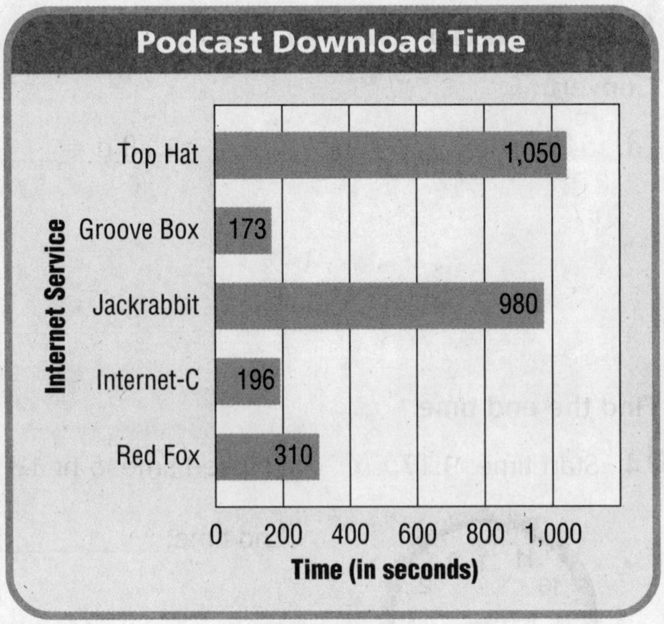

12. Which Internet services downloaded the podcast in less than 4 minutes?

13. H.O.T. Which service took the longest to download the podcast? How much longer did it take than Red Fox in minutes and seconds?

14. H.O.T. Which service was faster, Red Fox or Internet-C? How much faster in minutes and seconds?

15. Write Math **Explain** how you could find the number of seconds in a full 24-hour day. Then solve.

SHOW YOUR WORK

16. **Test Practice** Samit and his friends went to a movie at 7:30 P.M. The movie ended at 9:55 P.M. How long was the movie?

Ⓐ 2 hours 25 minutes

Ⓑ 2 hours 5 minutes

Ⓒ 1 hour 25 minutes

Ⓓ 1 hour 5 minutes

Name ____________________

Line Plots

COMMON CORE STANDARD CC.5.MD.2
Represent and interpret data.

Essential Question How can a line plot help you find an average with data given in fractions?

UNLOCK the Problem REAL WORLD

Students have measured different amounts of water into beakers for an experiment. The amount of water in each beaker is listed below.

$\frac{1}{4}$ cup, $\frac{1}{4}$ cup, $\frac{1}{2}$ cup, $\frac{3}{4}$ cup, $\frac{1}{4}$ cup, $\frac{1}{4}$ cup,
$\frac{1}{4}$ cup, $\frac{1}{2}$ cup, $\frac{1}{4}$ cup, $\frac{3}{4}$ cup, $\frac{1}{4}$ cup, $\frac{3}{4}$ cup

If the total amount of water stayed the same, what would be the average amount of water in a beaker?

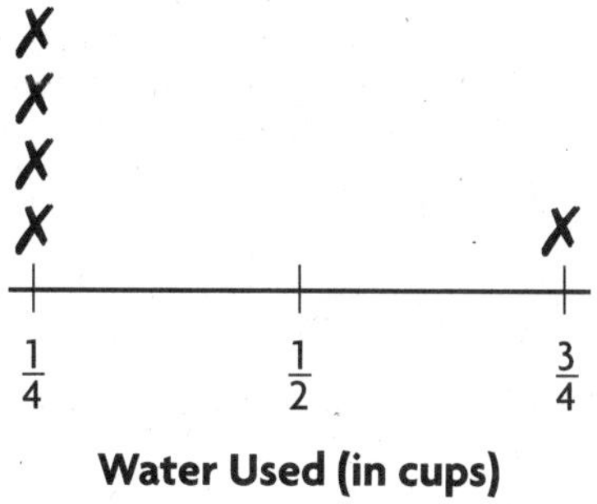

STEP 1 Count the number of cups for each amount. Draw an ✗ for the number of times each amount is recorded to complete the line plot.

$\frac{1}{4}$: ______ $\frac{1}{2}$: ______ $\frac{3}{4}$: ______

STEP 2 Find the total amount of water in all of the beakers that contain $\frac{1}{4}$ cup of water.

There are ______ beakers with $\frac{1}{4}$ cup of water. So, there are ______ fourths, or

$\frac{\quad}{\quad}$, or ______ $\frac{\quad}{\quad}$ cups.

STEP 3 Find the total amount of water in all of the beakers that contain $\frac{1}{2}$ cup of water.

There are ______ beakers with $\frac{1}{2}$ cup of water. So, there are ______ halves, or

$\frac{\quad}{\quad}$, or 1 cup.

STEP 4 Find the total amount of water in all of the beakers that contain $\frac{3}{4}$ cup of water.

$3 \times \frac{3}{4} = \frac{\quad}{\quad}$, or ______ $\frac{\quad}{\quad}$

STEP 5 Add to find the total amount of water in all of the beakers.

$1\frac{3}{4} + 1 + 2\frac{1}{4} =$ ______

STEP 6 Divide the sum you found in Step 5 by the number of beakers to find the average.

$5 \div 12 = \frac{\quad}{\quad}$

So, the average amount of water in a beaker is ______ cup.

Try This!

You can use the order of operations to find the average. Solve the problem as a series of expressions that use parentheses and brackets to separate them. Perform operations from inside the parentheses to the outer brackets.

$\left[\left(7 \times \frac{1}{4}\right) + \left(2 \times \frac{1}{2}\right) + \left(3 \times \frac{3}{4}\right)\right] \div 12$ Perform the operations inside the parentheses.

$\left[\frac{\square}{\square} + \square + \frac{\square}{\square}\right] \div 12$ Next, perform the operations in the brackets.

$\square \div 12$ Divide.

$\frac{\square}{\square}$ Write the expression as a fraction.

Example

Raine divides three 2-ounce bags of rice into smaller bags. The first bag is divided into bags weighing $\frac{1}{6}$-ounce each, the second bag is divided into bags weighing $\frac{1}{3}$-ounce each, and the third bag is divided into bags weighing $\frac{1}{2}$-ounce each.

Find the number of $\frac{1}{6}$-, $\frac{1}{3}$-, and $\frac{1}{2}$-ounce rice bags. Then graph the results on the line plot.

STEP 1 Write a title for your line plot. It should describe what you are counting.

STEP 2 Label $\frac{1}{6}$, $\frac{1}{3}$, and $\frac{1}{2}$ on the line plot to show the different amounts into which the three 2-ounce bags of rice are divided.

STEP 3 Use division to find the number of $\frac{1}{6}$-ounce, $\frac{1}{3}$-ounce, and $\frac{1}{2}$-ounce bags that were made from the three original 2-ounce bags of rice.

$2 \div \frac{1}{6}$ $2 \div \frac{1}{3}$ $2 \div \frac{1}{2}$

$2 \times \square = \square$ $2 \times \square = \square$ $2 \times \square = \square$

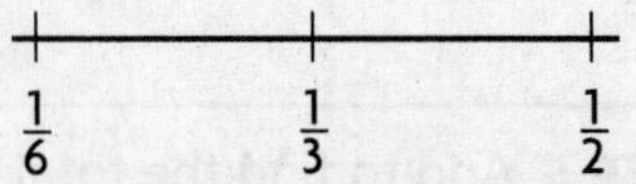

STEP 4 Draw an ✗ above $\frac{1}{6}$, $\frac{1}{3}$, or $\frac{1}{2}$ to show the number of rice bags.

MATHEMATICAL PRACTICES

Math Talk Explain why there are more $\frac{1}{6}$-ounce rice bags than $\frac{1}{2}$-ounce rice bags.

Name ________________________________

Share and Show

Use the data to complete the line plot. Then answer the questions.

Lilly needs to buy beads for a necklace. The beads are sold by mass. She sketches a design to determine what beads are needed, and then writes down their sizes. The sizes are shown below.

$\frac{2}{5}$ g, $\frac{2}{5}$ g, $\frac{4}{5}$ g, $\frac{2}{5}$ g, $\frac{1}{5}$ g, $\frac{1}{5}$ g, $\frac{3}{5}$ g,

$\frac{4}{5}$ g, $\frac{1}{5}$ g, $\frac{2}{5}$ g, $\frac{3}{5}$ g, $\frac{3}{5}$ g, $\frac{2}{5}$ g

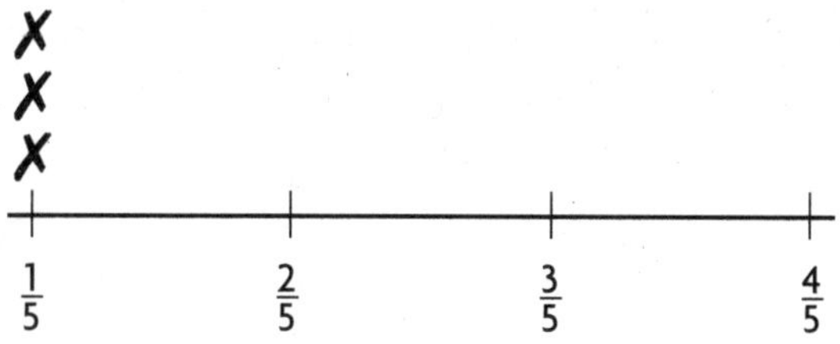

Mass of Beads (in grams)

1. What is the combined mass of the beads with a mass of $\frac{1}{5}$ gram?

   Think: There are ________ Xs above $\frac{1}{5}$ on the line plot, so the combined mass of the beads

   is ________ fifths, or ________ gram.

2. What is the combined mass of all the beads with a mass of $\frac{2}{5}$ gram?

   ____

3. What is the combined mass of all the beads on the necklace?

   ____

4. What is the average weight of the beads on the necklace?

   ____

On Your Own

Use the data to complete the line plot. Then answer the questions.

A breakfast chef used different amounts of milk when making pancakes, depending on the number of pancakes ordered. The results are shown below.

$\frac{1}{2}$ c, $\frac{1}{4}$ c, $\frac{1}{2}$ c, $\frac{3}{4}$ c, $\frac{1}{2}$ c, $\frac{3}{4}$ c, $\frac{1}{2}$ c, $\frac{1}{4}$ c, $\frac{1}{2}$ c, $\frac{1}{2}$ c

Milk in Pancake Orders (in cups)

5. How much milk combined is used in $\frac{1}{4}$-cup amounts? ________

6. How much milk combined is used in $\frac{1}{2}$-cup amounts? ________

7. How much milk combined is used in $\frac{3}{4}$-cup amounts? ________

8. How much milk is used in all the orders of pancakes? ____________

9. What is the average amount of milk used for an order of pancakes? ____________

10. H.O.T. **Describe** an amount you could add to the data that would make the average increase.

    ____

UNLOCK the Problem REAL WORLD

11. For 10 straight days, Samantha measured the amount of food that her cat Dewey ate, recording the results, which are shown below. Graph the results on the line plot. What is the average amount of cat food that Dewey ate daily?

$\frac{1}{2}$ c, $\frac{3}{8}$ c, $\frac{5}{8}$ c, $\frac{1}{2}$ c, $\frac{5}{8}$ c, $\frac{1}{4}$ c, $\frac{3}{4}$ c, $\frac{1}{4}$ c, $\frac{1}{2}$ c, $\frac{5}{8}$ c

a. What do you need to know? ______

______

______

b. How can you use a line plot to organize the information?

______

______

______

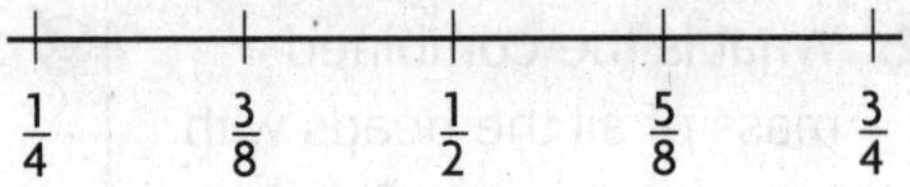

Amount of Cat Food Eaten (in cups)

c. What steps could you use to find the average amount of food that Dewey ate daily?

______

______

______

______

______

d. Fill in the blanks for the totals of each amount measured.

$\frac{1}{4}$ cup: ______

$\frac{3}{8}$ cup: ______

$\frac{1}{2}$ cup: ______

$\frac{5}{8}$ cup: ______

$\frac{3}{4}$ cup: ______

e. Find the total amount of cat food eaten over 10 days.

______ + ______ + ______ + ______ +

______ = ______

So, the average amount of food Dewey ate daily was ______.

12. ★ **Test Practice** How many days did Dewey eat the least amount of cat food?

Ⓐ 1 day

Ⓑ 2 days

Ⓒ 3 days

Ⓓ 4 days

Name ______________________________

Unit Cubes and Solid Figures

Essential Question What is a unit cube and how can you use it to build a solid figure?

COMMON CORE STANDARD **CC.5.MD.3a**
Geometric measurement: understand concepts of volume and relate volume to multiplication and to addition.

Investigate

You can build rectangular prisms using unit cubes. How many different rectangular prisms can you build with a given number of unit cubes?

Materials ■ centimeter cubes

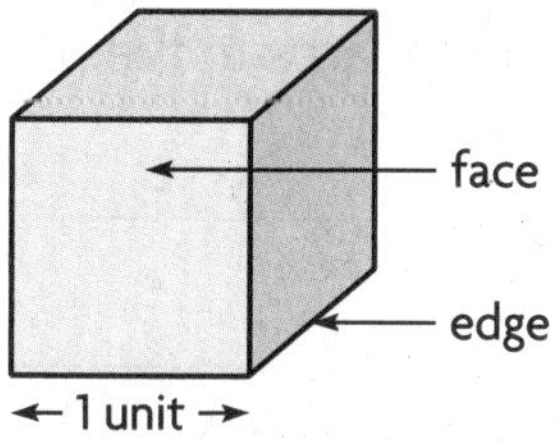

A **unit cube** is a cube that has a length, width, and height of 1 unit. A cube has ______ square faces. All of its faces are congruent. It has ______ edges. The lengths of all its edges are equal.

A. Build a rectangular prism with 2 unit cubes.

Think: When the 2 cubes are pushed together, the faces and edges that are pushed together make 1 face and 1 edge.

- How many faces does the rectangular prism have? ______
- How many edges does the rectangular prism have? ______

B. Build as many different rectangular prisms as you can with 8 unit cubes.

C. Record in units the dimensions of each rectangular prism you built with 8 cubes.

Dimensions		

So, with 8 unit cubes, I can build ______ different rectangular prisms.

MATHEMATICAL PRACTICES
Math Talk **Describe** the different rectangular prisms that you can make with 4 unit cubes.

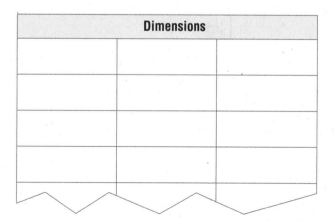

Draw Conclusions

1. **Explain** why a rectangular prism composed of 2 unit cubes has 6 faces. How do its dimensions compare to a unit cube?

______

______

______

2. **Explain** how the number of edges for the rectangular prism compares to the number of edges for the unit cube.

______

______

3. **Describe** what all of the rectangular prisms you made in Step B have in common.

______

______

Make Connections

You can build other solid figures and compare the solid figures by counting the number of unit cubes.

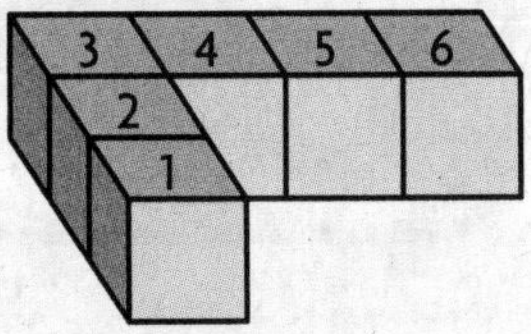

Figure 1

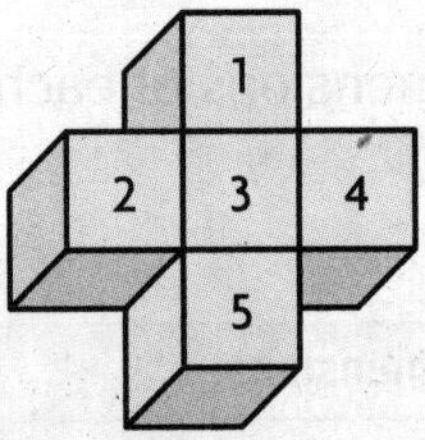

Figure 2

Figure 1 is made up of ______ unit cubes.

Figure 2 is made up of ______ unit cubes.

So, Figure ______ has more unit cubes than Figure ______.

- Use 12 unit cubes to build a solid figure that is not a rectangular prism. Share your model with a partner. Describe how your model is the same and how it is different from your partner's model.

______

______

Name ____________________

Share and Show

Count the number of cubes used to build each solid figure.

1. The rectangular prism is made up of ______ unit cubes.

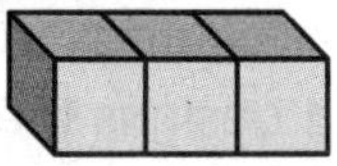

2. 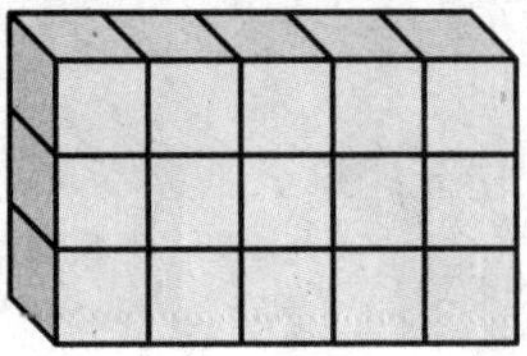

______ unit cubes

3. 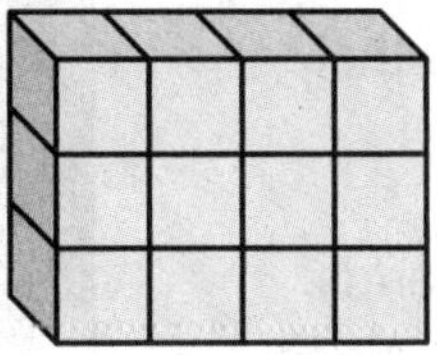

______ unit cubes

✓ 4. 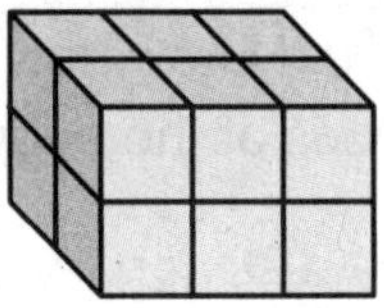

______ unit cubes

5. 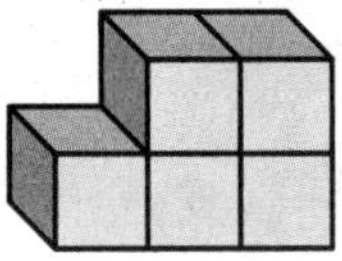

______ unit cubes

6. 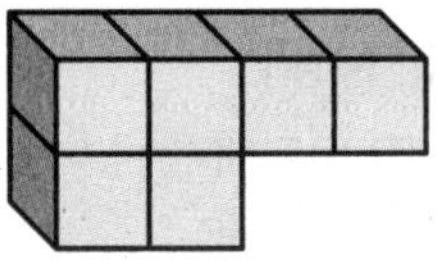

______ unit cubes

✓ 7. 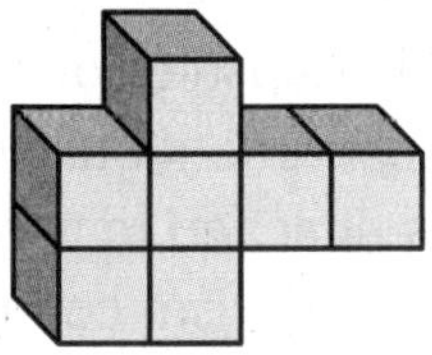

______ unit cubes

8. **Write Math** How are the rectangular prisms in Exercises 3–4 related? Can you show a different rectangular prism with the same relationship? **Explain.**

____

____

Compare the number of unit cubes in each solid figure. Use <, > or =.

9.  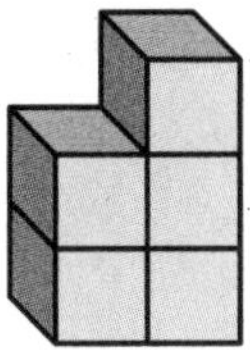

______ unit cubes ◯ ______ unit cubes

10. 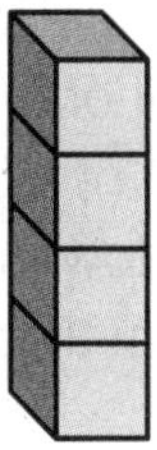 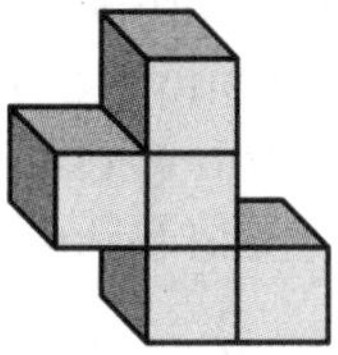

______ unit cubes ◯ ______ unit cubes

Connect to Art

Architecture is the art and science of designing buildings and structures. An architect is a person who plans and designs the buildings.

Good architects are both artists and engineers. They must have a good knowledge of building construction, and they should know how to design buildings that meet the needs of the people who use them.

The Cube Houses of Rotterdam in the Netherlands, shown at the top right, were built in the 1970s. Each cube is a house, tilted and resting on a hexagon-shaped pylon, and is meant to represent an abstract tree. The village of Cube Houses creates a "forest".

The Nakagin Capsule Tower, shown at the right, is an office and apartment building in Tokyo, Japan, made up of modules attached to two central cores. Each module is a rectangular prism connected to a concrete core by four huge bolts. The modules are office and living spaces that can be removed or replaced.

Use the information to answer the questions.

11. There are 38 Cube Houses. Each house could hold 1,000 unit cubes that are 1 meter by 1 meter by 1 meter. Describe the dimensions of a cube house using unit cubes. Remember that the edges of a cube are all the same length.

____

____

12. H.O.T. The Nakagin Capsule Tower has 140 modules, and is 14 stories high. If all of the modules were divided evenly among the number of stories, how many modules would be on each floor? How many different rectangular prisms could be made from that number?

____

Name ______________________________

Understand Volume

Essential Question How can you use unit cubes to find the volume of a rectangular prism?

COMMON CORE STANDARDS **CC.5.MD.3b; CC.5.MD.4** Geometric measurement: understand concepts of volume and relate volume to multiplication and to addition.

Investigate

CONNECT You can find the volume of a rectangular prism by counting unit cubes. **Volume** is the measure of the amount of space a solid figure occupies and is measured in **cubic units**. Each unit cube has a volume of 1 cubic unit.

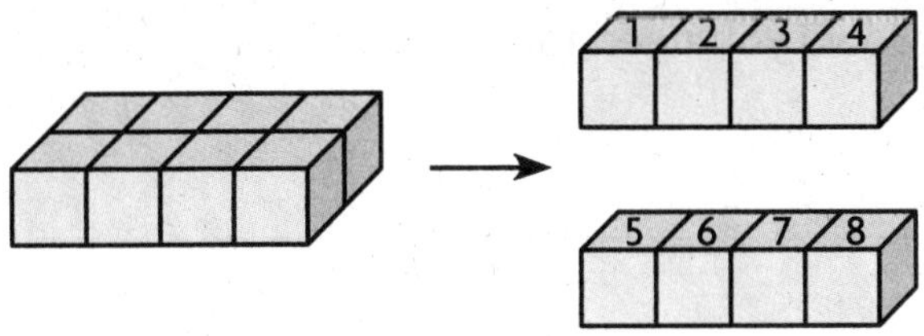

The rectangular prism above is made up of ______ unit cubes

and has a volume of ______ cubic units.

Materials ■ rectangular prism net A ■ centimeter cubes

A. Cut out, fold, and tape the net to form a rectangular prism.

B. Use centimeter cubes to fill the base of the rectangular prism without gaps or overlaps. Each centimeter cube has a length, width, and height of 1 centimeter and a volume of 1 cubic centimeter.

- How many centimeter cubes make up the length of the first layer? the width? the height?

  length: ______ width: ______ height: ______

- How many centimeter cubes are used to fill the base? ______

C. Continue filling the rectangular prism, layer by layer. Count the number of centimeter cubes used for each layer.

- How many centimeter cubes are in each layer? ______
- How many layers of cubes fill the rectangular prism? ______
- How many centimeter cubes fill the prism? ______

So, the volume of the rectangular prism is ______ cubic centimeters.

Draw Conclusions

1. **Describe** the relationship among the number of centimeter cubes you used to fill each layer, the number of layers, and the volume of the prism.

____

____

____

2. **Apply** If you had a rectangular prism that had a length of 3 units, a width of 4 units, and a height of 2 units, how many unit cubes would you need for each layer? How many unit cubes would you need to fill the rectangular prism?

____

Make Connections

To find the volume of three-dimensional figures, you measure in three directions. For a rectangular prism, you measure its length, width, and height. Volume is measured using cubic units, such as cu cm, cu in., or cu ft.

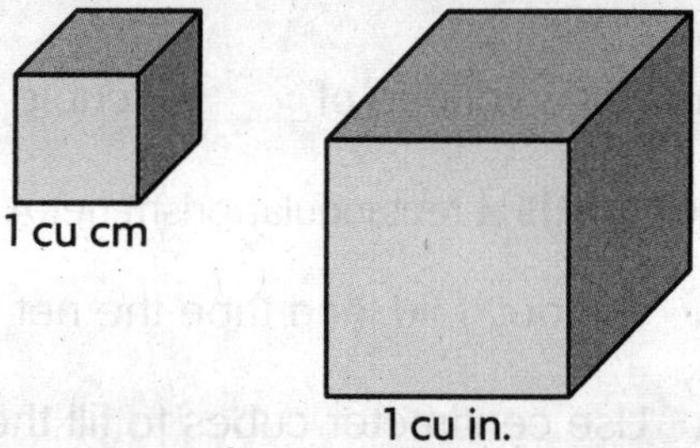

- Which has a greater volume, 1 cu cm or 1 cu in.? **Explain.**

____

____

Find the volume of the prism if each cube represents 1 cu cm, 1 cu in., and 1 cu ft.

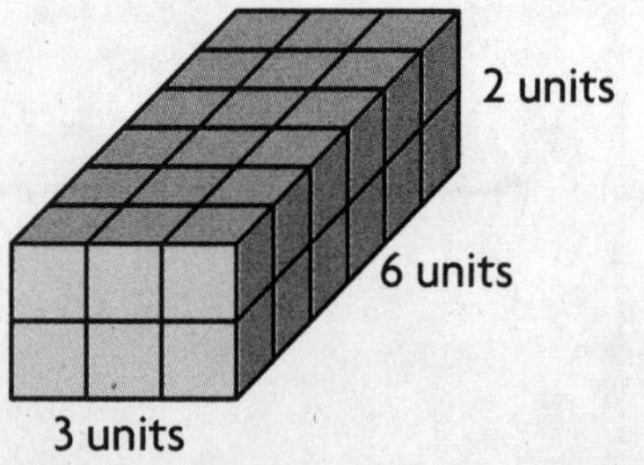

_____ cu cm

_____ cu in.

_____ cu ft

- Would the prism above be the same size if it were built with centimeter cubes, inch cubes, or foot cubes? **Explain.**

____

____

____

Name ______________________________

Share and Show

Use the unit given. Find the volume.

1.

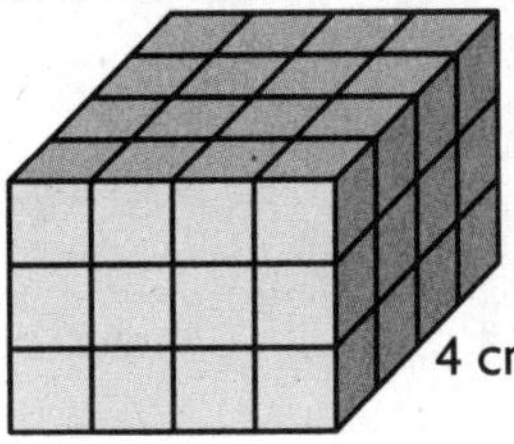

Each cube = 1 cu cm

Volume = ______ cu ______

2.

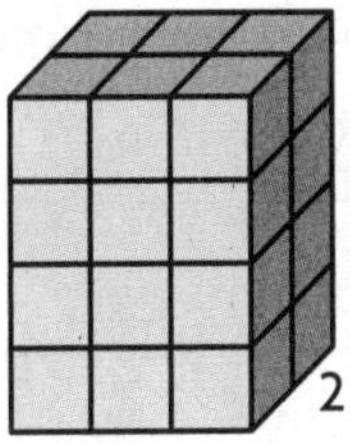

Each cube = 1 cu in.

Volume = ______ cu ______

3.

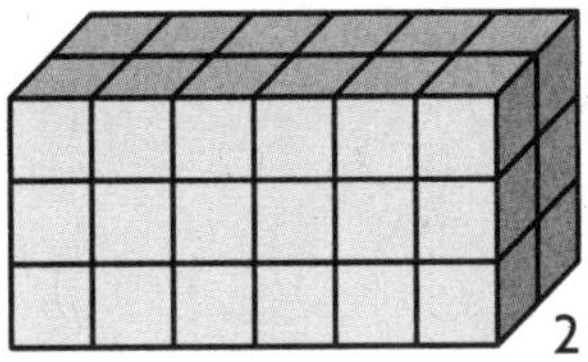

Each cube = 1 cu ft

Volume = ______ cu ______

4.

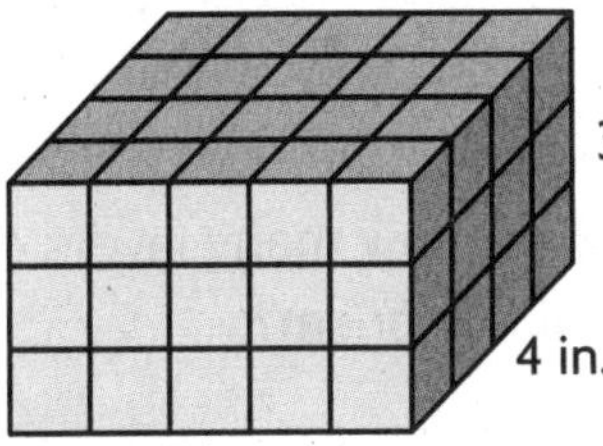

Each cube = 1 cu in.

Volume = ______ cu ______

Compare the volumes. Write <, >, or =.

5.

Each cube = 1 cu cm

Each cube = 1 cu in.

______ cu cm ◯ ______ cu in.

6.

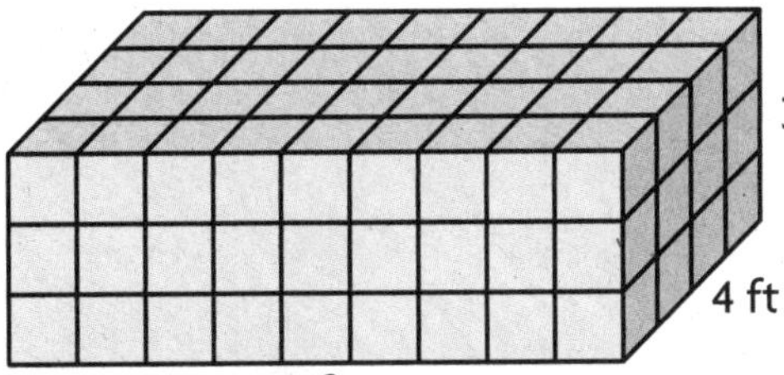

Each cube = 1 cu ft

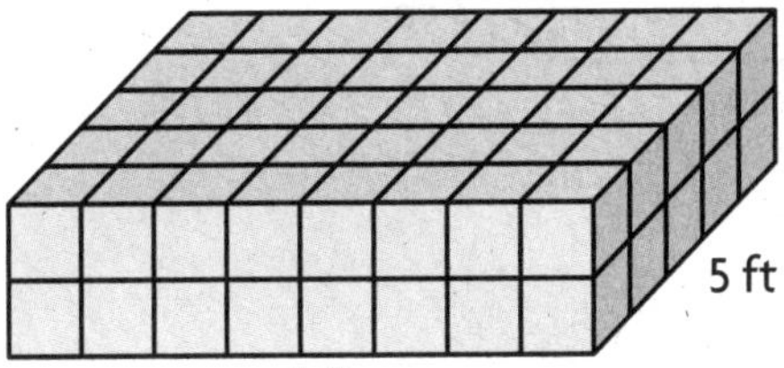

Each cube = 1 cu ft

______ cu ft ◯ ______ cu ft

Problem Solving REAL WORLD

SHOW YOUR WORK

7. **What's the Error?** Jerry says that a cube with edges that measure 10 centimeters has a volume that is twice as much as a cube with sides that measure 5 centimeters. **Explain** and correct Jerry's error.

____

____

____

____

8. H.O.T. Pattie built a rectangular prism with cubes. The base of her prism has 12 centimeter cubes. If the prism was built with 108 centimeter cubes, how many layers does her prism have? What is the height of her prism?

____

9. A packing company makes boxes with edges each measuring 3 feet. What is the volume of the boxes? If 10 boxes are put in a larger, rectangular shipping container and completely fill it with no gaps or overlaps, what is the volume of the shipping container?

____

10. **Test Practice** Find the volume of the rectangular prism.

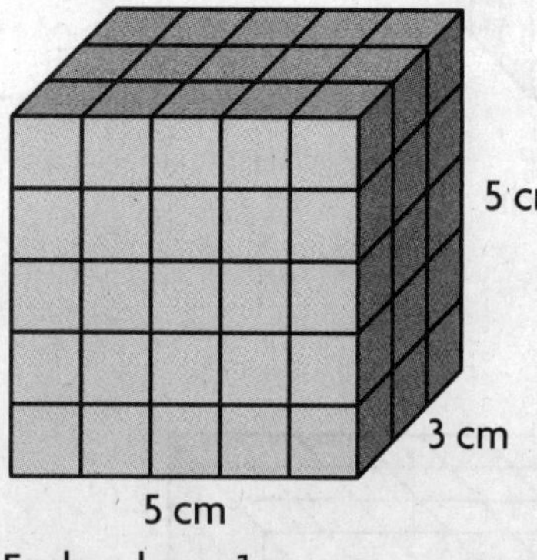

Each cube = 1 cu cm

Ⓐ 25 cubic feet

Ⓑ 25 cubic meters

Ⓒ 75 cubic meters

Ⓓ 75 cubic centimeters

Name ______________________________

Estimate Volume

Essential Question How can you use an everyday object to estimate the volume of a rectangular prism?

COMMON CORE STANDARD **CC.5.MD.4**
Geometric measurement: understand concepts of volume and relate volume to multiplication and to addition.

Investigate

Izzy is mailing 20 boxes of crayons to a children's-education organization overseas. She can pack them in one of two different-sized shipping boxes. Using crayon boxes as a cubic unit, about what volume is each shipping box, in crayon boxes? Which shipping box should Izzy use to mail the crayons?

Materials ■ rectangular prism net B ■ 2 boxes, different sizes

A. Cut out, fold, and tape the net to form a rectangular prism. Label the prism "Crayons." You can use this prism to estimate and compare the volume of the two boxes.

B. Using the crayon box that you made, count to find the number of boxes that make up the base of the shipping box. Estimate the length to the nearest whole unit.

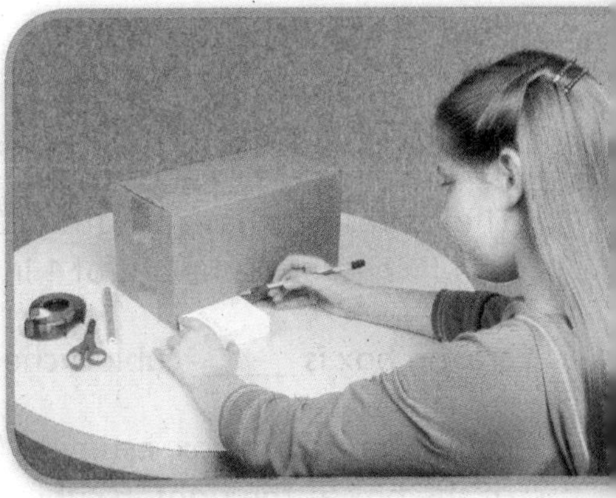

Number of crayon boxes that fill the base:

Box 1: ______________ Box 2: ______________

C. Starting with the crayon box in the same position, count to find the number of crayon boxes that make up the height of the shipping box. Estimate the height to the nearest whole unit.

Number of layers:

Box 1: ______________ Box 2: ______________

Box 1 has a volume of ______ crayon boxes

and Box 2 has a volume of ______ crayon boxes.

So, Izzy should use Box ______ to ship the crayons.

Draw Conclusions

1. **Explain** how you estimated the volume of the shipping boxes.

____

____

____

____

2. **Analyze** If you had to estimate to the nearest whole unit to find the volume of a shipping box, how might you be able to ship a greater number of crayon boxes in the shipping box than you actually estimated? **Explain**.

____

____

____

Make Connections

The crayon box has a length of 3 inches, a width of 4 inches, and a height of 1 inch. The volume of the crayon box is ______ cubic inches.

Using the crayon box, estimate the volume of the box at the right in cubic inches.

- The box to the right holds ______ crayon boxes in each of ______ layers, or ______ crayon boxes.
- Multiply the volume of 1 crayon box by the estimated number of crayon boxes that fit in the box at the right.

  ______ × ______ = __________

So, the volume of the shipping box at the right is about __________ cubic inches.

Name ____________________

Share and Show

Estimate the volume.

1. Each tissue box has a volume of 125 cubic inches.

   There are ______ tissue boxes in the larger box.

   The estimated volume of the box holding the tissue boxes is ______ $\times$ 125 = ____________ cu in.

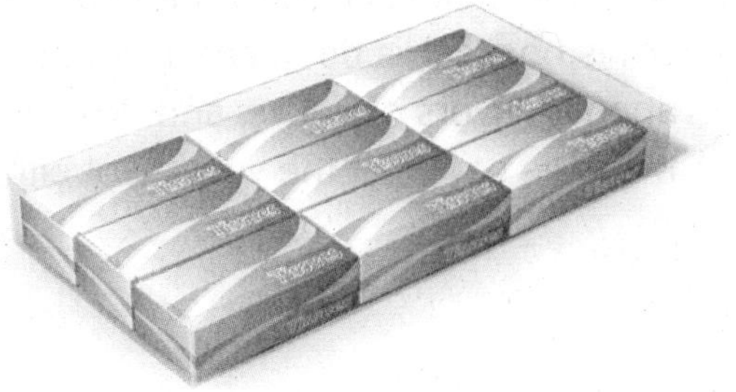

2. Volume of chalk box: 16 cu in.

Volume of large box: ____________

3. Volume of small jewelry box: 30 cu cm

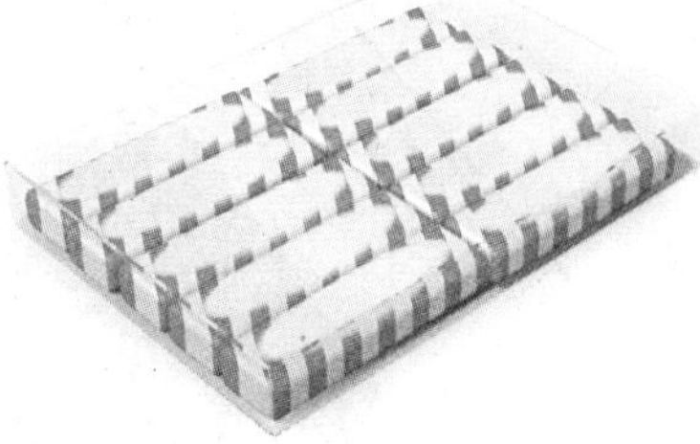

Volume of large box: ____________

On Your Own

Estimate the volume.

4. Volume of book: 80 cu in.

Volume of large box: ____________

5. Volume of spaghetti box: 750 cu cm

Volume of large box: ____________

6. Volume of cereal box: 324 cu in.

Volume of large box: ____________

7. Volume of pencil box: 4,500 cu cm

Volume of large box: ____________

Problem Solving REAL WORLD

H.O.T. Sense or Nonsense?

8. Marcelle estimated the volume of the two boxes below, using one of his books. His book has a volume of 48 cubic inches. Box 1 holds about 7 layers of books, and Box 2 holds about 14 layers of books. Marcelle says that the volume of either box is about the same.

- Does Marcelle's statement make sense or is it nonsense? **Explain** your answer.

Name ______________________________

Volume of Rectangular Prisms

Essential Question How can you find the volume of a rectangular prism?

COMMON CORE STANDARD CC.5.MD.5a
Geometric measurement: understand concepts of volume and relate volume to multiplication and to addition.

CONNECT The base of a rectangular prism is a rectangle. You know that area is measured in square units, or units^2, and that the area of a rectangle can be found by multiplying the length and the width.

The area of the base is ______ sq units.

Volume is measured in cubic units, or units^3. When you build a prism and add each layer of cubes, you are adding a third dimension, height.

UNLOCK the Problem REAL WORLD

Sid built the rectangular prism shown at the right, using 1-inch cubes. The prism has a base that is a rectangle and has a height of 4 cubes. What is the volume of the rectangular prism that Sid built?

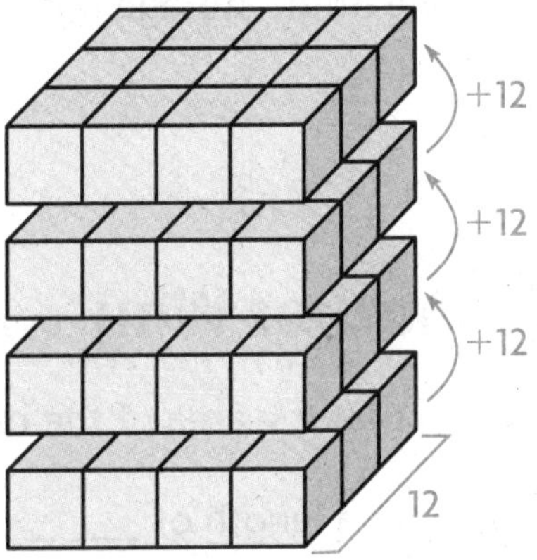

You can find the volume of a prism in cubic units by multiplying the number of square units in the base shape by the number of layers, or its height.

Each layer of Sid's rectangular prism is composed of ______ inch cubes.

Height (in layers)	1	2	3	4
Volume (in cubic inches)	12	24		

Multiply the height by ______.

1. How does the volume change as each layer is added?

____

____

2. What does the number you multiply the height by represent?

____

____

So, the volume of Sid's rectangular prism is ______ in.^{3}

Relate Height to Volume

Toni stacks cube-shaped beads that measure 1 centimeter on each edge in a storage box. The box can hold 6 layers of 24 cubes with no gaps or overlaps. What is the volume of Toni's storage box?

- What are the dimensions of the base of the box?

____

- What operation can you use to find the area of the base shape?

____

One Way Use base and height.

The volume of each bead is ______ cm^3.

The storage box has a base with an area of ______ cm^2.

The height of the storage box is ______ centimeters.

The volume of the storage box is

(______ × ______), or ______ cm^3.

Base area

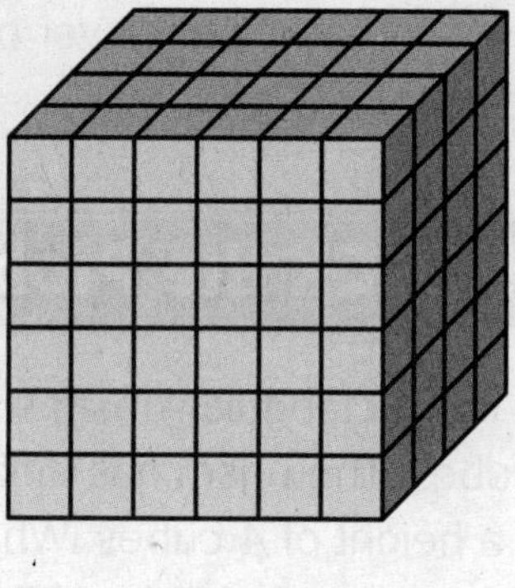

Another Way Use length, width, and height.

You know that the area of the base of the storage box is 24 cm^2.

The base has a length of ______ centimeters and a width of ______ centimeters. The height is ______ centimeters. The volume of the storage box is

(______ × ______) × ______, or ______ × ______, or ______ cm^3.

Base area

So, the volume of the storage box is ______ cm^3.

3. H.O.T. What if each cube-shaped bead measured 2 centimeters on each edge? How would the dimensions of the storage box change? How would the volume change?

____

____

____

Name ______________________________

Share and Show

Find the volume.

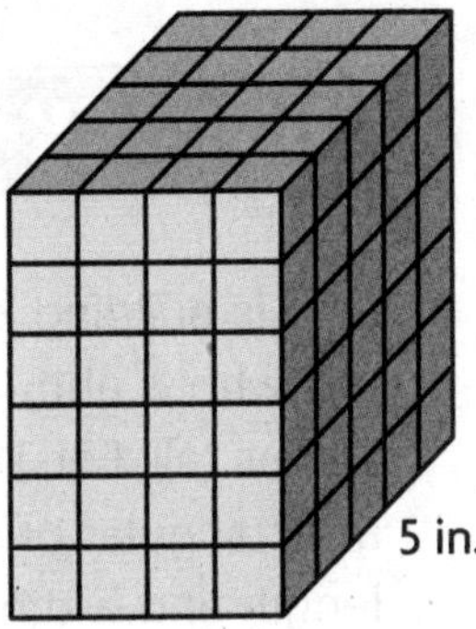

1. The length of the rectangular prism is __________.

   The width is __________. So, the area of the base is __________.

   The height is __________. So, the volume of the prism is __________.

2.

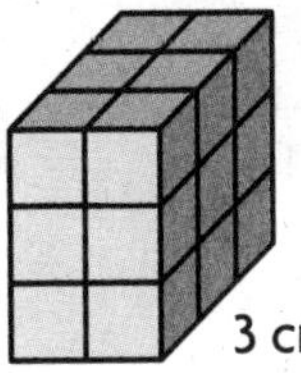

Volume: __________

3.

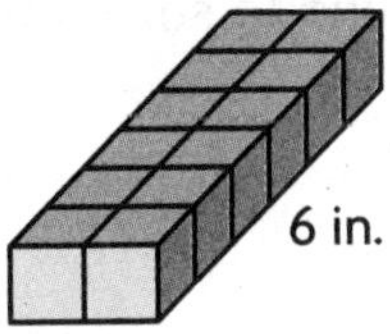

Volume: __________

MATHEMATICAL PRACTICES

Math Talk Explain why the exponent 2 is used to express the measure of area and the exponent 3 is used to express the measure of volume.

On Your Own

Find the volume.

4.

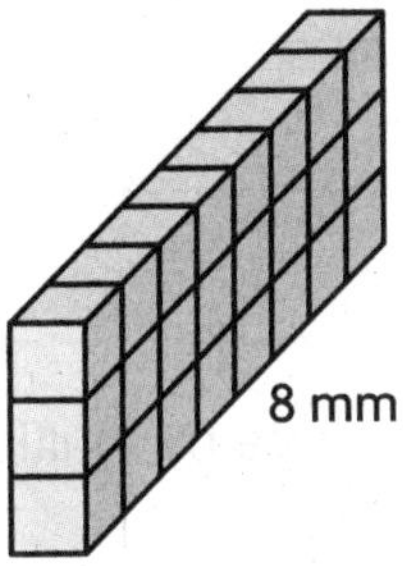

Volume: __________

5.

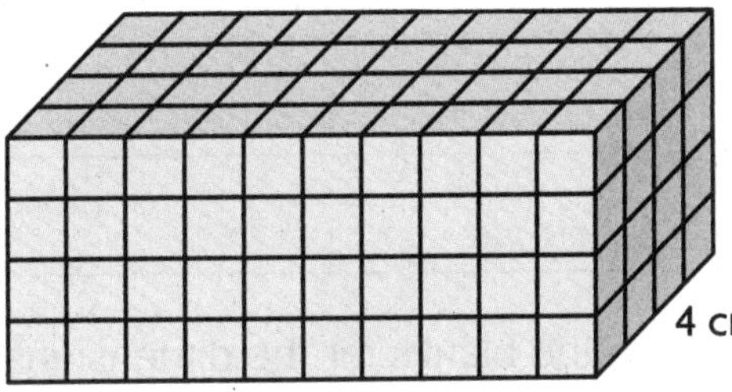

Volume: __________

6.

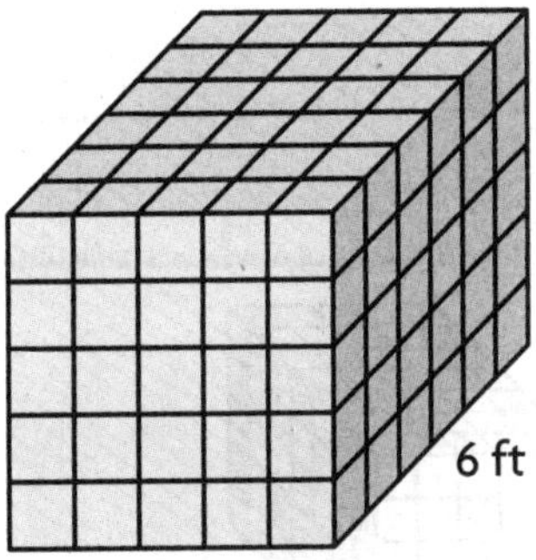

Volume: __________

7.

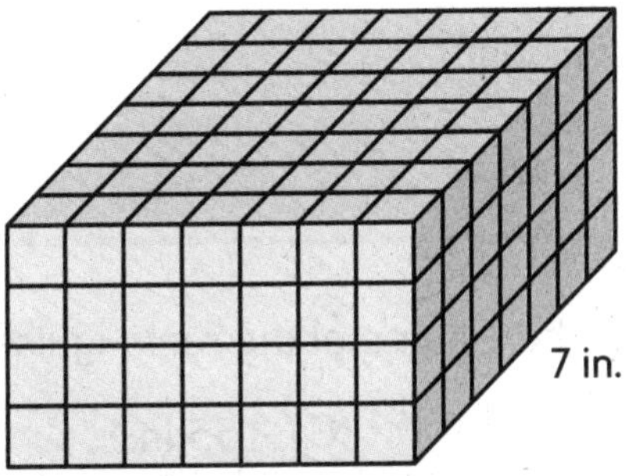

Volume: __________

UNLOCK the Problem REAL WORLD

TEST PRACTICE

8. Rich is building a travel crate for his dog, Thomas, a beagle-mix who is about 30 inches long, 12 inches wide, and 24 inches tall. For Thomas to travel safely, his crate needs to be a rectangular prism that is about 12 inches greater than his length and width, and 6 inches greater than his height. What is the volume of the travel crate that Rich should build?

a. What do you need to find to solve the problem?

____

____

b. How can you use Thomas's size to help you solve the problem?

____

____

____

c. What steps can you use to find the size of Thomas's crate?

____

____

____

d. Fill in the blanks for the dimensions of the dog crate.

length: __________

width: __________

height: __________

area of base: __________

e. Find the volume of the crate by multiplying the base area and the height.

_____ × _____ = _______

So, Rich should build a travel crate for Thomas that has a volume of __________.

9. What is the volume of the rectangular prism at the right?

Ⓐ 35 in.^{3} Ⓒ 155 in.^{3}

Ⓑ 125 in.^{3} Ⓓ 175 in.^{3}

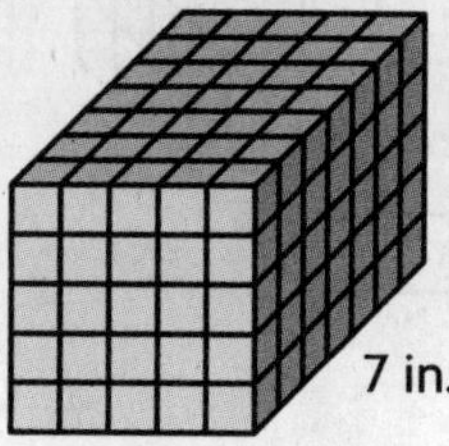

Name ____________________

Apply Volume Formulas

Essential Question How can you use a formula to find the volume of a rectangular prism?

COMMON CORE STANDARD CC.5.MD.5a; CC.5.MD.5b
Geometric measurement: understand concepts of volume and relate volume to multiplication and to addition.

CONNECT Both prisms show the same dimensions and have the same volume.

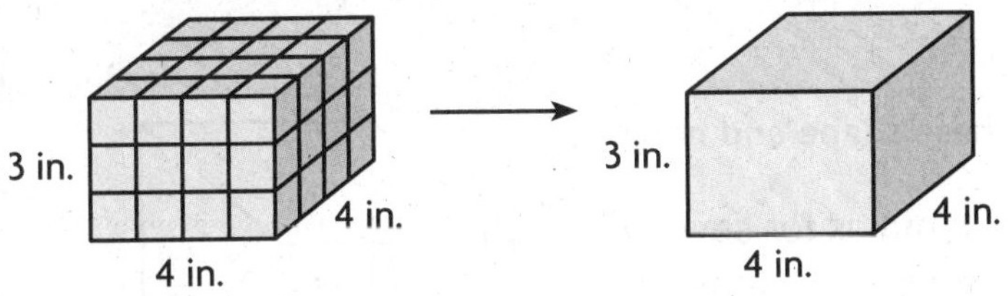

UNLOCK the Problem REAL WORLD

Mike is making a box to hold his favorite DVDs. The length of the box is 7 inches, the width is 5 inches and the height is 3 inches. What is the volume of the box Mike is making?

- Underline what you are asked to find.
- Circle the numbers you need to use to solve the problem.

One Way Use length, width, and height.

You can use a formula to find the volume of a rectangular prism.

Volume = *length* × *width* × *height*

$V = l \times w \times h$

STEP 1 Identify the length, width, and height of the rectangular prism.

length = ______ in.

width = ______ in.

height = ______ in.

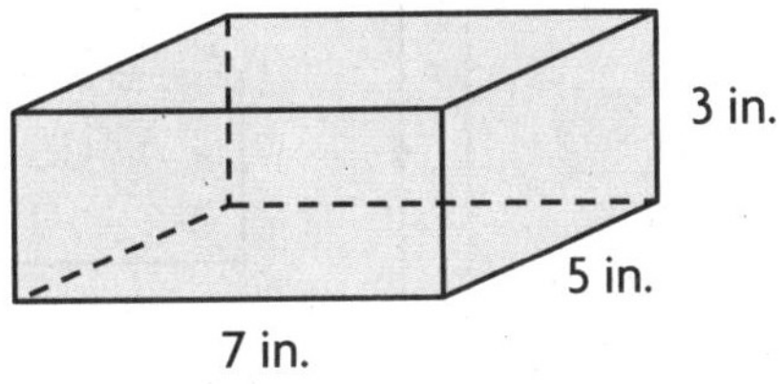

STEP 2 Multiply the length by the width.

______ × ______ = ______

STEP 3 Multiply the product of the length and width by the height.

35 × ______ = ______

So, the volume of Mike's DVD box is ____________ cubic inches.

MATHEMATICAL PRACTICES

Math Talk **Explain** how you can use the Associative Property to group the part of the formula that represents area.

You have learned one formula for finding the volume of a rectangular prism. You can also use another formula.

> *Volume* = *Base area* × *height*
>
> $V = B \times h$
>
> B = area of the base shape,
>
> h = height of the solid figure.

Another Way Use the area of the base shape and height.

Emilio's family has a sand castle kit. The kit includes molds for several solid figures that can be used to make sand castles. One of the molds is a rectangular prism like the one shown at the right. How much sand will it take to fill the mold?

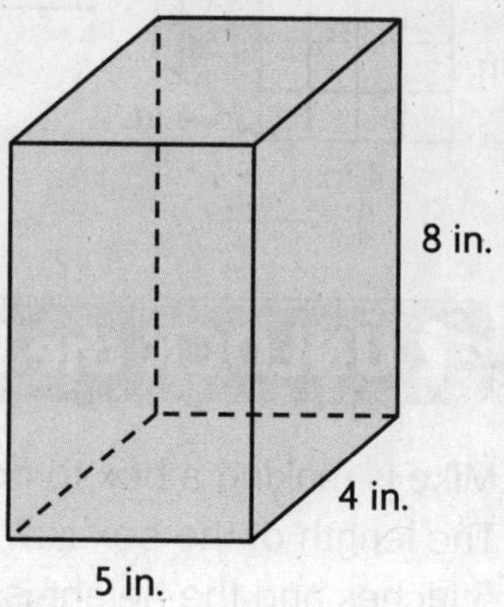

$V = B \times h$ — Replace B with an expression for the area of the base shape. Replace h with the height of the solid figure.

$V = (\_\_\_\_ \times \_\_\_\_) \times \_\_\_\_$ — Multiply.

$V = \_\_\_\_ \times \_\_\_\_$

$V = \_\_\_\_$ cu in.

So, it will take ______ cubic inches of sand to fill the rectangular prism mold.

Try This!

A **Find the volume.**

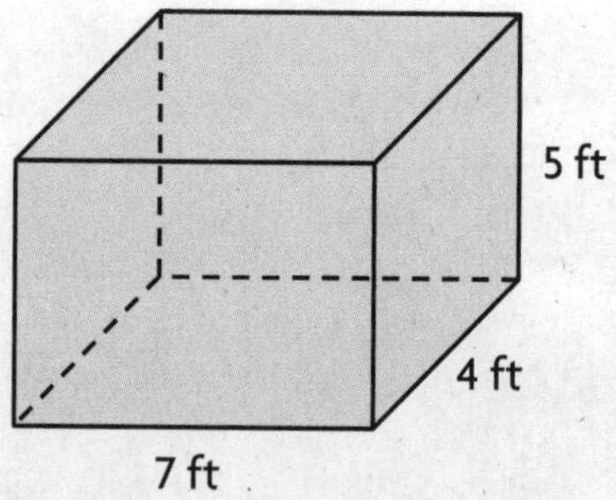

$V = l \times w \times h$

$V = \_\_\_\_ \times \_\_\_\_ \times \_\_\_\_$

$V = \_\_\_\_ \times \_\_\_\_$

$V = \_\_\_\_$ cu ft

B **Find the unknown measurement.**

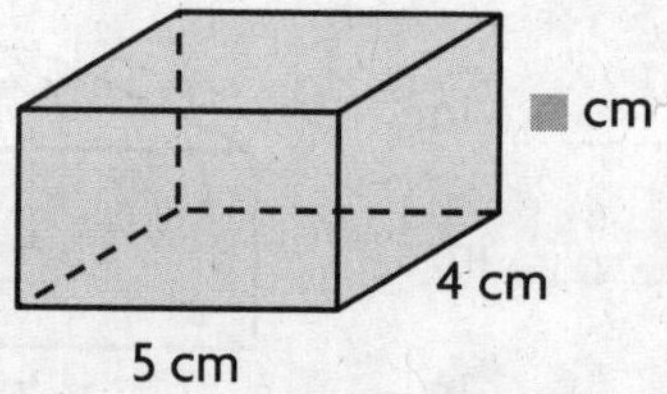

$V = l \times w \times h$

60 = ______ × ______ × ■

60 = ______ × ■

Think: If I filled this prism with centimeter cubes, each layer would have 20 cubes. How many layers of 20 cubes are equal to 60?

So, the unknown measurement is ______ cm.

Name ______________________________

Share and Show

Find the volume.

1.

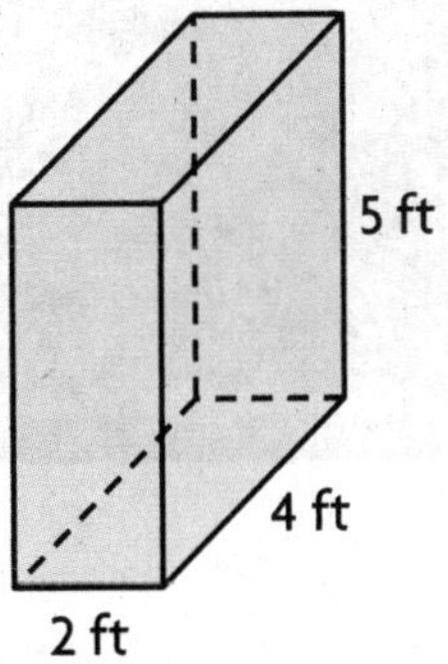

$V =$ ____________

2.

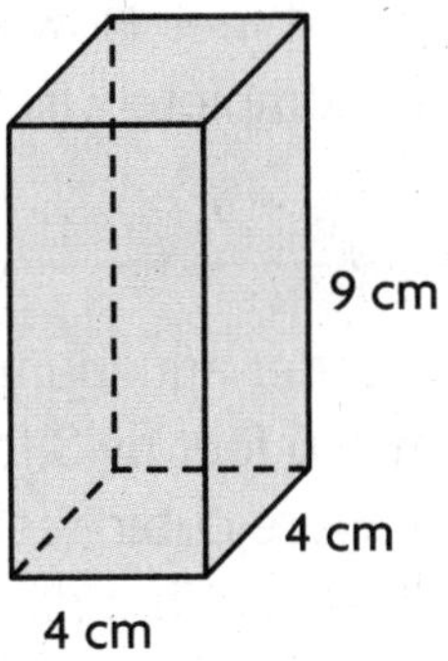

$V =$ ____________

On Your Own

Find the volume.

3.

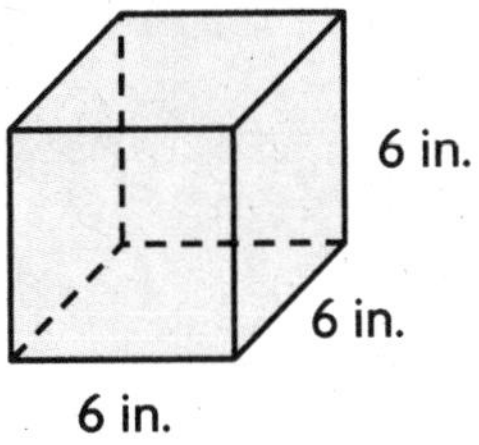

$V =$ ____________

4.

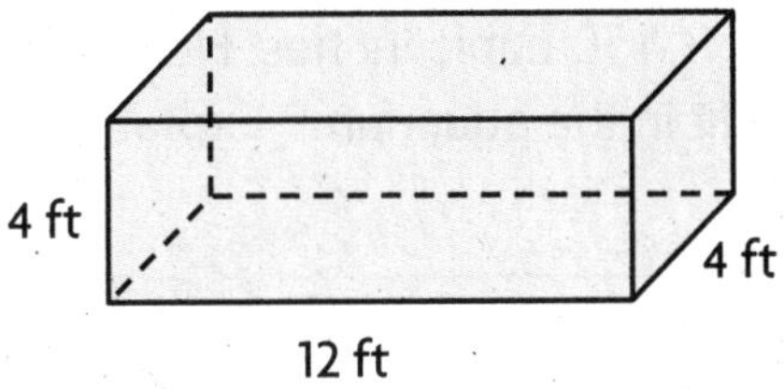

$V =$ ____________

5.

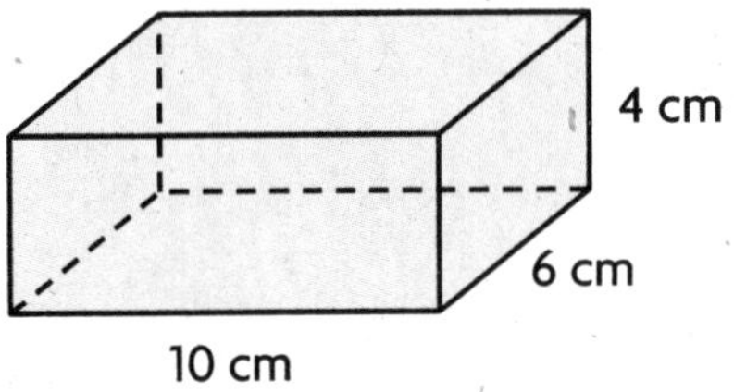

$V =$ ____________

6.

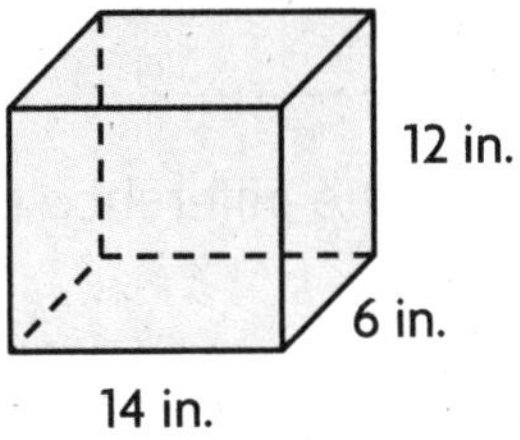

$V =$ ____________

H.O.T. **Algebra** Find the unknown measurement.

7.

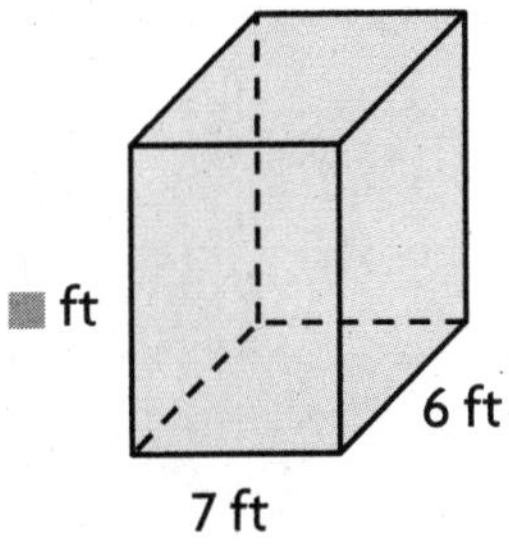

$V = 420$ cu ft ■ = ________ ft

8.

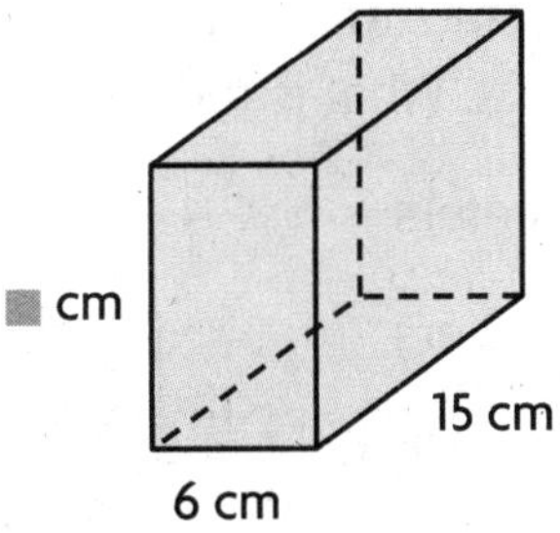

$V = 900$ cu cm ■ = ________ cm

Problem Solving REAL WORLD

9. The Jade Restaurant has a large aquarium on display in its lobby. The base of the aquarium is 5 feet by 2 feet. The height of the aquarium is 4 feet. How many cubic feet of water are needed to completely fill the aquarium?

____

10. The Pearl Restaurant put a larger aquarium in its lobby. The base of their aquarium is 6 feet by 3 feet, and the height is 4 feet. How many more cubic feet of water does the Pearl Restaurant's aquarium hold than the Jade Restaurant's aquarium?

____

SHOW YOUR WORK

11. H.O.T. Eddie measured his aquarium using a small fish food box. The box has a base area of 6 inches and a height of 4 inches. Eddie found that the volume of his aquarium is 3,456 cubic inches. How many boxes of fish food could fit in the aquarium? **Explain** your answer.

____

____

____

____

12. Write Math ▸ **Describe** the difference between area and volume.

____

____

____

13. ★ **Test Practice** Adam stores his favorite CDs in a box like the one at the right. What is the volume of the box?

Ⓐ 150 cubic centimeters

Ⓑ 750 cubic centimeters

Ⓒ 1,050 cubic centimeters

Ⓓ 1,150 cubic centimeters

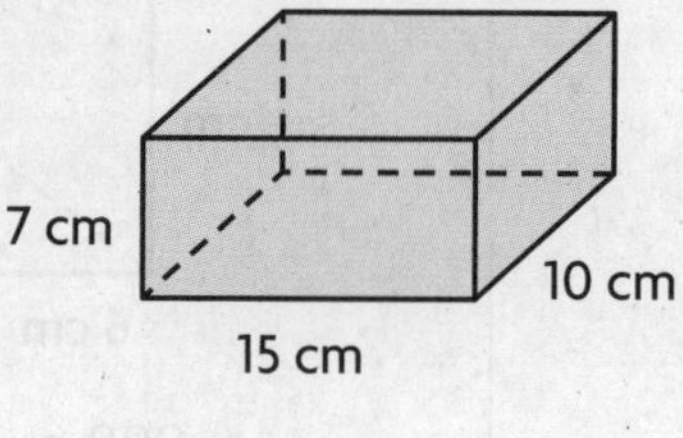

Name ______________________________

Find Volume of Composed Figures

Essential Question How can you find the volume of rectangular prisms that are combined?

COMMON CORE STANDARD CC.5.MD.5c
Geometric measurement: understand concepts of volume and relate volume to multiplication and to addition.

UNLOCK the Problem REAL WORLD

The shape at the right is a composite figure. It is made up of two rectangular prisms that are combined. How can you find the volume of the figure?

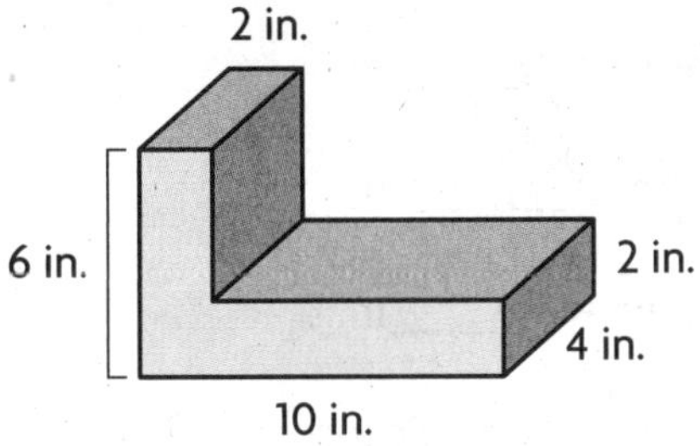

One Way Use addition.

STEP 1 Break apart the solid figure into two rectangular prisms.

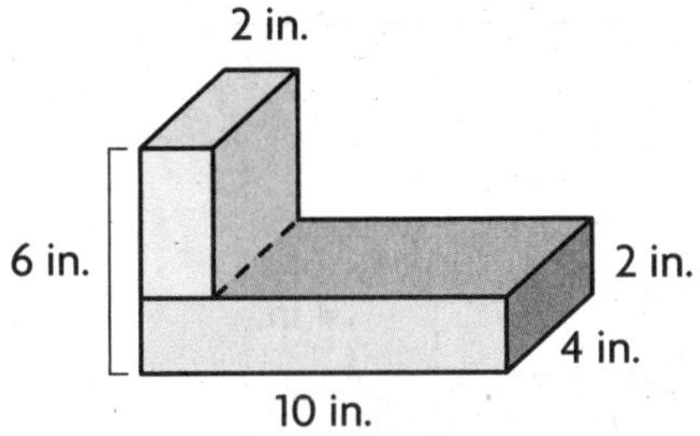

STEP 2 Find the length, width, and height of each prism.

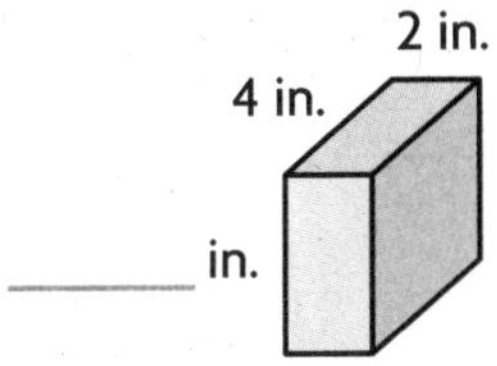

Think: The total height of both prisms is 6 inches. Subtract the given heights to find the unknown height. 6 − 2 = 4

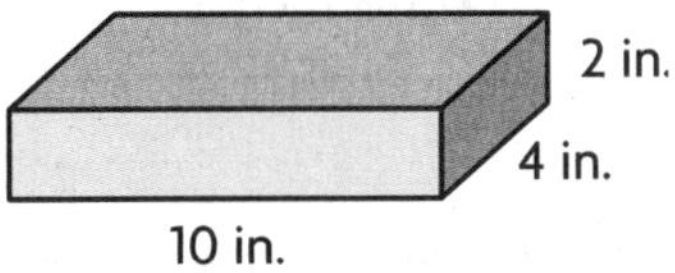

STEP 3 Find the volume of each prism.

$V = l \times w \times h$

$V =$ ______ $\times$ ______ $\times$ ______

$V =$ ______ in.^{3}

$V = l \times w \times h$

$V =$ ______ $\times$ ______ $\times$ ______

$V =$ ______ in.^{3}

STEP 4 Add the volumes of the rectangular prisms.

______ + ______ = ______

So, the volume of the composite figure is ______ cubic inches.

- What is another way you could divide the composite figure into two rectangular prisms? ______________________________

____

Another Way Use subtraction.

You can subtract the volumes of prisms formed in empty spaces from the greatest possible volume to find the volume of a composite figure.

STEP 1

Find the greatest possible volume.

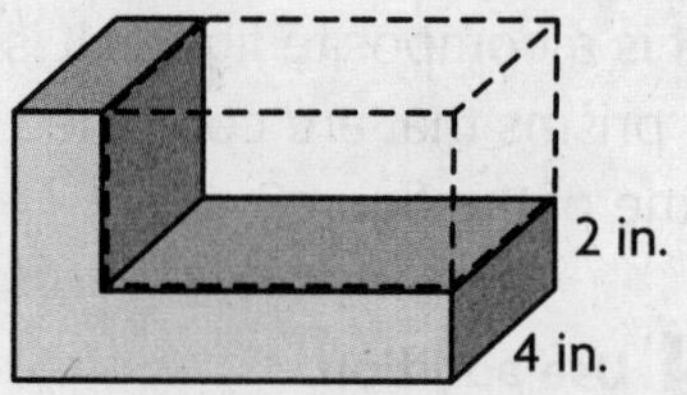

length = ______ in.

width = ______ in.

height = ______ in.

V = ______ cubic inches

STEP 2

Find the volume of the prism in the empty space.

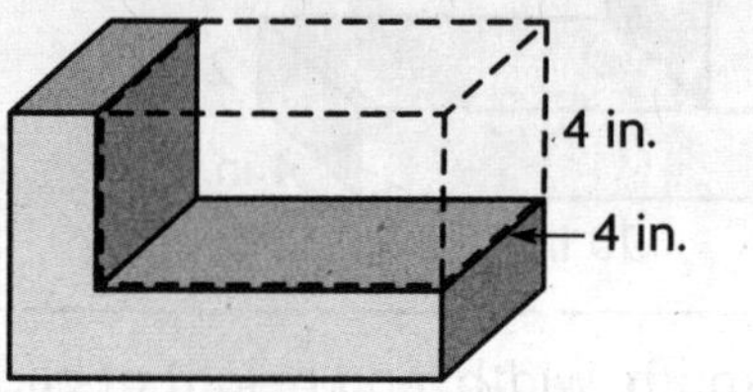

length = ______ in. **Think:** $10 - 2 = 8$

width = ______ in.

height = ______ in. **Think:** $6 - 2 = 4$

$V = 8 \times 4 \times 4 =$ ______ cubic inches

STEP 3

Subtract the volume of the empty space from the greatest possible volume.

______ − ______ = ______ cubic inches

So, the volume of the composite figure is ______ cubic inches.

Try This!

Find the volume of a composite figure made by putting together three rectangular prisms.

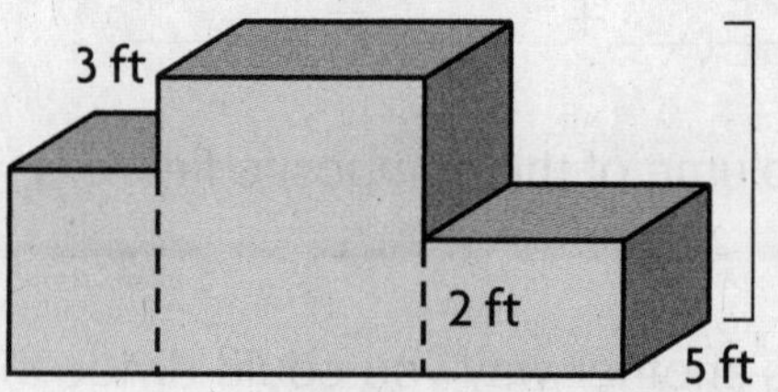

V = ______ × ______ × ______ = ______ cu ft

V = ______ × ______ × ______ = ______ cu ft

V = ______ × ______ × ______ = ______ cu ft

Total volume = ______ + ______ + ______ = ______ cubic feet

Name ______________________________

Share and Show

Find the volume of the composite figure.

1.

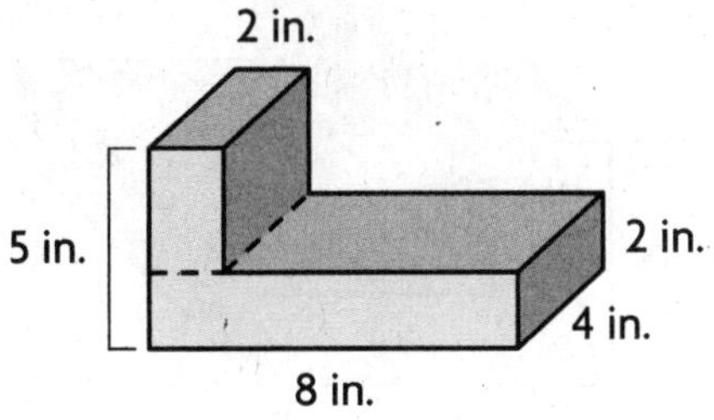

$V =$ ______________

2.

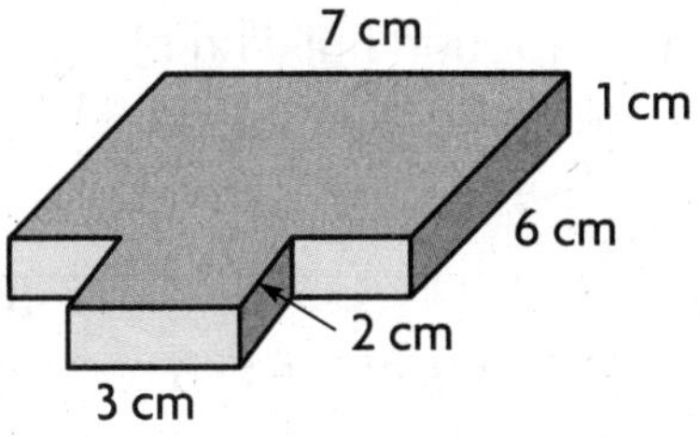

$V =$ ______________

On Your Own

Find the volume of the composite figure.

3.

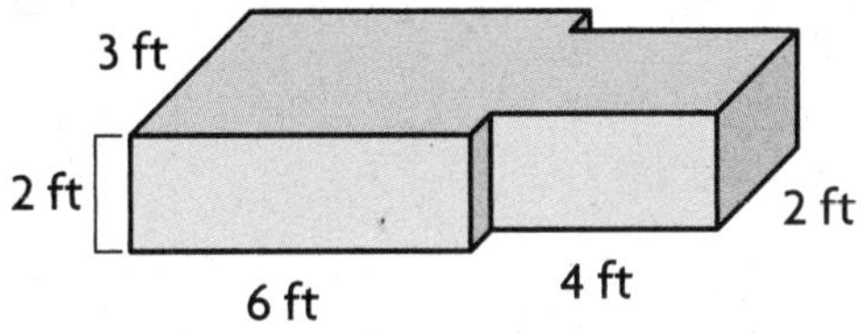

$V =$ ______________

4.

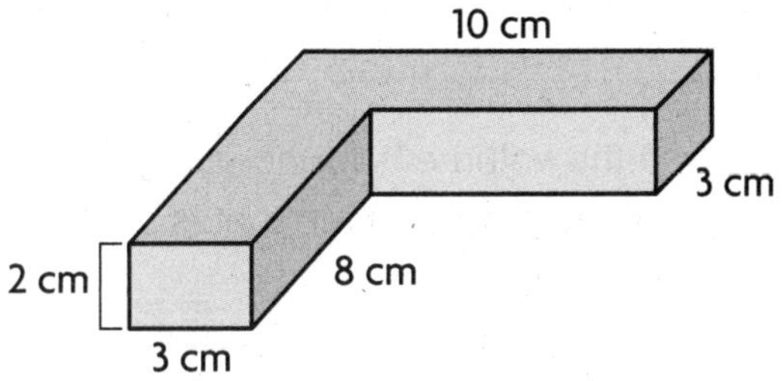

$V =$ ______________

5.

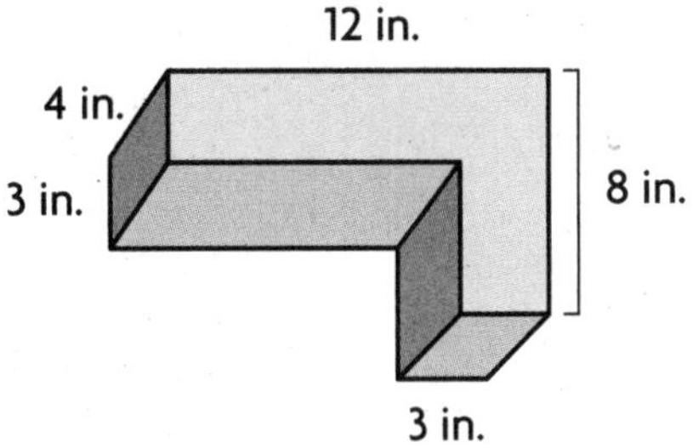

$V =$ ______________

6.

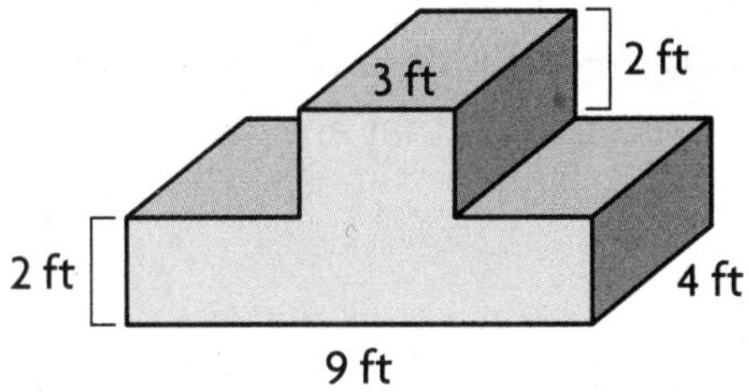

$V =$ ______________

7.

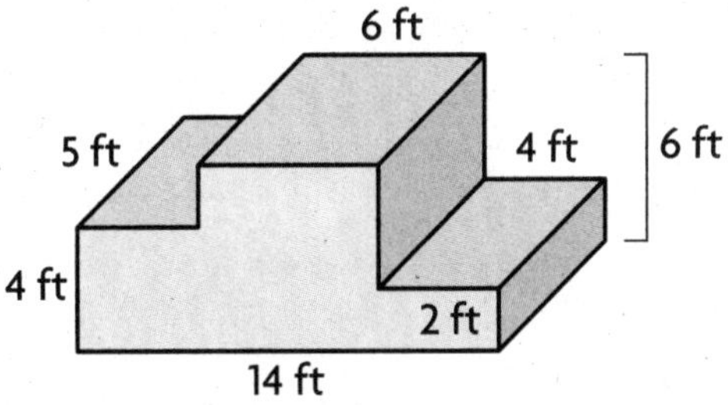

$V =$ ______________

8.

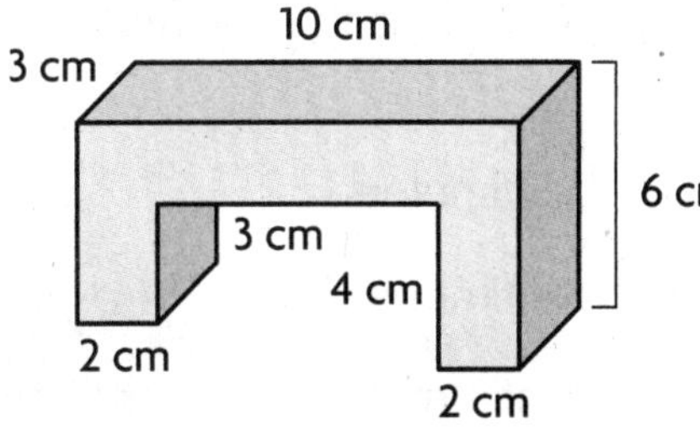

$V =$ ______________

Problem Solving REAL WORLD

Use the composite figure at the right for 9–11.

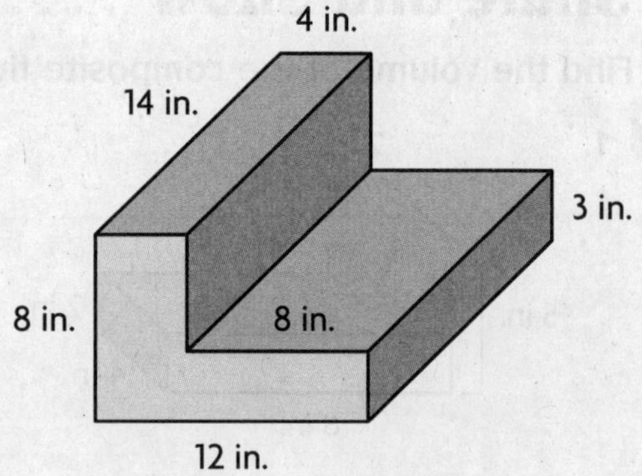

9. As part of a wood-working project, Jordan made the figure at the right out of wooden building blocks. How much space does the figure he made take up?

____

10. What are the dimensions of the two rectangular prisms you used to find the volume of the figure? What other rectangular prisms could you have used?

____

____

____

____

SHOW YOUR WORK

11. H.O.T. If the volume is found using subtraction, what is the volume of the empty space that is subtracted? **Explain.**

____

____

____

12. **Write Math** **Explain** how you can find the volume of composite figures that are made by combining rectangular prisms.

____

____

____

13. **Test Practice** What is the volume of the composite figure?

Ⓐ 126 cubic centimeters

Ⓑ 350 cubic centimeters

Ⓒ 450 cubic centimeters

Ⓓ 476 cubic centimeters

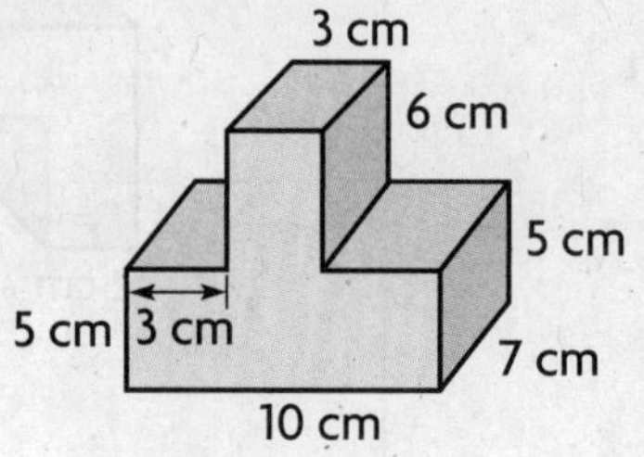

Name ____________________________________

Ordered Pairs

Essential Question How can you identify and plot points on a coordinate grid?

COMMON CORE STANDARD **CC.5.G.1; CC.5.G.2**
Graph points on the coordinate plane to solve real-world and mathematical problems.

CONNECT Locating a point on a coordinate grid is similar to describing directions using North-South and West-East. The horizontal number line on the grid is the **x-axis**. The vertical number line on the grid is the **y-axis**.

Each point on the coordinate grid can be described by an **ordered pair** of numbers. The **x-coordinate**, the first number in the ordered pair, is the horizontal location, or the distance the point is from 0 in the direction of the x-axis. The **y-coordinate**, the second number in the ordered pair, is the vertical location, or the distance the point is from 0 in the direction of the y-axis.

(x, y)

x-coordinate ↑ ↑ y-coordinate

The x-axis and the y-axis intersect at the point (0, 0), called the **origin**.

UNLOCK the Problem REAL WORLD

Write the ordered pairs for the locations of the arena and the aquarium.

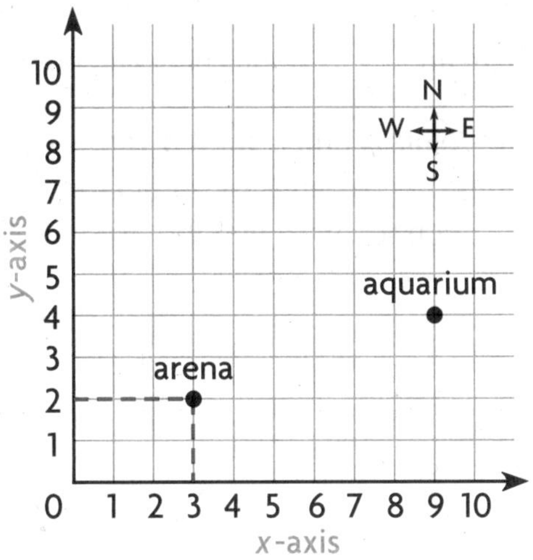

Locate the point for which you want to write an ordered pair.

Look below at the x-axis to identify the point's horizontal distance from 0, which is its x-coordinate.

Look to the left at the y-axis to identify the point's vertical distance from 0, which is its y-coordinate.

So, the ordered pair for the arena is (3, 2) and the ordered pair for the aquarium

is (______, ______).

- Describe the path you would take to get from the origin to the aquarium, using horizontal, then vertical movements.

____

____

Example 1 Use the graph.

A point on a coordinate grid can be labeled with an ordered pair, a letter, or both.

A Plot the point (5, 7) and label it *J*.

From the origin, move right 5 units and then up 7 units.

Plot and label the point.

B Plot the point (8, 0) and label it *S*.

From the origin, move right ______ units and

then up ______ units.

Plot and label the point.

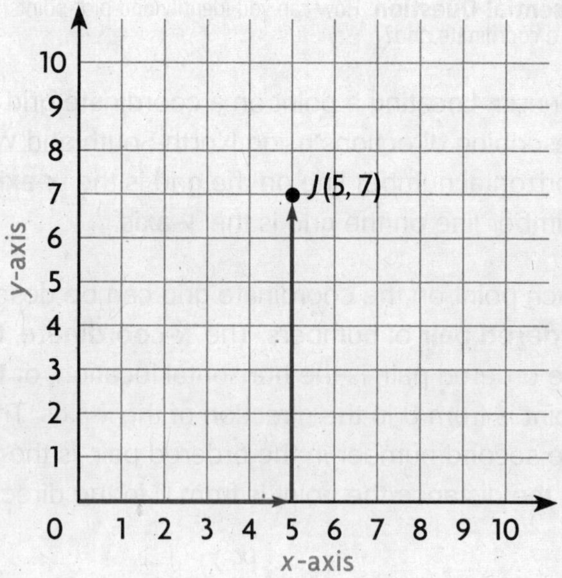

Example 2 Find the distance between two points.

You can find the distance between two points when the points are along the same horizontal or vertical line.

- Draw a line segment to connect point *A* and point *B*.
- Count vertical units between the two points.

There are ______ units between points *A* and *B*.

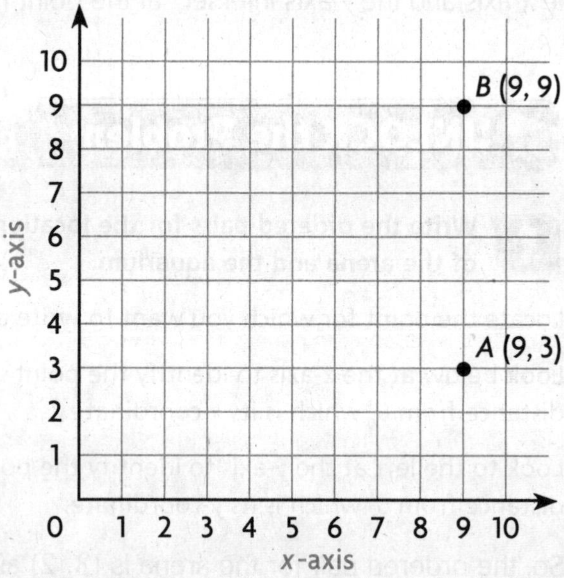

1. Points *A* and *B* form a vertical line segment and have the same *x*-coordinates. How can you use subtraction to find the distance between the points?

____

____

____

____

2. Graph the points (3, 2) and (5, 2). **Explain** how you can use subtraction to find the horizontal distance between these two points.

____

____

Name ______________________________

Share and Show

Use Coordinate Grid A to write an ordered pair for the given point.

1. *C* ____________
2. *D* ____________
3. *E* ____________
4. *F* ____________

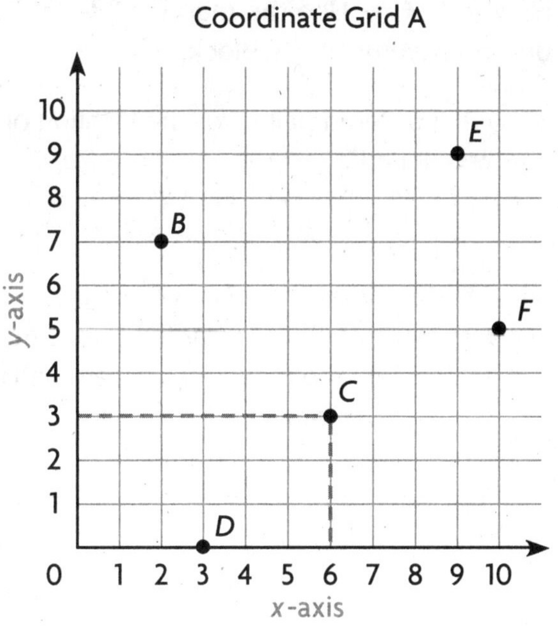

Plot and label the points on Coordinate Grid A.

5. $M(0, 9)$
6. $H(8, 6)$
7. $K(10, 4)$
8. $T(4, 5)$
9. $W(5, 10)$
10. $R(1, 3)$

Math Talk MATHEMATICAL PRACTICES Describe how to find the distance between point *R* and point *C*.

On Your Own

Use Coordinate Grid B to write an ordered pair for the given point.

11. *G* ____________
12. *H* ____________
13. *I* ____________
14. *J* ____________
15. *K* ____________
16. *L* ____________
17. *M* ____________
18. *N* ____________
19. *O* ____________
20. *P* ____________

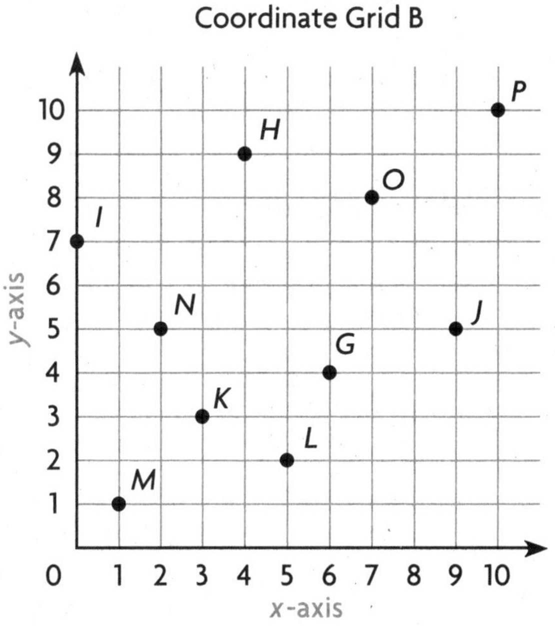

Plot and label the points on Coordinate Grid B.

21. $W(8, 2)$
22. $E(0, 4)$
23. $X(2, 9)$
24. $B(3, 4)$
25. $R(4, 0)$
26. $F(7, 6)$
27. $T(5, 7)$
28. $A(7, 1)$
29. $S(10, 8)$
30. $Y(1, 6)$
31. $Q(3, 8)$
32. $V(3, 1)$

Problem Solving REAL WORLD

Nathan and his friends are planning a trip to New York City. Use the map for 33–38. Each unit represents 1 city block.

Map of New York City

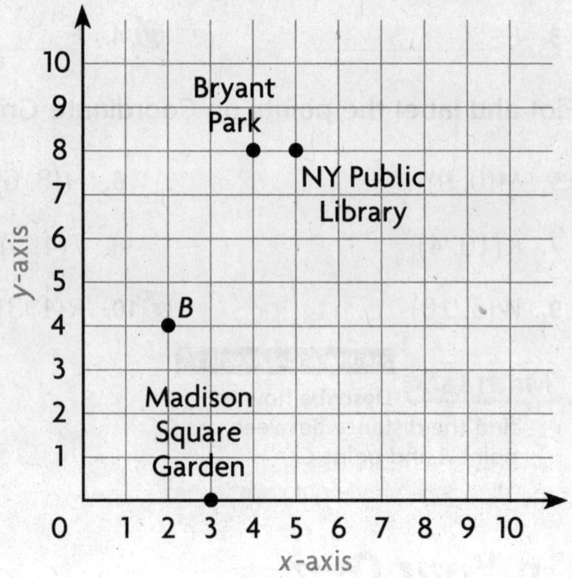

33. What ordered pair gives the location of Bryant Park?

____

34. H.O.T. **What's the Error?** Nathan says that Madison Square Garden is located at (0, 3) on the map. Is his ordered pair correct? **Explain.**

____

____

____

____

35. The Empire State Building is located 5 blocks right and 1 block up from (0, 0). Write the ordered pair for this location. Plot and label a point for the Empire State Building.

____

36. H.O.T. Paulo walks from point *B* to Bryant Park. Raul walks from point *B* to Madison Square Garden. If they only walk along the grid lines, who walks farther? **Explain.**

____

____

37. Write Math **Explain** how to find the distance between Bryant Park and a hot dog stand at the point (4, 2).

____

____

38. **Test Practice** Use the map above. Suppose a pizzeria is located at point *B*. What ordered pair describes this point?

Ⓐ (4, 2) Ⓑ (3, 4) Ⓒ (2, 4) Ⓓ (4, 4)

Photo Credits

KEY: (t) top, (b) bottom, (l) left, (r) right, (c) center, (bg) background, (fg) foreground, (i) inset

CC4 (tr) Creativ Studio Heinemann/Westend61/Corbis; CC8 (tr) Leonard de Selva/Corbis; CC13 Macduff Everton/Corbis; CC14 (tr) Phil Schermeister/Corbis; CC17 (tr) Bluemoon Stock/Getty Images; CC18 (tr) Richard McDowell/Alamy Images; CC22 (tr) Bernd Vogel/Corbis; CC28 (tr) Hill Street Studios/Getty Images; CC29 (tr) IML Image Group Ltd/Alamy Images; CC32 (cr) TongRo Image Stock/Alamy Images; CC33 (br) Anna Peisi/Corbis; CC36 (tr) Jonathan Daniel/Getty Images; CC40 (tr) Elizabeth Whiting & Associates/Alamy Images; CC42 (tr) Purestock/Getty Images; CC45 (tr) Corbis; CC53 artville/Getty Images; CC54 (tr) Ralph A Clevenger/Corbis; CC56 vasa/Alamy Images; CC58 (l) Andrew Paterson/Alamy; Kraig Scarbinsky/Getty Images; CC60 Compassionate Eye Foundation/Getty Images; CC69 (cr) Mike Powell/Getty Images; CC72 (tr) Image100/Corbis; CC73 (tr) Paul Street/Alamy Images; CC76 (tr) photodisc/Alamy Images; CC77 (tr) COMSTOCK Images/age fotostock; CC80 (tr) Juniors Bildarchiv/Alamy; CC82 (tr) comstock/Getty Images; CC84 (tr) Judith Collins/Alamy Images; CC93 (tr) image source/Getty Images; CC98 (cl) C Squared Studios/Photodisc Green/Getty Images; CC100 (tr) Imagemore Co., Ltd./Alamy Images; CC101 (cr) Alamy; CC106 (tr) Photodisc/Getty Images; CC118 PhotoDisc/Getty Images; CC120 (tr) Robert Maass/Corbis; CC122 (tr) Gary Ombler/Getty Images; CC125 (tr) Blend Images/Shalom Ormsby/Getty Images; CC129 (tr) Cutcaster.com/Lawren Lu; CC130 (tr) MIXA/Alamy Images; CC131 (tr) Colin Hawkins/Getty Images; CC133 FoodCollection/Superstock; CC134 FOOD/Alamy Images; CC140 C Squared Studios/Getty Images; CC142 (tr) William Leaman/Alamy Images; CC145 (cr) Jude Gibbins/Alamy; CC147 (cr) Graham Bailey/Alamy; CC148 (cr) Dr. Stanley Flegler/Visuals Unlimited/Getty Images; CC153 (tr) dbimages/Alamy Images; CC154 (tr) Comstock/Getty Images; CC164 (tr) PhotoDisc/Getty Images; CC165 (tr) Lawrence Manning/Corbis; CC169 (tr) Getty Images/PhotoDisc; CC170 (tr) Chris Ratcliffe/Alamy; CC177 (cr) Image Plan/Corbis; CC178 (r) Ingram; (l) C Squared Studios/Photodisc/Getty Images; CC181 (tr) digital vision/Getty Images; CC182 (tr) comstock/Getty Images; CC184 (tr) Brand New Images/Getty Images; CC186 (tr) Corbis; (br) Steve Gorton and Karl Shone/Getty Image; CC188 (tr) LianeM/Alamy Images; Judith Collins/Alamy Images; CC190 (tr) Brand X Pictures/Getty Images; CC192 (tr) jane burton/Getty Images; CC202 (tr) Christina Kennedy/Brand X Pictures; CC208 (tr) Brian Hamilton/Alamy Images; (cr) John Dakers/Corbis; CC216 (tr) Martin Ruegner/Getty Images; CC220 (tr) Imagebroker/Alamy Images.